AN IRRATIONAL HATRED
OF EVERYTHING

MY CONTINUING ODYSSEY AS
A WEST HAM FAN 2003–2018

AN IRRATIONAL
HATRED
OF EVERYTHING

ROBERT BANKS

WITH A FOREWORD BY PHIL PARKES

Biteback Publishing

First published in Great Britain in 2018 by
Biteback Publishing Ltd
Westminster Tower
3 Albert Embankment
London SE1 7SP
Copyright © Robert Banks 2018

Robert Banks has asserted his right under the Copyright, Designs and Patents Act
1988 to be identified as the author of this work.

ISBN 978-1-78590-404-2

10 9 8 7 6 5 4 3 2 1

A CIP catalogue record for this book is available from the British Library.

Set in Minion Pro

Printed and bound in Great Britain by
CPI Group (UK) Ltd, Croydon CR0 4YY

MIX
Paper from
responsible sources
FSC   FSC® C020471
www.fsc.org

FOREWORD

BY PHIL PARKES (WEST HAM UNITED AND ENGLAND GOALKEEPER)

When Rob asked me to write the foreword for his book, I read the draft with great interest and, to be honest, much sadness. It struck me that Rob is an ordinary bloke with an extraordinary love for West Ham United. But what also came across strongly was that his relationship with the club is strained and very similar to mine these days.

West Ham fans are among the best in the world. They are funny, intelligent and do not suffer fools gladly. Rob says that for him the club changed beyond recognition when John Lyall died in 2006 and I agree with him. Although John had left in 1989, his passing meant that a link with the past had gone for ever. John showed enormous faith in me, persuading the board to pay a world-record fee for a goalkeeper on a nine-year contract that would keep me at the club until I was thirty-eight. Even Manchester United found that too hot a deal to trump. And West Ham was a second-division club at the time, too. It was a statement of intent, the like of which we will never see again.

There have been a number of huge traumas at the club in the last fifteen years. The only thing that comes close to any of them during my playing days was when John told us he was leaving. The way that was handled was terrible, and while we accept that nothing lasts for ever, it was something that changed the club for ever.

The last fifteen years have seen so many calamities that it is hard to know where to start. Rob has chronicled these with his own brand of humour that will help you to remember them without wanting to tear the book up and throw it out of the window!

Rob talks of the West Ham Way and how difficult this is to define. Sam Allardyce could not understand it, but if he had taken a little time to get his head around the fact that West Ham fans can applaud their team off the pitch after a 4–1 defeat to Dinamo Tbilisi, they are just as entitled to boo a 2–1 victory over Hull City. But he felt West Ham fans should see things his way, not the other way around.

West Ham fans are no mugs. Yet they have been treated as such for too long now. The present board has made it impossible for me to attend in an official capacity, and I think it unlikely that I will return until they leave. David Gold is a West Ham fan, but I don't believe Sullivan is, whatever he may claim. As for Karren Brady, I think she's just a Karren Brady fan. I feel they set out from day one with the sole intention of moving from the Boleyn, one of the greatest football theatres in the world, to systematically destroy the club's identity, dressing it up as a huge move forward. Call it my irrational hatred. It's just my opinion.

I can only speak for myself, but I know many of the players I played with loved you, the West Ham fans, and wanted to perform for you every week. Today, things are different. Today, players earn so much they can happily sit on the bench, go out on loan or maybe not even make the squad. In my day you had to play to top up your money and it made you hungry, eager to show up every week. And if someone was hiding they would get a kick up the backside from Bill! That is the major difference and the reason why so many modern players have a poor attitude. Today's West Ham fans deserve better than that.

Football is some way down the pecking order for me these days. Like Rob, I understand perspective. I enjoy going to watch Alan Devonshire's national league side Maidenhead. They play football with a smile on their faces, and a hunger and passion that is so sadly lacking in modern professional football.

Rob told me he had intended this book to be positive, but he found it impossible. I see his point, but there is still a positive message that comes across.

I sincerely hope that with the new signings made this summer the team will give the Hammers and their amazing fans something to cheer about. With everything you have been through in the last fifteen years, you certainly deserve it.

AUTHOR'S NOTE

This is the fourth instalment in a series of books I started writing in 1994, but as it has been fifteen years since the last one, I have tried to make this one stand alone and appeal to those of you who may not have read the previous three volumes. *An Irrational Hatred of Luton* covered the period of my earliest memories as a Hammers fan from 1975 to 1995. *West Ham 'Till I Die* covered 1995 to 2000 and *The Legacy of Barry Green* covered 2000 to 2003.

In all four books the chapter headings take the form of a song title and a match selected from the period covered by the chapter. In this book, they are the titles of songs that were number one on the date of the match. Additionally, in this book, each chapter has its own 'irrational hatred', selected either by me or one of my friends.

There are some themes that run throughout all four books, so if something doesn't make sense it may be that I have assumed you have read the other three. That is not intentional. I wanted this volume to stand alone – but if you enjoy this tome do please take the time to check out the others, which can no doubt be picked up for a few measly coppers on eBay or Amazon.

INTRODUCTION

Gareth Southgate said just before England played Croatia in the World Cup semi-final on 11 July 2018 that recently, the country had experienced a lot of issues with unity, and that hopefully a successful England team would bring people together.

Southgate is a wise man. It's been nice to have something we can pretty much all agree on, if only for a few weeks. In the last few years we have had Brexit, the Scottish Independence referendum and a General Election, all of which caused massive divides between people, and particularly on social media, where people seem to think it's okay to get lairy, aggressive and downright rude.

The last fifteen years have been similarly divisive at West Ham. Terry Brown, the Tevez affair, the Icelandics, relegation, the move to the Olympic Stadium, the cancelled protest march. They are just the low-lights. The last three years in particular have been especially excruciating; it's been enough to make me want to avoid the news for fear of the next embarrassing story involving West Ham.

The period since 2003 has also seen massive changes for me personally. This book attempts to chronicle those changes alongside the events at West Ham to provide a narrative which will hopefully bring back some of your own memories: to help you recall where you were, who you were with, what happened that weekend.

It does not purport to be a definitive club history. You could write individual books on any of the subjects listed above; I have merely skimmed the surface to give you a flavour. Trying to cover every event in detail from the last fifteen years would be like trying to herd a thousand indifferent cats. And it would not be a fun read.

I do not claim to be West Ham's number one fan. You will notice from the narrative that these days I only go to home games and a handful of away matches. I'm comfortable with that. I served my time doing every home and away match during the 1980s and 1990s. It nearly broke me. For some, West Ham is the focus of their lives, and good luck to them. For others, they follow only from the armchair, and that's fine too. I fall somewhere in the middle, so hope that I am able to give a balanced view. For me, the club we support now is not the same club I fell in love with in 1975. Everything, and I mean *everything*, has changed.

The biggest difference that I've noticed has been the way fans interact with each other. The relationship has never been so fractious, and I put that down to the rise of social media. Before Facebook, Twitter and any number of web forums you may wish to mention, birds of a feather flocked together. There was no reason for fans of such differing backgrounds to exchange views. You knew your mates' opinions, and those of the people sat around you. You knew the opinions of those who wrote for the fanzines. If you disagreed, you put it down and forgot it – or in some extreme cases, you maybe started writing for the fanzine yourself.

Nowadays fans with very different perspectives exchange views and put forward opinions every day. It is no surprise there would be friction occasionally. West Ham fans come from a broad base geographically and demographically. We will not always see eye to eye, but we can unite a lot easier if the team is performing. And the team has a better chance of performing if we unite.

At the time of writing it does appear that funds are being found down the back of the sofa to facilitate a squad befitting a club with the average crowds we 'enjoy'. We have a manager with a proven track record who is widely respected throughout the game. We have a chance. That includes us as fans – we have a chance too.

What follows is a plea for everyone to put things in perspective. Football, contrary to what some believe, is a game. It is not a matter of life and death. There are so many things that people get uptight about. There are sixty-five of them in the chapter titles of this book. But, like the football played, none of them really matter. The game is important to all of us, but never more than our family and friends. It is not worthy of violence, bitterness, vitriol and hatred. Be tribal by all means. Be witty of course. Be considerate. But above all, be West Ham UNITED.

1

ROCKABYE

WEST HAM UNITED 0, MANCHESTER CITY 5
FA CUP THIRD ROUND, 6 JANUARY 2017

As soon as the draw had been made for the third round of the 2016/17 FA Cup, it became clear it would be our last game in the competition for twelve months. Manchester City were riding high and scoring for fun; West Ham playing an awkward brand of nervous football at the London Stadium that invariably ended in painful victory or humiliating defeat.

But hope springs eternal, as it has done for me since I first started supporting the Hammers in 1975, and I bought a ticket even though the game had the added negative factor of being played on a Friday night for the benefit of television.

My ticket arrived but I didn't use it. I didn't go. Not because of the way the team were playing. Not because I didn't enjoy the whole match day experience like we used to at Upton Park. Not because we were odds-on to get a good hiding. Not because I have become a bit flaky of late and any excuse not to go to the game will be grabbed. Not because it was a Friday night and on TV anyway.

I didn't go because my father was dying.

My sister called me on the Thursday morning to suggest I should take the day off work and come to see Dad as it seemed the end was near. It had been a difficult few weeks watching my father suffering from dementia and cancer, in obvious pain and slowly fading away.

The hospice delivered a special bed so we could nurse him at home, and that's what we did: me, my two sisters and my

1

mother taking turns to make sure he wasn't alone. Talking to him, playing him his favourite pieces of music, reminiscing about our childhoods. We knew we could not bring him back, but we wanted to try to make his last few hours as peaceful and pleasant as they could be.

By the time the Friday evening came around, we knew it would not be long. I thought long and hard about switching on the TV in his room, before deciding it was what he would want, to at least hear a West Ham game for the last time. As the fifth goal went in I was sure I saw a knowing smile furnish his lips. It would have been nice if we had been able to upset the odds. It would have been one last hurrah just for my dad. But it wasn't to be. He passed away a couple of hours later.

I didn't give the football a second thought. I watched the game with tears in my eyes and his hand in mine, just as it had been when he took me to my first game in 1978 – not because West Ham were laying down for another embarrassing pasting, but because I was losing my longest-standing, and best, friend. He was my biggest supporter, my inspiration, my hero.

The point? Just this: Bill Shankly was wrong. Football is not more important than life and death. I would love to have gone to one more game with my dad. But I would rather have him here with me in a world without football, than live without him in a world with it.

Football is only a game, after all. It is on the back pages of the newspaper for a reason. It doesn't really matter in the grand scheme of things. But we make it important because of what it means to us – it helps us to forget about what is on the front pages, and the more pressing issues in our own lives. Football, as with most hobbies, is just another elaborate way of wasting time. In that respect it does serve an important role, and a few days later when I met up with my two nephews before the game against Crystal Palace, we contrived to believe Andy Carroll's spectacular bicycle kick was a parting gift for Dad.

You may well ask then, given football is so rubbish and un-important, why am I writing another book about football? Why now, fifteen years after my last book, *The Legacy of Barry Green*? Anyone who has ever written a book with an audience of a few thousand rather than a few million will know it isn't for the cash.

I had always said I would not write another book unless it was a ghost-written autobiography or a novel. But I was on holiday, and this was a good time to reflect on the past and consider the future. Holidays are not what they used to be, though, with social media keeping you abreast of every minuscule rumour and news item around the club as long as you take the trouble to buy into it.

I was becoming tired of the daily diatribes about the team, about the board, about the new stadium and the constant looking back at how great things used to be and how terrible they are now. It was getting under my skin. I hated seeing the club I love portrayed in such a negative manner, it seemed, twenty-four hours a day, seven days a week. I firmly believed I could write a book that would be wearing its hat at a jaunty angle; poke fun at the way things are and point to a brighter future.

Then I actually started to write it and realised trying to put a positive spin on current events is virtually impossible.

So the book has morphed into something else. It has become a testament to the fact that no matter how hard you try to be positive about the current situation we find ourselves in, it is an impossible task. And the mood is such that until there are sweeping changes in the way the club is run, that will not change. I am not here to peddle doom and gloom – but to try to at least provide some gallows humour.

But I also wanted the book to point to our recent history. The history everybody loves and the traditions we remember so fondly. Was it really as good as we remember, or were we just as discontent (or maybe even more so) during the bond scheme protests? After relegation in 1989? After the baffling appointment of Glenn Roeder as manager? When the North Bank was demolished? What would social media as we know it today have made of those events?

The collision, and I use the word advisedly, of astronomical amounts of money in the English game, and astronomical numbers of idiots on social media, makes for a potent mixture. The game has a global audience and on social media you have a group of people who crave attention – regardless of whether they have a valid opinion or not.

Life is all about perspective. It's about seeing things from other people's point of view, comparing it to your own and taking something from it. It's about ranking things in order of importance and allocating your time accordingly. Recent events have shown West Ham has a fan base of broad background and diverse social and political views. We have to respect each other.

So brace yourselves for what follows. I will not be carrying any banners, calling for anyone to resign, moaning about the board or criticising the move. I simply don't understand why some people have to hate so much. I want to put some perspective on things. Perspective that, like many, I didn't know existed until I watched that final game with my father.

2

WHERE IS THE LOVE?

CARDIFF CITY 2, WEST HAM UNITED 3
LEAGUE CUP SECOND ROUND, 23 SEPTEMBER 2003
Unexpected item in bagging area. God,
I hate self-service checkouts.

The *Legacy of Barry Green* left matters in September 2003 with West Ham shepherded by caretaker-manager Trevor Brooking for a second time following the departure of the ill-fated and, well, just plain ill, Glenn Roeder. I was living in Bradford with my ex-wife. Not living with my ex-wife you understand, she is now my ex-wife. She wasn't then, although we weren't married at that point. Anyway, moving on. You will have the necessary background story if you read *The Legacy of Barry Green.* I won't repeat myself here. Suffice to say the 'unmentionable ex' was not too happy about the prospect of featuring in another book, so I will keep references to a minimum.

Alan Pardew, who had been impressive as manager of Reading, had agreed to move to Upton Park, but negotiations had been protracted with Reading chairman, John Madejski, reluctant to allow his clearly talented coach to go to a rival team. Although West Ham were Reading's rivals in terms of league position, you could not say the same about their status in the world of football overall. Pardew was coming – but Madejski wasn't going to make it easy for us. The matter went to court, but Reading failed in their attempt to prevent Pardew becoming West Ham's tenth full-time boss. His appointment was confirmed on 18 September 2003, but he wasn't able to take over first-team affairs until a month later.

Sir Trevor had taken up the reins again in the interim, having done so at the end of the 2002/03 season and narrowly failed to keep West Ham in the Premier League, despite taking 7 points from the 3 games he took charge of. Indeed the team had performed well over the second half of the campaign, losing only one of their last 11 matches. Unfortunately the loss was to Sam Allardyce's Bolton Wanderers, who ultimately finished 17th on 44 points, as we went down on 42. A draw in that game and we would have stayed up; but you could argue that failing to win a single home game until January meant we ultimately got what we deserved.

It seemed to me, though, that Roeder's days had been numbered even before his illness had necessitated Brooking's first caretaker stint, and the board felt they could not sack him while he still had such a high degree of public sympathy. So he started the 2003/04 campaign and the board waited patiently for him to make his first cock-up. They did not have to wait long. After an opening day win at Preston North End and a routine 3–1 win over Rushden and Diamonds in the second round of the League Cup, a goalless draw at home to probable promotion rivals Sheffield United was not a bad start. However, defeat at Rotherham United the following weekend signalled the end for Roeder. I felt personally he should have been given longer.

Brooking continued his impressive record as caretaker manager, ultimately losing just one game in the eleven he presided over in his second spell, and that was an ill-tempered match at Gillingham which saw Jermain Defoe sent off. Before that we had beaten both Bradford City and Reading 1–0 at Upton Park, and Ipswich Town and Crewe Alexandra away 2–1 and 3–0 respectively. Defeat at Gillingham left us in 4th place in the league with 16 points from 8 games.

Defoe had been causing the club headaches since handing in a transfer request before the dust had settled on West Ham's relegation. It seemed that the club's refusal to let him leave, when they had allowed the likes Glen Johnson, Joe Cole, Paolo Di Canio, Frédéric Kanouté and Trevor Sinclair to go, was causing the striker to act more than a little petulantly. He would be sent off three times that season, each of them seemingly deliberate. Although 15 goals in the 22 games he was involved in was an impressive return for someone supposedly in a strop.

At Ninian Park – yes, Ninian Park, Google it kids – West Ham faced Cardiff City in a third round League Cup tie. Cardiff were out of the traps quickly and were 2–0 up inside 25 minutes, both goals scored by Robert Earnshaw. Defoe kept West Ham in it with a penalty just before the break after David Connolly had been tripped in mid-air by Tony Vidmar. Defoe then scored twice in the second half, the first taking a deflection off soon-to-be Hammer Danny Gabbidon to leave Brooking not just defending the striker in the post-match press conference, but positively singing his praises. He said Defoe was committed. Many of us thought he should be.

The league game against Millwall passed relatively quietly, or rather, as quietly as a football match can pass with that many helicopters and police dogs present. David Connolly had been proving to be a popular figure at Upton Park, among the fans at any rate. He hadn't been afraid to make his point when he discovered that Glenn Roeder was starting the season with on-loan Liverpool striker Neil Mellor. He scored the opening goal against Millwall, finishing well after a jinking run. Summer signing Matthew Etherington hit a post and Kevin Horlock should have done better with a header before Millwall inevitably equalised.

When Defoe shot wide from a stupidly narrow angle, instead of cutting back to a much better placed Connolly, the glare Connolly gave Defoe was the biggest threat of violence that day. Maybe just as well that Defoe's two-match ban for his sending off at Gillingham was about to start.

Defoe had one more game before that ban started, a 3–0 win against Crystal Palace in which he scored a goal reminiscent of Pelé's famous dummy on Uruguayan goalkeeper Ladislao Mazurkiewicz in the semi-final of the 1970 World Cup. The difference here was that Defoe rounded the keeper without touching the ball and slotted home, whereas that old donkey Pelé fired wide. It helped Defoe's cause, I suppose, that the through ball was a backpass played by a hapless Palace defender. The other two goals came from Mellor, no doubt much to Connolly's chagrin.

'And what were you doing in the middle of all this, Banksy?', I hear my avid reader cry. You will have noticed I do not recall these games with eye-witness anecdotes. Well, it was proving a little tricky to attend games in 2003 for a number of reasons. Primarily it was a fiscal issue – I was skint – and the unmentionable ex and I had committed to rebuilding our kitchen, something which, much like our relationship, we were both completely unqualified to attempt. Second, and much less of an issue, was my geographical location: Bradford. This wasn't too much of a problem given that I retained the use of an away season ticket and was still able to get to a number of northern away games – but constraints on time and money were overriding.

The third issue was that when not ripping out old kitchen units, or counting pennies, I was working feverishly on *The Legacy of Barry Green*, which I had been writing on a laptop borrowed from the office on my ninety-minute commute to work and the equally dull journey back – table seat permitting.

I was working for the Co-operative Insurance Society (CIS) at its chief office in Manchester, monitoring the financial advice provided by its sales force. It was as exciting as it sounds. In an effort to temper my morning enthusiasm and to allow the adrenalin accumulated from the day job to dissipate naturally, I consumed myself on my journey in writing the book. I had the working title *The Rise and Fall of Rufus Brevett*, which I thought sounded suitably Dickensian – but it was vetoed by the publishers who felt that since Brevett was still in the squad it might have caused issues. Shame. I rather liked that title.

Speaking of Rufus, his part in the fracas at the end of the defeat to Bolton the previous April went punished by a fine of £1,000. Loose change to a professional footballer, and an indication that the FA accepted his assertion that he was sorry, and his behaviour was out of character. Brevett didn't appear for the Hammers again that season as he was out injured with a broken ankle. I could have got away with the title after all.

West Ham's England International goalkeeper David James retained his place in Sven-Göran Eriksson's squad, featuring in a 0–0 draw in Turkey, in doing so becoming the first player from the second flight to feature for the senior England team since Steve Bull in 1990.

Sky selected the away game at Pride Park for its Saturday evening game and quickly regretted it. The match had hardly any positives other than Don Hutchison's last-minute winner.

The detail of Pardew's contract meant that he still had to sit out two more home games before he could take over, against Norwich City and Burnley. After a 1–1 draw against Norwich City, with Peter Crouch cancelling out an Edworthy own goal, the Burnley game signalled Sir Trevor's final match in caretaker charge.

Despite the fact it was just that, temporary care, it was as though he was retiring all over again and many fans, me included, would have liked to see him take the role permanently. However, I was mindful of the way Billy Bonds had been treated previously, and also felt it might be better if he walked away with a record of one defeat in fourteen – a remarkable achievement for a man with no previous experience in the role.

Brooking had somehow managed to navigate his way through two spells as caretaker boss and still remain a legend. He had made it clear that he would not be returning, just as he had made that clear in 1983/84 when he said it would be his last season. He was never tempted to play on. The man is pure class.

David Connolly put West Ham 1–0 up against Burnley but the Clarets struck twice to take a 2–1 lead into the final minute. Both goals were seemingly avoidable and clumsily dealt with by David James. Don Hutchison repeated the trick he had performed at Derby by popping up with a last-minute goal to preserve Sir Trevor's record to allow him to hand over the reins to Alan Pardew with West Ham still in the hunt, sitting in 5th place in the table.

3

BE FAITHFUL

WEST HAM UNITED 3, WEST BROMWICH ALBION 4
FOOTBALL LEAGUE, FIRST DIVISION 8 NOVEMBER 2003
*If anyone tells you fitting a kitchen is easy, punch them
in the face. It's hard. Really hard. I hate it.*

Alan Pardew might have been able to help, having been a
window fitter in his time, but without him on speed dial, I
had to be satisfied with regular calls to Dad for advice. I decided
to let Pardew do what he does best – manage football teams.

However, his initial attempts at managing West Ham were
less than impressive. His first signing was not inspiring either.
Hayden Mullins may well have been Crystal Palace's player of
the season two years in a row, but in my view that didn't make
him a suitable candidate to run West Ham's midfield. He signed
initially on loan with a view to a permanent deal.

Pardew's first game was a 1–1 draw at home to Nottingham
Forest. Andy Reid fired a belter into the top corner and West
Ham, including debutant Mullins, equalised through Defoe's
ninth goal of the season to keep them in 5th place. Having waited
so long for Pardew to start, it was all a bit of an anti-climax.

Things didn't improve at Cardiff City in the next game, which
was again selected for live television and ended in a 0–0 draw
of the worst kind. Any luck with that Google search for Ninian
Park yet? Tottenham were up next in the League Cup, and a tense
atmosphere surrounded the whole area (as is often the case for
West Ham's games at White Hart Lane). Bobby Zamora scored
the only goal of the game, ironically but not completely surprisingly, his only goal for Tottenham Hotspur in 18 appearances.

Yet again the game itself took second stage to the knuckle-dragging salads who attach their allegiances to football clubs at times, with trouble reported from as early as mid-afternoon. The West Ham website stated afterwards that the troublemakers would be found and banned.

I'd heard it all before. I shrugged my shoulders and moved on as I had a ticket for Coventry City the following Saturday. I had worked in Nottingham with a bloke called Micky Maxwell, salt of the earth that man, and a mad keen Coventry City supporter. Although I had since moved north we were both still working for the CIS and he kept in touch. We arranged to meet for the Coventry game on 1 November. He sent me directions saying, 'Go straight over at the first island.' I was confused. I could see no islands anywhere. Just roundabouts.

I had a couple of beers and played a few frames of snooker with Micky in the local working-men's club where I was lightly teased by the other Coventry fans, but escaped with my life on the basis that I was with him. We bade each other farewell and went to our respective areas of Highfield Road where I witnessed a third draw in a row (it ended up 1–1). Jermain Defoe again scoring but West Ham failed to hold on to the advantage.

That was the last time I saw Micky Maxwell; he passed away shortly after that.

Three draws in a row was not going to get us into the play-offs, but we somehow clung on to 6th place, and, I reasoned, at least we hadn't lost. We had more draws than an IKEA warehouse. I was going to the home game against West Bromwich Albion the following Saturday, surely it would all click then?

Squad-wise, Robbie Stockdale, one of Roeder's on-loan summer recruits, was sent back to Middlesbrough from whence he came after picking up an injury in the cup defeat at White Hart Lane. Nobody shed any tears, least of all Stockdale himself. He joined Niclas Alexandersson who we had borrowed from Everton, and who had then returned after being similarly unimpressive.

It is always hard for any football club to achieve the balance between youthful enthusiasm and wise, old hands, especially when you have the added headache of injuries and players wanting to leave.

In that respect, I had always felt that our relegation in 2002/03 was down to a failure on the part of the management to prepare for the January transfer window, which was in place for the first time. The number of injuries caught everyone by surprise, and the club failed to consider the fact they could not bring anyone in until the new year. When you consider what glorious football we played at Upton Park against Arsenal in that 2–2 draw in August 2002 when we should have won 3–1 (Kanouté missed a penalty at 2–1), it showed we were capable. But then injuries, and a falling out between Roeder and Di Canio, really stitched us up, with Roeder resorting to playing Ian Pearce up front. When the window opened on 1 January 2003 we were able to bring in decent reinforcements in the shape of Les Ferdinand and Rufus Brevett – but the damage had already been done.

Social media was in its infancy still, and the level of anger towards both board and manager was not as obvious as it might have been in the same situation today. Terry Brown, the chairman, wrote a letter to shareholders immediately before the AGM addressing a number of points that had been raised, including the impact of the transfer window. He said:

> Firstly, we had to fund the second tranche of the transfer fees incurred in 2001 in respect of Hutchison, James, Řepka, Schemmel and Labant. Nick Igoe explained at the AGM that borrowings would escalate as a consequence of our outstanding transfer commitments. In financial terms those commitments in the summer of 2002 were £9m. We then incurred a further £1m in transfer and agents' fees and transfer levy in respect of Sofiane, van der Gouw, Breen and Cissé. Those players added £2m to the 2002/3 wage bill and contract renegotiations with Sinclair, Lomas, Pearce, Schemmel, Moncur and Winterburn added a further £2m to our 2002/3 costs. As a result of this financial outlay we were negotiating with our banks throughout the summer of

2002 and then suffered greatly by freezing ticket prices for the second year running when our rivals, such as Tottenham Hotspur, were increasing prices by up to 19%. Had we increased our ticket prices we would, undoubtedly, have been able to acquire the additional strikers we required. This is where the board and the fans part company. We believe the Club took enormous financial risks with £14m in the summer of 2002. Many supporters believe the Club suffered 'the effects of non-investment last summer'. Watching this activity were, of course, the banks with commitments of £48m during the course of the 2002/3 season and feeling most reluctant to see the additional expenditure go beyond £14m. In the end they acquiesced and the figure moved on to £17m when we made our January acquisitions.

Who would run a football club? It is easy to snipe from the sidelines and suggest that we should have invested more heavily in the squad in the summer of 2002, but the reality of the situation is that doing so would have either meant a hike in season ticket prices, which would not have gone down well, or financial penalties for over-borrowing compared to income. The board took a risk. It backfired. It is all horribly familiar. That gamble meant the board was left with little choice in the summer of 2003 but to sell the crown jewels.

As a result we found ourselves borrowing the likes of Matthew Kilgallon from Leeds, the aforementioned Alexandersson and Stockdale, as well as Wayne Quinn, from Newcastle (the latter being possibly the most effective of the three) and drafting in seasoned pros like Rob Lee and Kevin Horlock.

Brian Deane, a hardened veteran who had played for the likes of Doncaster, Leeds, Sheffield United and even had a spell at Benfica, joined on a free transfer from Leicester City. That was where we were at.

The Legacy of Barry Green had recently appeared on the shelves and the publishers arranged for a signing session at the club shop before the home game against West Bromwich Albion.

To save a few quid I decided to get the coach down to London for the game, confident that if I got an early one I would be there in good time to sign the 150 books Gary Firmager, the editor of the fanzine *Over Land and Sea*, had purchased, and spend a good hour at the club shop.

The journey was a nightmare however, and after being stuck in a traffic jam on the M1 we were then waiting for another hour at motorway services for the relief driver to turn up, who had been stuck in the same traffic jam. I wondered if Terry Brown also ran National Express.

The coach arrived at Golders Green at about 1 p.m. and I decided to cut my losses and jump on a tube train, arriving at Upton Park around 2 p.m. I hastily signed the books Gary had ordered, which, on reflection, was not a very kind thing to do given the amount of time he had invested in me over the years. But I also felt I owed it to the publishers to fulfil my obligations to them, so with the ink still wet on half of the books, I trotted off to the club shop.

It was gratifying to have so many people come and get their books signed, even more so when they brought copies of the other books too. It was hardly a queue out of the door, but enough people came to massage my ego and make me think the whole exercise had been worthwhile.

The publishers had arranged a seat for me in the press box, which was a bit of a hike from the shop. I just made my seat in time for kick-off and watched West Ham sweep into a 3–0 lead inside the first twenty minutes. Defoe scored in the 1st minute and Brian Deane notched a brace on his debut. This was a doddle. Finally it was clicking. Pardew was on course for his first win.

But then something happened. A mix-up between Christian Dailly and David James allowed Rob Hulse to pull one back. Dailly and James argued long after the incident; not a good sign. When Hulse added a second just before half time it felt, to me at least, that the game was already lost.

I trotted down the stairs in the West Stand to the tunnel area where I had been instructed to be at half time to conduct the 50:50 draw. Jeremy Nicholas, longstanding master of ceremonies on match day at Upton Park, had been a friend since I made three appearances on his Granada Talk show, pitting my West Ham wits against Ray Spiller 'The Statmaster' and narrowly failing on each occasion. He invited me to conduct the draw on the pitch at half time, an honour I could not refuse.

As I went back upstairs I felt an impending sense of doom overwhelm me. When the Baggies scored twice in the second half I was sickened, but not surprised. To add insult to injury, their equaliser was an own goal from Brian Deane. The winner came from Lee Hughes, who two weeks later was involved in a fatal road accident that would see him spend three years in prison for causing death by dangerous driving. Anyone can make mistakes, of course – but legging it from the scene was unlikely to earn him much sympathy.

Defoe was sent off in the first half, which did not help our cause, but we were winning at that stage. The team collapsed as soon as their first goal went in.

I traipsed back down Green Street feeling very low. I had started the day travelling on a £15 coach ticket. Then I had three hours of celebrity. Now I was walking back to Upton Park tube station having watched us throw away a 3–0 lead, and I felt completely hollow and anonymous. I had to struggle back up to Leeds on a coach, a prospect I did not relish.

The fallout from the game was severe. Defoe was facing a five-match suspension for two red cards in the space of a couple of months, and Pardew was left still searching for his first win. The players were arguing among themselves, and defensively we looked just as poor as we had twelve months previously.

The only positive I could see was that we had two weeks until our next game, away at Watford. But in the meantime, there was more trouble at board level.

A group of shareholders calling themselves 'Whistle' wanted to oust Terry Brown, finance director Nick Igoe and managing director Paul Aldridge at the AGM set for 8 December.

According to the BBC website, Whistle believed it had enough support to force a vote at the AGM, but the club insisted it was too late, offering instead to call an EGM for the proposed vote to take place.

To me this seemed like a confident move by the board – it could have hidden behind the rules of the Companies Act to wriggle out of facing a vote altogether but offered to arrange an EGM instead.

Whistle said in a statement on 7 November 2003:

> It is important that the directors are aware that we, the shareholders, are not satisfied in the way the company is being run. We strongly urge you to support the Motion by signing and returning the enclosed Notice of Motion to the company no later than 15th November 2003 and make every effort to attend the AGM to make your feelings known.

Familiar? Whistle wanted to install Trevor Brooking in place of Brown, Igoe and Aldridge, who they blamed for the club's £44 million debts, but on the surface there appeared to be little interest from Brooking in taking on such a role, just as there hadn't been in managing first team affairs. In any event, Brooking left his role as a non-executive director on 27 November to take up a new role at the FA as Director of Football Development.

Pardew's search for a first win continued with two more draws: first, a dull, muddy goalless affair against Watford at Vicarage Road. The weekend would be more memorable for Jonny Wilkinson's last-gasp drop goal which won the Rugby World Cup for England against Australia, and my spectacular effort at hanging the kitchen door.

The second was a 1–1 draw against Wimbledon in the bizarre surroundings of the National Hockey Stadium in Milton Keynes. Now there's a thought. Why on earth would any quasi-successful football team move stadium to a place not designed for football? Shocking.

In between the two games Marlon Harewood signed from

Nottingham Forest for £500,000. This was more like it, in my opinion. Harewood was a young, powerful, maverick striker, painfully popular with the Forest fans who were devastated to see him go. This was better than loaning someone who couldn't get into the Middlesbrough, Leeds or Everton first XI.

Harewood made his debut in the draw with Wimbledon and immediately looked at home, even if Wimbledon – who actually were at home – didn't.

I was looking forward to seeing him make his home debut against Wigan at Upton Park on 29 November. I had a signing session at the Newham Bookshop on Barking Road, without doubt one of the finest bookshops in the country, and this year celebrating its fortieth anniversary. It is as much a part of West Ham United's history as Nathan's or the Boleyn Pub. If you are ever in the area, and I know many of you do still go there, it is well worth patronising.

Not wanting to risk National Express coach travel again, I drove down, this time with the unmentionable ex, as my publishers, Goal!, had arranged for us to stay in one of the hotel rooms at the Boleyn Ground after the game. I met Steve Blowers and Tony MacDonald from Goal! in the bookshop and we had another successful signing session, but at 2 p.m. I was naturally feeling thirsty and we decided to squeeze in a few beers.

Steve and Tony had again arranged press passes for us in the West Stand upper tier. The passes were not numbered, so we sat where we liked and took up two front row seats.

Normally I would go and have a quick pee before a game starts, but we were running late and the game was about to kick off as we sat down, so I thought, I'll go when there was a quiet period during the first half.

The seats had little fold-down tables for the journalists to use, and no sooner had we taken our places than a man with a big suitcase full of broadcasting equipment plonked himself down in the aisle seat next to us and proceeded to set up like a radio ham. Aerials everywhere. The press box was beginning to fill up and I felt a little trapped, as my bladder began to fill and all around us people started broadcasting. There was a local radio station from Wigan behind us and Capital Radio to our left. All the seats to our right were occupied by people nattering away on the radio.

By the time Kevin Horlock had put us 1–0 up I was starting to feel a bit queasy and was in quite a bit of discomfort. I didn't feel I could disturb these guys mid flow: 'And there's a beautiful pass out to the right wing and oh, hang on a sec, I've just got to let this guy go past for a piss.' Doesn't work like that.

So I tied a knot in it and watched the minutes of the first half drag by. When Harewood's low, hard cross from the right side of the penalty area was bundled into his own goal by Wigan defender Jason Jarrett I let out an involuntary yelp, and probably a little bit of wee.

Tomáš Řepka got himself involved in a touchline spat with Wigan manager Paul Jewell and Matt Jackson got his marching orders with a straight red for a horrendous two-footed challenge on Hayden Mullins two minutes before the break. While both were entertaining, I was mindful of the fact this would undoubtedly result in unwanted additional minutes at the end of the half.

When the half time whistle blew, I climbed over the poor Capital Radio commentator and headed for the bogs with a bladder the size of a watermelon. Funny how after all that, you can't always go? I did though; enough to irrigate the Sahara Desert for a month. We picked less confined seats for the second half and were able to enjoy seeing Harewood score the third from the penalty spot and a sublime fourth, lobbing the goalkeeper when put through. Both goals came after Wigan had been reduced to nine men, Lee McCulloch sent off on 50 minutes for a second bookable offence.

As for me at half time, it seemed that now the seal had been broken, so to speak, the wins for West Ham would start to flow.

After attending the post-match press conference, I went downstairs to check into the West Ham hotel. We would not be able to take our room until about 8 p.m. as the rooms were executive boxes by day on a Saturday. They had to wait for the guests to leave, then clean all the prawn sandwiches off the carpet and turn it into a hotel room. I wanted to check in and get the key so we could go off for a bite to eat and come back later.

As I stood in the queue, who should be in front of me, but none other than Sir Geoff Hurst. I have never been one to strike up conversations with anyone in a queue, let alone people who have scored hat-tricks in World Cup finals, so I said nothing. When he got to the front of the queue the receptionist looked at him for about five seconds and asked: 'What's your name sir?'

I let out an involuntary snort. Sir Geoff turned around and smiled at me, shrugging his shoulders. I couldn't resist. 'Terrible isn't it, Martin? Can't get the staff.' He frowned and went back to the receptionist.

'Hurst,' he said.

The West Ham hotel was very comfortable, and I had the surreal experience of waking up, pulling back the curtains and seeing Upton Park right there in front of me. My only criticism would be that the branded towels were so thick I couldn't shut my suitcase.

The chance for early revenge against West Bromwich Albion was spurned after taking a 1–0 lead at the Hawthorns through a spectacular Brian Deane strike, only to have it cancelled out by an equally spectacular Hayden Mullins own goal. So far, Mullins was not impressing me, but Harewood looked to be a good prospect; just as well, as it seemed almost certain that Jermain Defoe would not be around come the end of January, confirmed somewhat indiscreetly by chairman Terry Brown at the AGM which, predictably enough, ended with everyone in the same place they started in.

Defeat at home to Stoke in the next game deepened the gloom: the team lacked balance and drive, and seemed bereft of ideas. And going 2–0 down at home to Sunderland in the next game did not help. Jason McAteer and John Oster scored after, dare I say it, calamitous mistakes by David James. He, too, looked to be on his way, and I could not have been happier at the prospect at that time.

West Ham were showing occasional flashes of brilliance but no consistency. Against Sunderland they turned around the 2–0 deficit to win 3–2, courtesy of two goals from Defoe and a late winner from Ian Pearce. Sixteen-year-old Chris Cohen made his first team debut in the second half and the future, for a while at least, looked bright: the Hammers were just eight points behind the leaders West Bromwich Albion, who had mysteriously dropped points at home to Crewe.

But the inconsistencies that would mar Pardew's first two seasons returned with a 1–1 draw at Walsall. Jermain Defoe was again sent off and, in the end, West Ham did well to earn a point.

This being Defoe's third red card of the season he was facing a lengthy ban of 5 games. The club appealed, unsuccessfully. This was hardly surprising, as none of the red cards appeared to be erroneous and Defoe simply seemed to prefer not playing until he could get his move. God help the rest of the First Division had he been entirely focused, because even with a half-arsed attitude he managed 15 goals from his 22 appearances.

The inconsistency I mentioned previously had stopped. We finally achieved consistency by failing to win all but 2 of Pardew's first 13 games. The unlucky 13th was the Boxing Day home fixture against Ipswich Town. After taking the lead through Defoe, Ipswich striker Pablo Couñago scored twice, first from the penalty spot, and shortly after from open play, both goals coming in the last ten minutes.

I had been in London for Christmas and had been at the game, shaking my head as I walked away from Upton Park and thinking that promotion was a distant dream. West Ham should have been the force to be reckoned with in the league that year, but they still struggled on with the likes of Kevin Horlock in midfield and a bench that consisted of a half-fit Don Hutchison, a half-talented Neil Mellor and the hardly talented Robbie Stockdale, who had returned on loan from Middlesbrough to highlight our desperate shortcomings.

Something had to change. Pardew had to be allowed to design the team himself and make signings. That meant something had to give. That meant selling Jermain Defoe to Tottenham. He played his final game in a West Ham shirt at the City Ground, Nottingham, on 28 December 2003. Naturally, he scored, as he did in his first game at Walsall in September 2000. Overall his career record at West Ham was impressive. In just over three years he had made 72 starts and 33 sub appearances (a total of 105) and scored 41 goals. Say what you like about him, that was a good return. I only mention his sub appearances because he scored 10 goals coming on from the bench. I'm not sure if that's a club record, but it has to be up there.

Defoe encapsulated everything that was apparently wrong with the modern game. There had been controversy around him right from the start as he joined our youth ranks from Charlton Athletic and cannot therefore technically be described as 'home produced', although 'home finished' might be a suitable epithet.

His handling, or, it seems, his representatives' handling of his situation following relegation did not endear him to the crowd. For his final eight months at the club his relationship with the fans was fractious at best. Although Defoe has gone on to have two spells at Tottenham, he has also shown himself to be a decent man and accepted his shortcomings over the way he behaved at West Ham, unlike his predecessor Paul Ince, who failed to realise exactly what he had done wrong in our eyes and steadfastly refused to apologise.

Defoe's relationship with young Bradley Lowery, the Sunderland fan who tragically died from cancer aged six in July 2017, cannot have failed to soften even his hardest critic.

In December 2003, however, we still had mixed feelings as he scored his final goal in the 2–0 win at Nottingham Forest, with Marlon Harewood bagging the opener against his former club.

2003 ended with West Ham in 7th and, somehow, despite failing to win 15 of our opening 26 league games, we were still in reach of a play-off place, with funds to come and badly needed new blood to be injected.

4

TAKE ME TO THE CLOUDS ABOVE

BRADFORD CITY 1, WEST HAM UNITED 2
FOOTBALL LEAGUE FIRST DIVISION, 7 FEBRUARY 2004
Dad's Army. *Seriously BBC, is that the best*
you can do on a Saturday night?

2004 kicked off with a third round FA Cup tie away at Wigan. Not the most inspiring of prospects, but West Ham won 2–1 with Hayden Mullins's first for West Ham and David Connolly stepping up to replace Defoe – and not seeming to whinge about it too much. Rightly so: not being in the team at the expense of a Defoe or a Harewood was a totally different matter to being dropped to the bench for an on-loan Mellor.

Wigan had not covered themselves in glory on the ticketing front, insisting that West Ham fans could pay on the turnstile, then twenty-four hours before kick-off stating it was an all-ticket match. As it turned out, fans were able to purchase tickets over the telephone through West Ham and collect them at the ticket office at the JJB. A storm in a teacup really.

The draw for the fourth round paired us with temporary Premier League side Wolverhampton Wanderers at Molineux, the game moved to the Sunday to avoid potential clashes between West Ham and Millwall fans, who had been due at Telford on the same day. Madness.

Our progress in the league continued to be an unmitigated disaster, and we suffered another home defeat, this time to Preston North End. After taking the lead, this time with a very well-taken strike by David Connolly, we still lost 2–1. It almost seemed that taking the lead was a dangerous thing to do, particularly at home.

In an effort to release funds, England goalkeeper David James was sold for Manchester City in a deal supposedly valued at around £1.5 million and Ian Pearce was allowed to go to Fulham, after allegedly falling out with Alan Pardew. Defenders Andy Melville and Jon Harley came in the other direction. Anthony Barness also joined on loan from Bolton Wanderers, but was recalled twenty-four hours later by Sam Allardyce citing a defensive crisis. Defoe remained at West Ham but seemed certain to leave once he had served out his suspension. For now, at least, his chickens appeared to be coming home to roost.

I had recently been in touch with my old mate Simon Smith (minus his amazing dancing bear). You will remember he was a serving soldier based in Bosnia at the time my first book came out. He wrote to me to tell me how much he enjoyed it and we remained friends. He was a bit down on his luck, and we arranged to meet at the game at Bradford City on 7 February. Simon had been back in touch after showing me some rather unpleasant comments on the unofficial West Ham website Knees Up Mother Brown (KUMB) about my last book and inviting me to respond.

I managed to squeeze in West Ham's visit to Sheffield United on 17 January. Melville and Harley made their debuts in the Saturday evening kick-off that had been switched for Uncle Rupert's benefit. It was strange. I was still making quite a few games, but it wasn't enjoyable. I drove to the game on my own. I went straight to the game and came straight home afterwards. The unmentionable ex thought she was being accommodating by allowing – even suggesting – that I go to more games, but she didn't understand that watching football is about more than just attending and observing the match.

To me, the match has always been the focal point of the day, but not necessarily the most enjoyable part. It is the reason friends gravitate towards each other. The thing we all had in common. But the enjoyable part was the camaraderie, the banter. I had none of that after moving north. The unmentionable ex did not understand that I had no desire to park up at a quarter to three to watch the game then come home at a quarter to five. And as for watching a game on television, why on earth would I want to watch all that talking beforehand and afterwards? Going over it again and again. This is not a trip to the cinema where the most enjoyable part of the experience will be the film. Football is not like that. It's the overall experience, the creation of memories. People either get it or they don't. It's nothing to do with your gender, it's to do with the way your brain is wired.

Although the game at Bramall Lane was exciting, it was just the game; there were no pre-match beers, no taking the piss, no in-jokes and no clowning around. Well, there was a bit, mainly in West Ham's defence. We came from behind and raced into a 3–1 lead, with goals from Harewood, Carrick and a screamer on his debut from Harley. But the defensive fragilities exposed themselves again, and after pulling it back to 2–3, Sheffield United had a penalty saved by goalkeeper Steven Bywater, given his chance after the departure of James. That just served to energise the Blades further, and they threw the kitchen sink at us in added time and grabbed an equaliser through Phil Jagielka. I left the ground dejected, got straight in the car and went straight home.

Three more goals followed at Wolves, but this time it was enough to win the game, and we finished on 3–1. As at Bramall Lane the score was 3–1 at the end of the first half, but this time it stayed that way. West Ham were then to be paired in the last 16 with either Premier League Fulham or Everton, who had to replay their fourth-round tie.

Before the Wolves game Pardew made a double signing from Wimbledon, picking up their highly rated youngsters Nigel Reo-Coker and Adam Nowland. They were cup-tied and unable to play against Wolves, but made their debuts in the home game against Rotherham at Upton Park on 31 January. The game finished 2–1 to West Ham, and I found myself thinking that perhaps now we had the right blend of young new blood and experience to take us forward.

Transfer deadline day saw the expected departure of Defoe to Tottenham, and at the time we thought they deserved each other. Bobby Zamora came to us in a player-plus-cash deal and again we were underwhelmed. Jobi McAnuff, another promising teenager followed, and became the third player to join from Wimbledon in as many weeks.

Such is the blur surrounding my life at that time that I struggle to remember what happened pre-match against Bradford City at Valley Parade. It was my 'home' game and I had been eagerly anticipating it for weeks. I remember going to the game with the unmentionable ex, but other than that it's all a bit hazy. That is what happens when you don't have enough alcohol before the game, see?

West Ham won the game 2–1 with Zamora making his debut and scoring the first and making the winner for Harewood. We were a bit more whelmed than we had been before the game. After the match we met up with the unmentionable ex's friend Becky, a season ticket holder at Valley Parade, her boyfriend Johnny and Simon Smith (minus his… you get the picture). Simon kipped on our sofa and I took him back to his car the next morning. I don't think I have seen him since in person, but we have kept in touch. He called me after he was fired from *The Apprentice* in 2008. I thought, I know that bloke, he's kipped on my sofa!

The win at Valley Parade saw us creep back into the play-off spots but the inconsistency was the only consistent thing about West Ham at that time. A 0–0 draw in the fifth round of the FA cup against Fulham at their temporary home of Loftus Road (a game in which almost nothing noteworthy happened other than another ticketing fiasco) set us up for a winnable replay at Upton Park. I don't know if it was the prospect of another trip to Old Trafford in the sixth round or a conscious decision to 'concentrate on the league', but a game we could have won was lost 3–0 after goals from Brian McBride, Barry Hales and a certain Luís Boa Morte. After the departure of David James, Stephen Bywater was the only senior goalkeeper remaining at the club, so Pardew brought in Portsmouth and former Newcastle goalkeeper Pavel

Srníček on loan as cover. Pavel was a good keeper, but made only 3 appearances against Millwall, Derby and Crystal Palace before moving on to Beira-Mar in Portugal. Srníček tragically died from a heart attack suffered while out jogging in December 2015. He was just forty-seven years old.

In between we drew at Carrow Road against Norwich, with Marlon Harewood quickly becoming a favourite after scoring a great goal with a tremendous drive from outside the box. Zamora scored again in a home win against Cardiff before taking on Burnley at Turf Moor.

Burnley, like Sheffield, Leeds and Manchester, was a nice easy ground for me to get to from Bradford, and as I worked in Manchester I had a number of Burnley supporters as colleagues and I was invited by one of them, Stephen Green, to stay at his place the night of the game, and by Duncan Spencer to drink at Burnley Cricket Club, which he had once represented, before the game. Bit of a dark horse was our Duncan. It was only when chatting to him some years later I found out he made 92 not out for Burnley against Accrington in June 1991 when playing against a young Shane Warne. He also racked up a half-century against him later the same season.

I always find games against Burnley and Aston Villa away a little confusing, especially as we were playing in the navy-blue away kit that I had yet to welcome into my heart. David Connolly scored from the penalty spot to earn another draw.

Still in 5th place and still looking good for the play-offs, but another draw, this time 0–0 at home to Walsall, was causing unrest and nervousness among the fans. Mind you, 33,177 turned up to watch the Walsall draw; the fans deserved Premier League football even if the team didn't.

The 29,818 who turned up the following Tuesday were treated to a 5–0 thumping of Wimbledon, which was hardly surprising as we had nicked their three best players over the previous few weeks, and they were destined to finish bottom of the league. A hat-trick from Matthew Etherington and one apiece from Reo-Coker and Zamora sealed victory and pushed

West Ham up to 3rd, which hardly seemed merited, but other than West Bromwich Albion and Norwich City, everyone else in the league seemed hell-bent on failure. It was a question of who would be the least crap in the run-in.

Home form turned out to be the key. We won 4 and drew 1 of our remaining 5 home games, 4–2 against Crewe, 2–1 against Gillingham, 0–0 against Derby County, 2–0 versus Coventry City and 4–0 against Watford. Away form was atrocious though, and apart from a 2–0 win at Stoke City on 27 April we contrived to lose 2–0 at Sunderland and Reading, 4–1 at Millwall and 1–0 at Crystal Palace.

On the final day of the league campaign a Brian Deane goal gave us a 1–1 draw at Wigan and secured 4th spot. Somehow.

The play-offs it was then. More by luck than judgement, it has to be said, and as a result of being slightly less rubbish than twenty other teams. Ipswich were slightly more rubbish than us and were our semi-final opponents, while Sunderland who were slightly less rubbish than us had finished 3rd on 79 points, 5 ahead of us, and faced Crystal Palace who had finished 6th, but of all the teams in the play-off spots Palace had the best run of form going into the competition with six wins and only one defeat in their final 8 matches.

That turned out to be crucial, and despite finishing 6 points behind Sunderland after 46 league games, Palace beat Sunderland over two legs to reach the final.

We faced Ipswich at Portman Road and looked tired as we lost the first leg 1–0.

I could not make the second leg or any potential final as I was due to go off on holiday to Santorini. I asked for regular text updates from friends attending the second leg. We had arrived at our accommodation late after long delays and, as Santorini was two hours ahead of the UK, by the time the game entered its final phase I was in bed, with my phone set to ring when I got an update. I will never forget the ringtone that night. It played the theme tune from *Phoenix Nights*, and now every time I hear that I think of the play-off semi-final against Ipswich in 2004.

It rang three times. Once for the fantastic drive by Matthew Etherington to level the scores, once for the towering header by Christian Dailly that put us ahead on aggregate and once to confirm the game had ended 2–0 and we had gone through 2–1.

What the phone didn't tell me was about the atmosphere that night, about how special the goals had been or and how sad I was going to be in years to come that I had not been there.

The same cannot be said for the final, played at the Millennium Stadium in Cardiff on 29 May. I was still in Santorini, but was confident of finding a bar that would be showing the game. Alas not. I had found the FA Cup final between Manchester United and Millwall the weekend before, albeit with Greek commentary, but the day before the play-off final I spent a fruitless afternoon wandering up and down the main strip in Kamari trying to find a bar that would be showing the game.

Technology in 2004 was not quite as advanced as now, and the internet, while available on my phone, appeared more like the old teletext format and cost a small fortune every time it connected.

The day of the game, it clouded over after two weeks of almost unbroken sunshine. I had a sense of foreboding.

I tried to occupy myself reading, listening to music, pacing up and down and basically making a complete nuisance of myself, but in the end I could wait no longer and logged in to find we had lost 1–0. A pretty poor game by all accounts and in the end, our inconsistency over the course of the season meant we probably deserved no more. But it's always hard to lose a final, and the manner of the victory over Ipswich in the semi-final meant that losing in Cardiff was a bitter pill to swallow for the thousands who had made their way there.

Fortunately, as I have said before, football is about more than the ninety minutes, and those I have spoken to since still talk about the three Millennium Stadium dates in 2004–06 as being among their most treasured memories in football.

As for me, I will always have the *Phoenix Nights* ringtone.

5

THUNDERBIRDS

WEST HAM UNITED 1, READING 0
FOOTBALL LEAGUE CHAMPIONSHIP, 10 AUGUST 2004
When people say, 'Can I get?' instead of
'May I have?' I really hate that.
'Can I get a cappuccino please?'
'No, I work here; I'll get it for you.'

With the play-off final taking place on 29 May and the 2004/05 season due to start on 10 August there was not much time for the team to feel sorry for itself.

Pardew spent the summer revising the squad. David Connolly went off to Leicester City. Michael Carrick confirmed he would not be signing a new contract and would be leaving. He was being courted by a number of clubs including Portsmouth and West Bromwich Albion, but no deal had materialised before the start of the season. Brian Deane was allowed to leave. Kevin Horlock also moved on. Jobi McAnuff signed for Cardiff City after the start of the season for £300,000.

Coming in were goalkeeper Jimmy Walker, midfielders Luke Chadwick and Carl Fletcher, and forward Serhiy Rebrov. None of them exactly got the fans excited.

The signing of Teddy Sheringham was also greeted less than enthusiastically by Hammers fans. Many could not see the point of replacing the ageing Deane with another player nearing retirement, particularly given his connections with Millwall, Tottenham and Manchester United. It was going to take some work for Sheringham to win over sceptical fans. However, he made the right noises on the official website:

I'm delighted to be here. I spoke with Alan Pardew last season when he was manager at Reading and was very impressed with him, so when the chance came to join him at West Ham United I jumped at it.

'I was a Hammers fan as a youngster and stood on the old North bank with my big brother watching the likes of Alan Devonshire, Ray Stewart, Billy Jennings and Graham Paddon.

'So, to get the opportunity of playing for this great club after all these years is an honour and I'm sure I will enjoy the season helping the team to achieve their promotion goal.

Okay Teddy, whatever.

I have to admit I was also guilty of thinking this was a colossal waste of time. Sheringham had signed on a free transfer and was therefore likely to be on a significant wedge. Like many others I felt he was likely to only be good for an hour of most games and probably be injured for most of the season. I didn't like him. I didn't like the fact he had been at Millwall previously, I didn't like the way he always looked like he had just got out of bed. I just didn't like him.

The team that lined up at Filbert Street on the opening Saturday of the season therefore was:

Bywater, Řepka, Brevett, Dailly, Melville, Reo-Coker, Mullins, Etherington, Rebrov (McAnuff), Sheringham (Cohen), Harewood (Zamora).

Pardew was beginning to mould a team with his own signings, but it seemed to me those signing on the whole were not good enough, and we still had the likes of Dailly, Brevett and Melville in defence who were reliable, although ageing, and not exactly pacey. Řepka was always an accident waiting to happen. Mullins was still yet to impress.

I wasn't exactly fired with enthusiasm for a push at promotion when the game ended 0–0. Dion Dublin was sent off on his debut for Leicester, and even before Brevett followed him an hour later West Ham failed to capitalise on their advantage on a very hot afternoon.

The board continued to scratch at the irritation that was WHISTLE, although suing three of its members did seem a little over the top. Shareholder and WHISTLE member Barrie Abrahams and two others were served writs for libel, having been plainly critical of the board in an open letter. Despite the costs involved in preparing a defence, WHISTLE vowed to carry on in its fight to oust the incumbent.

The following Tuesday saw the opening home game of the campaign against Reading. This also looked like ending 0–0 until Luke Chadwick provided the only real bit of magic of the evening, cutting in from the right to pull the ball back for Sheringham to score his first goal for West Ham. Always loved that Teddy Sheringham.

Tottenham continued to assemble a team of former Hammers. The sincerest form of flattery I suppose. Carrick finally left for White Hart Lane, joining former team mates Frédéric Kanouté and Jermain Defoe. The value of the deal was thought to be around £3 million as it was undisclosed. This seemed low even for fourteen years ago, given Carrick's pedigree.

However, he had spent a year in the second flight not pulling up any trees, and we were under pressure to sell as he had indicated he would not sign a new deal the following year. It was £3 million now or nothing in twelve months.

The optimistic mood following an unbeaten start with no goals conceded was shattered the following Sunday by a 1–3 defeat at home to Wigan Athletic. The defence was still causing headaches. It was clear we could not continue with the ageing legs of Andy Melville and Rufus Brevett in front of an inexperienced goalkeeper like Stephen Bywater. But no new defensive signings came.

At Gresty Road the following week West Ham raced into a 3–0 lead. There was, it seemed nothing wrong with the offensive aspect of the team, a brace from Sheringham and a screamer from Brevett putting West Ham 3–0 up at the break. But as the game wore on the defensive frailties returned and Dean Ashton, who had been a target for Pardew in the summer, scored twice for Crewe to reduce the arrears and leave us hanging on.

Despite only one defeat in the opening four league fixtures enthusiasm among the fans was hard to find. In the Carling Cup, West Ham entertained Southend United in the second round. Although the game was won comfortably 2–0 with both goals from Marlon Harewood, the crowd was only 16,910 with 4,000 accounted for by the visitors.

It didn't help that there seemed to be a game every other day, and the quality was less than top notch. I reasoned it was nothing to worry about too much and recalled being in a crowd of just 10,896 in October 1983 when West Ham beat Bury 10–0 in a League Cup match. There wasn't anything much wrong with the entertainment provided by that team.

The 2004 Olympic Games in Athens were in full swing and the game against Burnley the following Saturday coincided with Kelly Holmes winning her second gold medal. It seemed most had decided to stay at home to watch that instead, as the attendance struggled at just over 22,000. Those who were there saw Adam Nowland score his first and only goal for West Ham in a 1–0 win.

There was so much to be positive about. We had played 5 league games, won 3, drawn 1 and lost 1. We had also won the only cup match placed before us. But despite that reasonable record, it was just that: reasonable. Only good enough for 6th place in the table. West Ham fans quite rightly expected better.

It seemed that we were due for more of the same from the previous season, one step forward and two steps back. A step back at Coventry on the August bank holiday Monday as Sheringham scored again but we succumbed 1–2, followed by a morale-boosting win at promotion rivals Sheffield United, Sheringham scoring again and Harewood also scoring on a beautifully sunny afternoon in South Yorkshire. What should have been an easy home victory over Rotherham came next. The Millers were destined to finish bottom of the league on just 29 points, but we made rather hard work of it, only winning 1–0.

Another draw at home to Ipswich saw new signing Malky Mackay score the opener, only for it to be cancelled out yet again. Teddy Sheringham missed a first half penalty and we had a couple of efforts cleared off the line, but it wasn't enough to win. The game had a little extra spice to it, following Ipswich captain Jim Magilton's pre-match comments, suggesting that Alan Pardew had adopted a big club mentality since joining West Ham, which wasn't merited.

In hindsight, it would appear that Pardew was something of a cocky character. Steve Bacon, the former club photographer, certainly did not mince his words in his autobiography, saying that Pardew used to call himself 'the King'. Jeremy Nicholas was similarly disparaging in his book.

Magilton said of Pardew:

> No disrespect to Reading, he went to a bigger club with higher expectations and suddenly he found his voice and developed automatic gums … I think Alan Pardew makes a lot of noise.

Ipswich had the last laugh with Couñago once again spoiling the party, as he had done the previous Boxing Day. The Ipswich team that day, managed by Joe Royle, had last season's midfield regular Kevin Horlock in the starting eleven.

The League Cup continued with a 3–2 win over Notts County at Upton Park, again followed by a meagre crowd of just 11,111 who saw Zamora score twice and a goal for Serhiy Rebrov. Chelsea awaited at Stamford Bridge in the fourth round.

We faced Nottingham Forest at the City Ground, losing 1–2 to a last-minute goal from Marlon King, leaving us back in 6th place in the table, something a 1–1 draw up the road at Derby the following Wednesday did not improve on. Chris Powell, Calum Davenport and Malky Mackay had all been drafted into defence, but with the exception of Davenport who was just twenty-two, the others were ageing defenders seeing out their playing careers and, as far as I could see, had little to offer.

October began with a 1–0 win over Wolverhampton Wanderers at Upton Park. Teddy Sheringham came on as a sub for Bobby Zamora and grabbed the winner 15 minutes from time.

It was a superb goal, chipping the ball on the run over the leg of a young Joleon Lescott, and finishing smartly in the bottom corner. The win pushed us back up into 5th, but the league table was shaping up with Wigan and Sunderland looking already like favourites for automatic promotion. Something would have to change dramatically if West Ham were to finish in the top two.

With London winning the right to stage the Olympics in 2012, eight years hence, speculation was rife that after the games, the purpose-built stadium might be taken over by West Ham or Tottenham Hotspur. The *London Evening Standard* reported the views of then Mayor of London, Ken Livingstone, on 6 October, however:

> In a bid to help attract other international events to the city, officials have abandoned plans of leasing the stadium in the way the Commonwealth Stadium in Manchester passed to Manchester City in 2002.
>
> 'Sadly, West Ham will not get the stadium,' Livingstone told a London 2012 fringe meeting. 'Instead, we will scale the stadium down to around 25,000 or 30,000 seats and treat it as an athletics facility.'
>
> Livingstone believes that a lasting athletics legacy in the capital would be a more attractive option for International Olympic Committee members when they come to examine London's bid in February.
>
> 'It will engage the IOC because it's the sort of facility that will attract world-class sporting events to London in the future,' he said.
>
> The mayor, whose office has agreed to underwrite the upkeep of Olympic facilities after the games in order to ensure the bid leaves a viable legacy in London, said the stadium would also house a sports academy.

And many people said thank God for that.

The unmentionable ex and I had sold the flat and moved into a two-bed terrace around the corner, which appeared to be a step up, but in fact turned out to be a nightmare. The cellar flooded every time it rained and the garden at the back provided a right of way for all the other neighbours, which some assumed meant their kids could also use it as a playground. Soon after moving in we knew it was not going to be home for very long. Sold a dream, delivered a nightmare.

I had also had enough of commuting from Bradford to Manchester every day, and although I loved working for the CIS I said my farewells and went off to work for a local family-run firm who packaged and distributed payment protection insurance plans for secured loans. PPI seemed okay, no problems there – what could possibly go wrong?

6

RADIO

*'He gave 110 per cent.' How can anyone possibly
give more than everything? Preposterous.*

I made my first game of the season, meeting up with Stuart the
QPR fan and his son Callum at the Argyll Arms at Oxford
Circus for a few pre-match pints. Stuart the QPR fan has been a
constant friend for nearly thirty years now. Although we don't
see each other very often, whenever we meet up it's like we just
saw each other last weekend. We also met his friend and former
neighbour Mike 'I nearly died' McManus, who had earned the
nickname on the occasion of Callum's christening when he cut
his lip on a chipped mug and continued, throughout the day, to
remind us of the sacrifice he had made to be present.

With me living in Bradford and Stuart in Peterborough it
was always going to be difficult to see each other on a regular
basis, but any QPR v. West Ham fixture was always pencilled
into the diaries quickly when the fixtures were released. Back
then there was less likelihood of plans being disrupted by Uncle
Rupert, so we were able to enjoy our pre-match pints and head
off to the game at 3 p.m. on the Saturday, like we always used to.

Sadly, the match was nothing to write home about. QPR had
just been promoted and gave us a bit of a battering to be fair.
How it only ended up 1–0 I don't know, but we offered virtually
nothing in attack, and the familiar stench of Deep Heat, Sana-
togen and Werther's Originals wafted across every time one of
our defenders creaked past.

Two home games followed, and two victories. First up Stoke City and a 2–0 win courtesy (mostly) of Harewood, with a falling shot on the turn and Sheringham flicking on a low, hard cross with the back of his heel. Then a routine 3–1 win over Gillingham, for whom a youngster by the name of Matt Jarvis came on as a substitute.

The League Cup tie at Stamford Bridge had been eagerly awaited, not necessarily because we felt we would get a result, but because it was a chance to have a pop at former players Lampard, Cole and Johnson. Maybe not so much Cole and Johnson, but certainly Lampard had made himself unpopular with West Ham fans by failing to show any loyalty to the club when his dad and uncle were shown the door. He was on the next train out.

Chelsea reaped the benefits of West Ham investing years nurturing a lazy, luxury player in its midfield so he could become world class, just in time for him to fuck off and play for the Blues.

The Chelsea fans had also had their noses put out of joint because we had been allocated the whole of the lower tier of the Matthew Harding stand. Some season ticket holders had to move to accommodate us and they didn't like it one little bit. As the game wore on and the likes of Cole, Lampard, Arjen Robben, Scott Parker, William Gallas and Mateja Kežman could not find a way through, the tension started to mount. However, Kežman eventually took a chance to make it 1–0 and, despite battling bravely, we never really looked like scoring. The highlight of the evening, however, was a penalty save by Jimmy Walker from Fat Frank. Řepka had made a suicidal challenge on Robben in the box and looked surprised when a penalty was awarded. Robben just looked for his legs. Years later in his autobiography, Řepka admitted he once deliberately gave away a penalty while playing in the Czech Republic, to ensure former club Sparta Prague did not win the league. It all starts to make sense now. As if further evidence of his madness were needed, he was sentenced to six months in prison by a court in Brno, Czech Republic in August

2018 for posting adverts offering sexual favours from his ex-wife. It seems he lived his life the same way he played football: recklessly and with scant regard for anyone else.

Walker saved, making him an instant cult hero; the West Ham fans cheered, but only an Anton Ferdinand effort that clipped the bar in the final minute showed any signs of forcing extra time. In the end it was comfortable for the Blues – more so than the scoreline suggested.

At Plymouth Argyle, Steve Lomas found himself on the score-sheet for the first time in over two years, but again it was only good enough for a 1–1 draw. Cardiff then thumped West Ham 4–1 at Ninian Park. This was a result out of the blue, pardon the pun. Cardiff had been struggling at the foot of the table and had been without a win in 5 matches. You know who they needed to play. Harewood brought it back to 3–1 from the penalty spot, but former Hammer Jobi McAnuff ended the rout.

An early chance for revenge against QPR was taken, winning at home 2–1 with goals from Marlon Harewood sandwiching an equaliser from Kevin McLeod.

Still we sought consistency and still it evaded us. The next game at home to Brighton ended in defeat without scoring. Then Millwall beat us again at the New Den, a game notable only for the sole appearance of Argentinian Mauricio Taricco at left-back (although curiously wearing the number nine shirt). Taricco lasted just 27 minutes before sustaining an injury which we did not know at the time would end his career. Generously, Taricco agreed to rip up his contract. Not many players would show such attitude today. I am sure his insurers looked after him, but nevertheless, he could have taken every penny the club owed him had he chosen to.

Taricco had been brought in because Davenport was injured, so then Darren Powell came in on loan to replace him from Crystal Palace. He had also made his debut at Millwall, and made his home debut against Watford scoring in a 3–2 win that had seen West Ham 0–2 down. A step forward, which was followed by another step forward with a 2–0 win against high-flying Sunderland at the Stadium of Light, but then a disappointing home draw with Leeds United and defeat away at Preston. Still, somehow we were in 6th place, and even more surprisingly, we were in with a shout of the play-offs, but it all seemed highly unsatisfactory.

7

DO THEY KNOW IT'S CHRISTMAS?

WEST HAM 3, NOTTINGHAM FOREST 2
FOOTBALL LEAGUE CHAMPIONSHIP, 26 DECEMBER 2004
People who start the answer to a question with the word, 'So'.
'How did you get here today?'
'So, we took the A23…'
Boils my piss, it really does.

I went down for London to visit my family for Christmas alone, as was now becoming routine, and as I drove back up the motorway on Boxing Day I listened to match reports of a 3–2 win over Nottingham Forest, but it was hard to feel the elation of another home win grasped from the jaws of defeat when the radio was also giving out such devastating news about the tsunami hitting countries surrounding the Indian Ocean.

Waves of between 50 and 100 feet smashed into the coastlines of countries including India, Sri Lanka, Thailand, the Maldives and Malaysia, causing devastating damage and huge loss of life. It is still not known how many people died as a direct result of the impact of the aftermath, but estimates are around 230,000. It was not a day for congratulating myself on my football team winning 3–2.

I made it down to Rotherham a few days later for the game at Millmoor. It was dire. As mentioned previously, Rotherham were appalling that season, but took a 2–0 lead and only two late penalties earned us a point. West Ham finished 2004 in 7th, outside the play-off places. 2005 was going to have to offer up something better if we were to win promotion.

It started positively enough with a 2–0 win at Ipswich but

then Sheffield United came to Upton Park and turned us over by the same score. The third round of the FA Cup saw us pitted against Norwich City at Upton Park. Norwich had been promoted the season before but were struggling; it showed as we won 1–0 with a Harewood goal. The indifferent form continued though. A 4–2 reverse at Molineux against Wolves saw Paul Ince score, much to our displeasure, then a 2–1 loss at home to Derby County, which I watched in a pub in Yorkshire with a fellow Hammer I had bumped into quite by chance. West Ham here, as they say, West Ham there.

8

LIKE TOY SOLDIERS

SHEFFIELD UNITED 1, WEST HAM UNITED 1
FA CUP 4TH ROUND REPLAY, 13 FEBRUARY 2005
(SHEFFIELD UNITED WIN 3–1 ON PENALTIES)
The Jeremy Kyle Show. Utter tripe. And while I'm at it, tripe too. What
possible excuse can there be for eating tripe in the twenty-first century?

The fourth round of the FA Cup saw us drawn at home to Sheffield United. This was well before the days when there was bad blood between the two clubs, but I still hated them. Right from the time we were 2–0 up at Bramall Lane in 1994 and lost 3–2. It was never a corner in the last minute. I'm telling you now. Anyway. The cup game ended 1–1, Harewood's opener equalised in the second half by Phil Jagielka, as he had done a year before. That meant a replay at Bramall Lane, which meant I could go, as Sheffield was just down the road from me.

In the interim we beat Cardiff 1–0 at Upton Park, Carl Fletcher heading a late winner from a Chris Powell cross. Uninspiring, but a vital win, nonetheless.

I went to Bramall Lane with my brother-in-law to be, Andy. He was a Liverpool fan, but despite that took a keen interest in the Hammers through me. So when I told him I had a spare ticket for the game he jumped at the opportunity to come with me, and the unmentionable ex was happy I had a reliable chaperone.

Now I have said in the past how much I hate rolling up at the game fifteen minutes before kick-off and leaving straight after. You will recall I said I like the build-up, the camaraderie, the banter. Well that day I got more than my fair share as we arrived in Sheffield at 10.30 a.m., anticipating an 11.30 kick-off for the benefit of television. As I parked the car I noticed how quiet it was. We arrived at Bramall Lane and the place was deserted. I wondered if I had got the date wrong. Turned out I had merely got kick-off time wrong. It was 4.30 p.m., not 11.30 a.m. Bollocks.

So we kicked our heels waiting for the pubs to open, but in the knowledge that I couldn't indulge too much as I had to drive home. It was a long few hours, made worse by the match going into extra time following yet another 1–1 draw, then a penalty shoot-out which we inevitably lost. The Blades had taken an early lead through Andy Liddell, but on 63 minutes West Ham levelled through a Sheringham penalty after Chris Morgan fouled Marlon Harewood in the box. Morgan was sent off so we had a one-man advantage for the rest of normal time and the whole of extra time, but could not find a way through.

Sheringham then missed his spot kick in the shootout, as did Carl Fletcher and Harewood. Mark Noble scored our sole penalty. Among the successful Sheffield United scorers was Jon Harley, who had scored such a belter for us at Bramall Lane the year before.

Still, a good day of bonding with my soon-to-be brother-in-law, but it wasn't enough, amazingly, to persuade him to switch allegiances. On the journey home I consoled myself that in the fifth round we had been due to face Arsenal at Highbury, something I felt at that stage was best avoided. Concentrate on the league and all that.

This seemed to be the message coming across as the next two league games yielded 6 points with a 5–0 thrashing of Plymouth Argyle at Upton Park and a 1–0 midweek away win at Gillingham. Harewood opened the scoring from the spot against Plymouth, seemingly more accurate without the pressure of a shoot-out. The Plymouth keeper Luke McCormick then diverted the ball into his own goal and Malky Mackay stabbed home a third. Sheringham grabbed a late brace for the most comprehensive win of the season so far.

Gillingham were a different proposition, fighting for their lives at the foot of the table, but the Hammers settled any nerves with Harewood scoring after 13 minutes.

Just when it seemed we would find a run of decent form, we hit another sticky patch and failed to win any of the next 5 games. I went to the Leeds match at Elland Road, travelling the eight miles from Bradford by bus, to see us fairly comprehensively beaten despite Gavin Williams grabbing an unlikely equaliser in spectacular style. The game ended 2–1 to Leeds, but it easily could have been more. We were kept in for half an hour after the game, at which point I was shepherded onto a bus heading to the city centre. I had an almighty struggle persuading the police at Leeds Station I did not require a southbound train the London, but a local bus to Bradford. My London accent did not help, but eventually producing my driving licence with my Bradford address persuaded the plod I was not a threat to society and could be allowed through the cordon.

We lost again to Preston North End for the third time in a row, 2–1 at home, then again to Reading 3–1 at the Madejski. Both these teams were play-off rivals, and following the Reading defeat, we found ourselves in 7th place wondering how we were going to make the top six. And if we did creep in, how would we fare given we had lost so meekly to our close challengers?

The question found no answer following a 1–1 draw at home to Crewe Alexandra and a 2–2 draw at home to Leicester City. We entered April still in 7th, needing a remarkable turnaround in form if we were to stand any chance of promotion.

9

LYLA

Halls of fame. Especially ones which leave out your favourite.

We experienced a remarkable turnaround in form.

Key to this, in my opinion, was the burgeoning partnership of a young centre-back pairing of Anton Ferdinand and Elliott Ward. Ferdinand, of course, was Rio's younger brother, and it was clear he was a talented footballer (even if not to the extent of his older sibling). Ward was another youth-team product who had made his debut in the League Cup win over Southend in August, but did not make his league debut until the 3–1 loss against Reading in March.

Ward and Ferdinand immediately seemed to have a telepathic understanding. This was vital. We already had a good forward line, but we had leaked goals through a creaky and ageing defence all season. Now we had two centre-backs both aged twenty. While experience counts for a lot, sometimes you just have to spend ninety minutes running around a lot.

By the time we faced automatic promotion hopefuls Wigan at the JJB Stadium on 2 April, the defensive line-up had been established with the youthful Ward and Ferdinand in the middle, the experienced Chris Powell at left-back and the nutter that was Tomáš Řepka at right-back.

Řepka was developing something of a cult status at West Ham, which I could not quite fathom. To me he was a walking liability, a red card waiting to happen. A penalty just waiting to be awarded. But Hammers fans love a bit of commitment. It's true we adored Billy Bonds and Julian Dicks before Řepka. But they had talent to make up for an occasional lack of discipline. Řepka was alright at Championship level, but I didn't rate him any higher.

We produced a morale-boosting win at Wigan with Harewood and Sheringham grabbing one each in a 2–1 victory. If you count the draws at home to Crewe and Leicester we only lost one of our final 10 games, and that was to champions Sunderland. But in the meantime, we were still 7th.

I travelled to Burnley unaware of the run we were about to go on. Sheringham walked the ball into an empty net late on to send us into delirium. Coventry were dispatched 3–0 in the next game, which made it 3 wins on the spin. Millwall were their usual awkward selves and stubbornly saw out a 1–1 draw at Upton Park, meaning we did not beat them in any of the four matches we played against them in that period in the second flight.

A 1–0 win against Stoke at the Britannia Stadium picked up the form again – but still we remained 6th. It was between us and Reading for 6th place, and Reading did not blink. They finally lost a match at Cardiff on 23 April, the same day we garnered a point at Brighton, which put us both on 70 points with a goal difference of +10. West Ham sneaked into 6th on goals scored.

The game at home to Sunderland was on a Friday night, and the 2–1 reverse meant we temporarily dropped back into 7th on goal difference. We had to wait and see what Reading did at home to Wolves on the Saturday. Somehow, our closest rivals contrived to lose 1–2 at home to a Wolves team who had nothing to play for. So without playing we sneaked back into 6th.

It came down to the final day. West Ham away at Watford and Reading away at Wigan. The odds were stacked in our favour with Wigan looking to seal promotion in style and Watford wallowing around in 18th place. But this is West Ham we are talking about. All we had to do was match Reading's result. A win still would not guarantee a play-off spot even though we were in 6th place. If Reading won by a bigger margin than we did, they could still take the final available place.

As it happened Reading got spanked 1–3 at Wigan so it didn't matter what we did, as long as we didn't lose at Watford by 3 or more. In the end we won 2–1 at Vicarage road with goals from Harewood from the spot and our new centre-half sensation, Anton Ferdinand.

Now for Ipswich in the play-offs once again.

This time though, we were the in-form team going into the matches, but clearly, as Ipswich had finished 3 places and 12 points ahead of us, missing out on automatic promotion by just 2 points, they had every right to be pissed off when we raced into a 2–0 lead in the first leg of the semi-final at Upton Park, with Harewood and Zamora netting in an exhilarating first 15 minutes which convinced me we were on our way to the final. But despite further chances being created, Ipswich were not killed off and a challenge from, ahem, Tomáš Řepka resulted in a free kick on the edge of the box for Ipswich in the last minute of the first half. Řepka's outstretched leg, the post and Jimmy Walker in goal combined to contrive a goal which did nothing to ease the nerves of the West Ham faithful at half time.

Joe Royle brought on former Hammer Darren Currie, who put in a number of teasing crosses, one of which was eventually converted by Shefki Kuqi.

With the match ending up 2–2, the return leg at Portman Road four days later was looking far from easy. In the event the Hammers won 2–0 with a brace from Bobby Zamora that consisted of two enormously contrasting goals. The first was a simple tap in; the second an exquisitely weighted lobbed volley that quite frankly left me speechless.

That goal has to go down as one of the best ever scored by a West Ham player, particularly give the significance of the occasion. For me, it is up there with Di Canio's strike against Wimbledon, the precision of which was pure class. Unfortunately, Zamora wasn't able to replicate that kind of effort on a regular basis, but when he did get it right it often resulted in a goal of the highest quality.

So West Ham won the tie 4–2 on aggregate and faced Preston

North End in the play-off final at the Millennium Stadium in Cardiff on 30 May. The fact that Preston had completed the double over West Ham and finished one place and two points above us in the league meant nothing as we went head to head in the one-off final.

The game sold out quickly. I was in the country for once, but had been unable to obtain a ticket through the usual channels, not having been a season ticket holder since the 2000/01 season. I had to content myself watching the game in the New Inn in the village of Idle, a suburb of Bradford which boasted an Idle Working Men's Club.

I cannot say I recall much about the game other than it was a cagey affair, and I was not among friends in the pub that day. Not because it was full of Preston fans – the folk of Bradford had no axe to grind either way as a team from Lancashire may as well come from Mars as far as they are concerned.

But at the same time they could not understand my glee, and certainly did not appreciate being showered in beer as Zamora swept home Matthew Etherington's cross for what proved to be the winning goal on 57 minutes to set up a nervous final half an hour.

On the final whistle the relief was palpable. I went home to my two-up two-down in Bradford, feeling distinctly homesick. But I had no time for that. I was getting married.

10

DARE

WEST HAM UNITED 4, ASTON VILLA 0
PREMIER LEAGUE, 12 SEPTEMBER 2005

When you go into an empty restaurant and they ask if you have booked. When you say no, they tut, shake their head and survey an empty dining room. Then offer you the worst table. Hate that.

Preparations for the wedding had been underway for some time, consuming almost every evening and weekend in some shape or form: checking out venues, trying on suits, hassling people.

I had my concerns, I think it's fair to say, that I was making a mistake. On reflection I think the unmentionable ex felt the same way, but we both felt this was a gamble worth taking if we were to survive. Bit daft in hindsight. If your house is on fire you don't put it out by hosing it down with petrol.

Stuart the QPR fan was to be my best man as I had been for him some years before, and he arranged my stag weekend in London, the plan being for drink, football, curry and friends, although not necessarily in that order.

As luck would have it, not only had West Ham been promoted to the Premier League, but we were due to play the opening fixture of the 2005/06 season at Upton Park against Blackburn Rovers. That would be the focus of the Saturday. I managed to secure tickets in the East Stand for me, my dad, my nephew Mark, Stuart the QPR fan, brother-in-law Andy and Dr George Sik, friend and author of *I Think I'll Manage* and *In Ma Head, Son* – both critically acclaimed books on sports psychology.

Andy and I took the train from Leeds early on Saturday morning and Stuart met us on the same train at Peterborough before we dumped our kit at the hotel in Holborn and headed east to the Millers Well pub opposite East Ham town hall. As a season ticket holder in the '90s it had been our favoured haunt pre-game. Mark had taken my dad there to meet us, we had a few beers and staggered off down the Barking Road in good spirits, ready to see the first game of a new era, for me and for West Ham.

Meanwhile at West Ham, transfer activity in the summer had been limited. I had been so impressed with the defensive partnership of Elliott Ward and Anton Ferdinand, but clearly Pardew didn't really rate Ward and brought in centre-backs Danny Gabbidon and James Collins from Cardiff City and left-back Paul Konchesky from Charlton Athletic. Goalkeeper Roy Carroll also signed from Manchester United, meaning the defence had been almost completely restructured. Another goalkeeper, Shaka Hislop, joined on a free transfer from Portsmouth for his second spell. Christian Dailly was also given a new contract, which hinted to some that Ward was not really in Pardew's plans.

The signings of Collins and Gabbidon just did not make sense to me. They were both playing for Cardiff City, who had finished 16th in the Championship the previous season. Sure, they were both Welsh internationals, but then so was Vinnie Jones. A closer inspection of the statistics, however, showed Cardiff's problems lay elsewhere; they actually conceded five goals fewer than West Ham over the course of the season. They clearly needed to invest in strikers.

Konchesky looked like a shrewd buy; I had seen him play before and had been impressed. He had also been a West Ham season ticket holder as a youth, and clearly had a desire to do well.

The right-back position remained a worry, though, as no replacement had been signed for Tomáš Řepka, who I had assumed would move on. He didn't.

In midfield we signed Yossi Benayoun, an Israeli international from Racing Santander. Apparently his missus had persuaded him to choose West Ham over Bolton, who had also had interest in him. Sensible lady. Benayoun looked, on paper at least, like a clone of Eyal Berkovic, the Israeli attacking midfielder signed by Harry Redknapp with much success in 1997. Benayoun was slightly different, he had a much slighter frame and operated a bit wider, but he still looked like a great prospect.

No strikers were signed, but I was confident the combination of Harewood, Zamora and a sparingly used Sheringham would serve us well.

In the end, the departures list was significantly longer than the arrivals. Out went Stephen Bywater, Don Hutchison, Andy Melville, Rufus Brevett, Yousef Sofiane, Steve Lomas, Luke Chadwick and Serhiy Rebrov. It seemed Pardew had ridden his luck a little bit with the ageing defence in the Championship, and only stumbled across a winning formula in the final few games. Now he had to freshen things up or face instant relegation. I felt before the season started he had done this to good effect.

The Blackburn game took place on Saturday 13 August 2005, our party of six making up part of the 33,305 crammed into Upton Park who were responsible for an impressive atmosphere as the game started. Despite this, West Ham, frankly, looked overwhelmed. We went behind to an Andy Todd goal that was swept in from a few yards out following a badly defended corner. We looked ragged and disorganised. Whatever was said at half time, though, did the trick.

In fact, not only was this the typical 'game of two halves', but it actually seemed as though West Ham had silently switched all 11 players at the end of the first forty-five minutes. They came out and blew Blackburn away with a breathtaking display of football conducted by Yossi Benayoun. Sheringham scored the first right after the break, then further goals from Reo-Coker and Etherington wrapped up a 3–1 win nobody would have predicted at half time.

We walked back to the tube station in the knowledge we were joint top after one game, and Charlton, having won 3–1 at Sunderland, were only top alphabetically.

The Saturday night of my stag weekend was unremarkable, and that was exactly how I had asked for it to be. Beer, curry, a club and a taxi back to the hotel. By ourselves.

The following morning I had a hangover the like of which I have not had since. I looked and felt dreadful. Stuart the QPR fan did not look much better, nor did Dr Sik or Andy. I drank coffee and stared at the breakfast in front of me, but I really just wanted to throw up.

We walked it off a bit, heading for Kings Cross to take the train back to Leeds. Dr Sik suggested a swift hair of the dog in the Flying Scotsman. I really didn't fancy it but everyone else seemed keen. Then I realised what he meant as he asked the barmaid if the 'entertainment' was still on.

My god, what a dump. It really was hair of the dog as a less-than-enthusiastic stripper did her thing then waved a pint glass in front of me. It was all I could do not to be sick into it.

With that image in my head we headed back off to Leeds, upgraded to first class and drinking all the coffee GNER could throw at us, before facing the unmentionable ex, who was bound to have had a terrible time on her hen weekend. It was just the way it was.

The following Saturday a creditable 0–0 draw at Newcastle followed, Konchesky unfairly sent off for a sliding tackle in which he clearly (on replays at least) got to the ball first. He was sent off for his tackle on Jermaine Jenas for denying an obvious goal-scoring opportunity. This was later rescinded, and I assumed it was not because the tackle was clean, but because it had been Jenas, and therefore it clearly hadn't been a clear goal-scoring opportunity.

Back down to earth the following Saturday, our first defeat of the season was to Sam Allardyce's Bolton Wanderers, 1–2 at Upton Park. But after three games it was looking like we could handle ourselves in the Premier League, and there was little to worry about.

The wedding on the other hand was giving me plenty to worry about, although we had wisely planned it to coincide with an international break over the weekend of 4–5 September 2005. Don't ask me the exact date, I have largely excluded it from my memory. But my abiding recollection from the whole weekend was just how nice total strangers were to us. The wedding was at a large hotel in Bradford that is oft-frequented by golfers. Everyone who saw us smiled and wished us good luck. Little did they know how much we would need it.

Our honeymoon was in Rhodes. The choice of hotel was spot on, although it did not have the facility to show the home game against Aston Villa on 12 September, which was a terrible lapse in planning on my part. I had known for some time it would be the *Monday Night Football* game on Sky, but somehow failed to check what channels were available at the hotel. Being an all-inclusive establishment, they had bled the life out of every other local restaurant in the area, so we had to travel some distance to find a bar showing the game. But find one we did, and I watched as Marlon Harewood grabbed a hat-trick and Benayoun stroked home a delightful fourth in a 4–0 win. I lifted a glass to all of them. The next day I developed a barking cough, which I assumed was down to the air conditioning in the hotel room, but a visit to the local quack confirmed it was in fact chronic bronchitis.

This was, of course, my fault. So I spent a few days in the shade, reading and listening to England win the Ashes on the radio, and accepting the blame for ruining the honeymoon. I'm such a bastard.

The good form on the pitch continued with a 2–1 win at Craven Cottage, which moved us up to 4th in the table and we progressed in the League Cup with a 4–2 win over Sheffield Wednesday at Hillsborough. Loan signing Jeremey Aliadiare was among the scorers before disappearing in a puff of mediocrity.

Earlier in the year I had changed my job and was now working in central Leeds. My work with the firm making PPI policies did not go well, as they were not receptive to the idea that they might have to curb some of their sharper practices in order to comply with the new regulations. They had employed me to ensure they were compliant, but didn't like what I was saying. It was a horrible job, made bearable by a good friendship with the IT director, Jon, and a flirtatious relationship with one of the clerks, Emma. I gave a training session one day on a particularly bland subject and sent a circular e-mail out apologising for the tedium. She sent me an email back saying, 'Don't worry it had its compensations' (it even had a winky face).

We flirted like bonkers after that, mainly by e-mail, often exchanging thoughts on the management. This was not terribly professional, but I saw no harm. I was also copied into a number of other e-mails critical of the management. When Jon was asked to leave for speaking out of turn, they trawled through all my e-mails and decided I should be put on a disciplinary for failing in my role as compliance officer by not notifying them of these negative comments.

I was put on gardening leave. When the day of the hearing came around it was all done very officially, in the boardroom. They were panicking. They knew I was about to recommend sweeping changes they didn't want to make. They also knew I had successfully applied for a job with a claims management company and were worried I would be using my inside knowledge against them. They had also seen the saucy e-mails.

They went through the charade of retiring to deliberate, and came back to say they would have to let me go. I went back to my office to find all my stuff already boxed up, so I'm not sure quite how much deliberation was involved. Didn't get so much as a snog from Emma.

While I was obviously disappointed to be sacked for the first time in my life, I felt I hadn't done anything particularly wrong, and I also knew that given what was about to happen in the world of PPI, my career would last significantly longer than theirs.

I joined Keypoint Claims in the summer of 2005 at its offices in Leeds, handling complaints about mis-sold endowment policies. The owners had advertised for a week on TV in the middle of *Coronation Street* and hadn't quite counted on the thousands of calls they would receive. By the time I joined they were already peering over the snow-topped peaks of their backlog. I had a job on.

It was great though. I loved every second. A wonderful bunch of people from all walks of life; I also made some great friends and had a manager who believed in me. It makes a huge difference.

11

HUNG UP

TOTTENHAM HOTSPUR 1, WEST HAM UNITED 1
PREMIER LEAGUE, 20 NOVEMBER 2005
*The word 'awesome'. Especially when used
to describe something far from it.*

I'm trying something different this evening. It's 16 April 2018 and, as I write this, West Ham are playing Stoke City. So I should really be there. But as you can see, it's 16 April and I have to have this book finished by 31 May. So far, I'm only up to 2005, so I'm in deep shit. For that reason I'm at home writing, with one eye on the TV. I will keep you updated, but as it stands, it's just been one big Manchester City love-in.

But for now, let's get back to September 2005. It was remarkably nice to get into late September approaching a fixture against Arsenal at Upton Park feeling safety was already pretty much assured. The game finished 0–0 with few opportunities for either side. It was a professional job, and I was starting to think maybe Pardew was the man. After two seasons at a lower level failing to achieve any level of consistency, I felt that now he had the opportunity to spend some money on better-quality, younger players, he could really show us what he was capable of.

Key to this was little Yossi Benayoun. The diamond from Dimona, as literally no one seemed to call him, had injected a little bit of creativity into the squad. Master of an angled pass, his head-up passing ability meant the team always had a bit of an edge to it, and even if they went behind, always looked like they might get something out of a game.

That was the case at the Stadium of Light as West Ham fell

behind to a goal from Tommy Miller, but Benayoun again made the difference, salvaging a 1–1 draw.

I drove along the M62 for the game at the Etihad, or rather, the City of Manchester Stadium as it was known then. We lost the game 2–1, but I was struck by the facilities at City's new ground, which had been built to host the Commonwealth Games and was, therefore, an athletics stadium. When compared to Maine Road, of course, it had the soul and character of a caravan site. But it was a cinch to park at and to drive away from; the surrounding area didn't make you fear for your safety, and the catering and other facilities were a distinct improvement. Why couldn't West Ham have the stadium due to be built for the 2012 Olympics? Moving stadium however was not high on the agenda as Terry Brown was re-elected chairman at the AGM.

It seemed astonishing, given the kerfuffle caused by the WHISTLE campaign, that of the 14 million votes available only 350 were cast against Brown returning as chairman in one of the quietest annual meetings in recent memory.

It was starting to look as though people didn't really care about what went on at board level as long as the team was winning.

And win they did in the next game, which I also managed to attend. The 2–1 win over Gareth Southgate's Middlesbrough was back home at Upton Park. I had a front row seat in the Bobby Moore Upper, but as with the City game the week before, I had driven straight there, watched the game and drove straight home. It's no way to experience your match day. I saw West Ham dominate, but they had to wait until just past the hour to get the breakthrough, which was provided by Teddy Sheringham. An own goal from Chris Riggott doubled the lead – and was no more than we deserved. The late consolation from Boro meant the scoreline did not reflect how dominant we had been.

But it was hard to pick holes when, as a newly promoted side, we had consolidated 9th place in the league and did not show any signs of being in bother.

If we had a bogey team at that time it was without a doubt Sam Allardyce's Bolton Wanderers. Bolton had sent us down, effectively; in 2003 they had also inflicted our only home defeat of the season to date and then dumped us out of the League Cup at the Reebok stadium on 26 October. No matter. It was Bolton. We didn't beat Bolton. Move on.*

We travelled to Anfield in good shape, seeking our first win there since September 1963, over forty-two years before. We were hopeful, but it would have to be forty-three.

The home game with West Bromwich Albion, however, showed how far we had come. It was another late show, and another goal from Sheringham to take all 3 points. Although we had the youth of Harewood and Zamora up front, sometimes the wise head of Sheringham was needed to show everyone the way. I was glad to have been so wrong about the decision to sign him.

Away at Tottenham we appeared to be heading for defeat, trailing 1–0 going into the final minute. But this team had proved it was made of sterner stuff, and a corner swung in from the left was nodded in by Anton Ferdinand for his first Premier League goal. The visiting supporters understandably went potty.

The next game was at home to Manchester United, who had just lost one of their greatest heroes in George Best. It was indeed tragic that Best had lost his battle against alcoholism. His death was actually caused by a kidney infection brought on by the drugs he was taking to prevent rejection of his recently transplanted liver. Some said he acted foolishly and selfishly by continuing to drink after being given a second chance with a new liver. But I say let he who is without sin cast the first stone. Anyone who has ever battled depression or addiction will know things are not always black and white.

Was George Best Manchester United's greatest ever player? Was he the greatest player ever? I doubt both. Massively

---

* Still West Ham 0, Stoke 0 after 22 minutes. Absolutely nothing to report; looks like a friendly. I'll keep you posted if anything happens.

talented, that's for sure, but a flawed genius. He certainly earned the respect shown to him by the Upton Park crowd that afternoon, who saluted him in the manner to which he had become accustomed.

Matthew Etherington was hardly in the mould of George Best, but he showed the Manchester United defence a clear pair of heels tearing down the left flank in the first minute and putting a perfectly weighted cross for Harewood to sweep in at the near post. But Manchester United would ultimately produce a result for George Best. Wayne Rooney and John O'Shea scored in the second half to give them a 2–1 win.[†]

It would be tempting to say this was the inconsistency we had experienced in the Championship for the previous two seasons, but this was the Premier League. It was unrealistic to expect us to go on winning – or even unbeaten – over a prolonged period; the quality of the opposition would dictate that. But we entered December in 9th position, which was more than we could have dreamed of at the start of the campaign. Inconsistency is a state of mind. We would win only two more games before the end of the year, but we would end the year in 10th place on 26 points with some brilliant performances and, if consistency was the goal, we had at least found it in levels of performance, even in defeat.[‡]

---

†   Fucking hell, Joe Hart spilled again. West Ham 0, Stoke 1. Pissed off now.
‡   Yes! Andy Carroll, 1–1. About time.

12

THAT'S MY GOAL

NORWICH CITY 1, WEST HAM UNITED 2
FA CUP THIRD ROUND, 7 JANUARY 2006

People who squeeze through a closing door
before letting it close in your face. Twats.

We came from behind to beat Birmingham at St Andrew's. Emile Heskey gave the Blues the lead, but soon afterwards Zamora scored one of the goals of the season. He flicked the ball over his head, shuffled it from right to left then nutmegged the keeper at the near post to equalise. Harewood scored the winner in first-half injury time with a comparatively mundane ping-pong of a goal after Etherington had cut back from the by-line when it looked like it may have gone out.

Annoyingly we could not carry the good form forward to Ewood Park, as we were beaten 3–2. Zamora scored again to put us 1–0 up against a Blackburn side which had not scored in almost five-and-a-half hours of football (though it was Mark Hughes's side, go figure), but as with so many teams experiencing a drought, a game against West Ham provides the outlet. Paul Dickov netted from the spot, and then put Blackburn 2–1 up after a sliced clearance from Dailly fell kindly for him. West Ham then scored a fabulous equaliser – Benayoun broke down the left, played Zamora in, onside by a hair's breadth, and he set up a cross at the far post that Harewood simply could not refuse.

2–2 would have been a fair result, but poor defending allowed Shefki Kuqi to grab an underserved winner. It was harsh, but I reasoned we had played well. This was enjoyable. This, to me, was what following West Ham was like at its best. We might not win every week, but we had some great players and we gave it a good old go. I could not fault them.

At Goodison Park we came from behind again to win 2–1. This was extraordinary. Our record at Goodison was almost as bad as our record at Anfield, but we had at least won in living memory – if you were older than eighteen, of course. Everton, tidy and efficient at home under David Moyes, took the lead through James Beattie, but a David Weir own goal and a third successive strike from Zamora gave the Hammers victory, in what was a third away game in a row – and I'm still not quite sure how that happened.

In each of those away fixtures we scored 2 goals, which was a measure of our performance levels and work rate. Against Newcastle at Upton Park on 17 December we also scored 2 goals, but call it inconsistency, or call it coming up against better teams with better players: they had Michael Owen, who got 3. Newcastle won 4–2 in the end, with Alan Shearer scoring one as well.

Portsmouth was a strange venue for Boxing Day, not exactly local, but the fixture computer never seemed to worry about that sort of thing; we picked up a point in a 1–1 draw. West Ham had to use all three substitutes before half time with Řepka and Mullins needing to be replaced, and then Danny Gabbidon, who had replaced Řepka, suffered a reaction to a previous injury and had to be replaced himself by Christian Dailly. Future Hammer Gary O'Neil then put Pompey 1–0 up and West Ham were creaking. In the second half James Collins pinched an equaliser, and Harry Redknapp's Portsmouth had Laurent Robert sent off for a second yellow – but by that point both sides had settled for a point.

Two disappointing results followed with a now tradition-al home defeat by Wigan Athletic and a reverse by the same scoreline, 2–0 at The Valley against Charlton. The Wigan defeat could not be explained by anything other than the fact it was just Wigan. The Charlton game, however, was probably the worst display of the season. Despite a couple of chances cleared off the line by Charlton we never really looked like scoring, but it was our seventh fixture of the month, with five of them away from home. The team was entitled to look a bit jaded.

Chelsea came to Upton Park on 2 January 2006 with the swagger of a team destined to win the league by 13 points. They duly disposed of us 3–1.

The FA Cup match at Carrow Road was interesting for a number of reasons. We had played Norwich while we were a Championship side the year before at the same stage and beat then Premier League Norwich 1–0. Now the roles were reversed. Who would have the desire? Well, as it turned out, it was us. It seemed this would be a good opportunity to have a good cup run: unless the wheels fell off in a dramatic way we were unlikely to get involved in a relegation fight, and we were similarly unlikely to qualify for Europe. So a tilt at the FA Cup seemed a distinct possibility. We won 2–1 on this occasion and goals from Hayden Mullins and Bobby Zamora put us through to face Blackburn at Upton Park in the fourth round.

The transfer window had opened, which was just as well as the existing squad was stretched with injuries, and the players had started to look tired. Tomáš Řepka had apparently set his heart on leaving, having agreed a three-year deal with Sparta Prague in his native Czech Republic. I'd set my heart on it too. I still didn't understand what people saw in him. Rumours circulated that we were in for the highly rated Norwich City striker Dean Ashton. Now this, I was excited about. I had seen him get two for Crewe against us the season before and I had seen him play for Norwich; he impressed me with his strength and eye for a goal. But other, bigger clubs were also in for him, so I did not hold out much hope.

The squad travelled wearily again to Villa Park, and again came from a goal down to win 2–1 against our claret and blue rivals, with the pairing of Zamora and Harewood providing the finishes. They had a happy knack of finding the net and were probably the best striking partnership we had enjoyed seeing in the top flight since Lee Chapman and Trevor Morley enjoyed a brief Indian summer in 1993/94.

Řepka made his final appearance for West Ham in a televised home match against Fulham at Upton Park on 23 January. The game will best be remembered from a footballing perspective for Anton Ferdinand's pirouetted opener and Yossi Benayoun's delightful wedge shot over the goalkeeper in a 2–1 victory. But the images remaining from that game are those of Tomáš Řepka on his lap of honour after the game with tears in his eyes, collecting scarves and mementos from the fans who had stayed to demonstrate to him that some, at least, appreciated him. After seeing what it meant to Tomáš to play for West Ham, I have to admit my attitude softened a little bit, and he is one of those players I now remember fondly in retrospect, but did not care for at the time.

A fourth successive win in all competitions came with a 4–2 win over Blackburn Rovers in the FA Cup, meaning we had a really good shot at a decent cup run, as long as we didn't draw Wigan at home or Bolton away…

Highbury. Scene of triumph and disaster for West Ham in unequal measure since, well, forever. I had seen Leroy Rosenior's header in 1989. I had seen Mike Small's smash-and-grab in 1990. I had seen Don Hutchison slide in at the far post in 1995. I had seen Les Sealey play up front. Now it was all to come to an end with a move to a purpose-built concrete bowl a few yards up the road. How could they give up their heritage and tradition in ruthless pursuit of the football dollar? Quite easily, it turned out. How many times have they won the league since?

Arsenal had a decent side and were looking to play every game like a cup final, but they could not live with West Ham that night. It didn't help that they had Plaistow-born Sol Campbell playing in defence like he was wearing concrete boots. Bobby Zamora turned him inside out for our second after Nigel Reo-Coker had put us 1–0 up. Campbell was substituted at half time and left the stadium, disappearing for a week. He left Arsenal that summer to seek a 'fresh challenge', which as we all know means dropping down a division or two. He remains, however, one of only six Englishmen to have scored in a Champions League final, and the way West Ham destroyed him personally in the space of forty-five minutes should not be underestimated.

Arsenal pulled one back and, in the Great Northern pub in Thackley, I started to wobble. But Etherington smashed in a third and Arsenal's late second was nothing more than a consolation. Five in a row and still Sunderland and Birmingham to come at home, and Dean Ashton was also on his way. But first we had to deal with a loss.

13

IT'S CHICO TIME

MANCHESTER CITY 1, WEST HAM UNITED 2
FA CUP SIXTH ROUND, 20 MARCH 2006
When bar staff ask, 'Who's next?' Like there is any chance people
on the other side of the bar will be honest about it.
They should know who's next.

Dean Ashton had made his debut at Highbury in the 3–2 win, but made his much-anticipated full debut at home against Sunderland on 4 February. Sunderland couldn't buy a win and were rooted to the bottom of the table with a paltry 9 points and just 2 wins all season. They were paying the price for having Barry Green as captain.

Despite their lowly position, the crowd of 34,745 at Upton Park that day witnessed a difficult afternoon, which was not as easy as the majority would have predicted. It should have been even easier as Sunderland had Stephen Wright dismissed in the first half for momentarily forgetting he was playing football and thinking he was playing rugby. But Barry Green had the defence well marshalled for once.

Eventually Dean Ashton made the breakthrough on 80 minutes, bundling home a Marlon Harewood shot, then Paul Konchesky fired in a second near the end, which gave the scoreline more respectability than it probably deserved. Another 3 points, a sixth win in a row. The footballing gods were looking down on us and smiling. But then they took one of our greatest sons.

Ron Greenwood died on 9 February 2006. He had been West Ham United manager between 1961 and 1974. In that period he transformed the club into a major force, winning the FA Cup in 1964, and making West Ham only the second English club to bring home a European trophy: they successfully beat 1860 Munich in the final of the European Cup Winners' Cup in 1965. Three of his protégés of course went on to win the World Cup the following year. But Ron Greenwood was significant to West Ham for more than that. It was not just what he achieved on the pitch, but how he revolutionised the club off it.

Forward-thinking in terms of strategy and training methods, he brought West Ham to the cutting edge of modern football at that time, using tactics such as the near post cross, which was perfectly executed by Geoff Hurst on so many occasions for West Ham and, of course, for England in 1966. It would be fair to say England owed much of its success in 1966 to Ron Greenwood.

Despite showing such ingenuity and capacity for change, Greenwood seemed to rather rest on his laurels after 1966, and became unpopular among some West Ham fans for much of the period after that as he inexplicably failed to adapt to the changing face of football in the 1970s.

He took over the England national team in 1977 following the departure of Don Revie, but could not prevent the failure to qualify for the 1978 World Cup, and although England qualified for the then eight-team European Championships in 1980, they did not progress beyond the group stage. The World Cup in Spain in 1982 was one of England's better campaigns, ending the tournament undefeated, but eliminated due to getting a 0–0 draw against Spain, whereas West Germany had beaten them 2–1 in the second-phase pool matches.

Greenwood laid a firm foundation for Bobby Robson to work with from that point on. He was a master of his trade and despite his failings in the latter years at West Ham, he will always be a club legend. And, you might argue, a national legend. Despite this, the powers that be at the Premier League did not deem his passing worthy of a minute's silence at every Premier League ground. Yet bizarrely, George Best, Northern Ireland international, was deemed worthy of such an endorsement.

As the players took to the pitch for the televised game against Birmingham City, West Ham organised an impeccably observed minute's silence before seeing off the Blues 3–0 to win their seventh straight game and push into the top six. Ron would have been proud.

The preparation could not have been any better as we travelled to the Reebok for what I fully expected to be our FA Cup exit. Our record against Sam Allardyce's Bolton was not good in recent years: their awkward, physical, direct style clashed badly with our mode of play, whatever that had been over the last few years. No one was entirely sure.

I went to the game thinking if we could get past Bolton then we had a realistic shot at winning the competition. I clung on to the fact a dull 0–0 draw was worth the journey so I could say, 'I was there.' But on reflection, I really wish I had saved my money.

Everton came to Upton Park similarly awkward and difficult to beat. Although we had won at Goodison in December, that was the exception proving the rule. Everton again proved a tough nut, and we had to settle for a 2–2 draw. Harewood scored with a smart shot on the turn from the edge of the box and Ashton from a precise left-foot strike, twice putting the Hammers in front, only for Osman and Beattie to equalise respectively.

Still, West Ham were unbeaten in 9 matches in all competitions, which, for a newly promoted side in the Premier League was impressive. That came crashing down to the ground, guess where? The Reebok. Maybe West Ham had an eye on their cup replay against the same opposition. Maybe we were trying to lull Bolton into a false sense of security. It might even have been the dreaded curse of the Manager of the Month award which Alan Pardew had received for February. Whatever it was, 1–4 was taking it a bit far. Not to worry, bad day at the office, put it down to experience.

We did just that, but made hard work of the replay against Bolton at Upton Park on 15 March. We got a little bit of luck with an own goal from Jussi Jääskeläinen opening the scoring, but Bolton seemed to take charge from there and equalised after Reo-Coker gave the ball away in midfield. Kevin Davies then had far too much time and space to get in a strike from the edge of the box. The tie went into extra time and eventually Marlon Harewood netted a scarcely deserved winner, sticking a weary leg out in front of the Bolton defender to loop the ball past Jääskeläinen. No one cared about that. How many times had we lost games we hadn't deserved to? How many times had we gone out in the cup to teams who nicked a lucky one? The only person who seemed genuinely bothered was Bolton manager Sam Allardyce, who was spitting feathers in the post-match press conference. It seemed the FA Cup still mattered to some people. He was probably on for a bonus. We had played Bolton five times that season and this was the only win. We deserved it.

The effort of getting past Bolton had its effects both mentally and physically, as West Ham capitulated a few days later at home to Harry Redknapp's Portsmouth. Pompey blew West Ham away with poor Jimmy Walker in goal not having a sniff at any of the three shots whistling past him before half time. The Hammers were made of stern stuff at that time and in the second half they came out swinging with both fists. Harewood belted a shot against the bar so hard that if it was still there it would still be shaking. Konchesky also hit the upright with a great shot, but thankfully this time Sheringham was on hand to tuck away the rebound. Just when it looked like we might have a fight-back on, Portsmouth grabbed a fourth which made Yossi Benayoun's beautifully crafted effort somewhat academic.

The focus was on the City of Manchester Stadium as the quarter-final against the Cityzens kicked off the following Monday for live broadcast on the BBC. West Ham, while not dominating, certainly carved out the better chances. Dean Ashton produced a piece of individual skill up there with the best I have witnessed in the last twenty years. The ball was pinged around between Ashton, Reo-Coker and Etherington without them really having it under full control. Ashton took the ball on, beat two men and hit a hard, low left-foot shot that was in the net before David James could say 'calamity'.

In the second half City had Chinese midfielder Sun Jihai sent off for raising his hand to Matthew Etherington. It wasn't so much a slap, or a punch, more something Dick Emery's Mandy might have been proud of as she said, 'Ooh you are awful, but I like you!' It was harsh, but them's the rules.

With a one-man advantage West Ham should have dominated, but still made hard work of it. With Christian Dailly injured the City players refused to put the ball out and paid the price for their unsporting behaviour as Nigel Reo-Coker nicked the ball and crossed it in to Benayoun, who hit a pass across the six-yard box that had Dean Ashton's name written all over it.

West Ham were in the FA Cup semi-finals for the first time in fifteen years. Musampa pulled one back for City, but it wasn't enough. We were through to the last four.

Despite playing on the Monday we still didn't know who we would face as the remaining quarter-finals were settled over the next three days. On the Friday we went into the hat with Liverpool, Chelsea and Middlesbrough.

14

CRAZY

LIVERPOOL 3, WEST HAM UNITED 3
FA CUP FINAL, 13 MAY 2006
(LIVERPOOL WON 3–1 ON PENALTIES AFTER EXTRA TIME.)
I'm not racist but… [Insert racist comment here].

Despite the great run in January and February 2006, West Ham still found themselves only in 9th place after another win, 2–1 away at Wigan on 25 March. I say 'only', but I think most Hammers fans would have ripped your arm off for 9th in March, followed by an FA Cup semi-final. The season had already surpassed the wildest dreams of even the most optimistic.

Wigan were our modern-day Wimbledon. We could not beat them at home, but quite often managed to turn them over at their place. Manchester United, on the other hand, continued to turn us over home and away. Although it felt like we beat them in 1995 to allow Blackburn to pip them to the title, it was still only a 1–1 draw and we had yet to beat them since the formation of the Premier League in 1992.

We would have to wait another year as we lost 1–0 at Old Trafford the following Wednesday, then dropped two more points in a 0–0 draw with Charlton Athletic the next Sunday. It seemed we had one eye on the FA Cup semi-final as we prepared over Easter by losing 4–1 at Stamford Bridge, sneaked past Manchester City at home 1–0, courtesy of a Shaun Newton goal, then lost to our cup opponents 2–0 at the Riverside. Comfortable in the league with 49 points, we were in no danger of relegation and seemed to approach the game against Middlesbrough as nothing more than a dress rehearsal.

With many West Ham fans still getting over the shock of losing Ron Greenwood, the next day we lost a man who, for me, embodied West Ham entirely. John Angus Lyall passed away on 18 April 2006 at the ridiculously young age of sixty-six.

It is hard to quantify how much Lyall and Greenwood put in to making the club what it became. Before them there had been no trophies. If they had not been part of our club who knows if there ever would have been? For me, Lyall was the bigger loss because Greenwood had already left his managerial post when I started watching West Ham. Other managers came and went, but John Lyall was always there while I was growing up. He was a father figure to some of us – and to many of the players as well.

He had played under Greenwood but was forced to retire after a serious knee injury in 1964. After taking on various roles at the club he eventually worked his way up to take over the reins from Greenwood in 1974/75, winning the FA Cup in his first season. He took us to the final of the European Cup Winners' Cup the following season, and it was clear he had a philosophy of playing fluid, attacking football. His teams, like Greenwood's before him, were a joy to watch, even if they could occasionally be rather generous to the opposition.

Despite relegation in 1978 the board kept faith in Lyall, and they were repaid with one of the most memorable five-year spells in the club's history: winning the FA Cup against Arsenal at Wembley in May 1980, getting promoted with a record points total, and reaching the League Cup Final in 1981. Consistently finishing in the top half, they produced some terrific football and eventually achieved a record 3rd place in 1986.

But after that the wheels started to loosen significantly. It seemed to me that Lyall, having been connected with the club for so long, suffered from the same issues Arsène Wenger had to deal with at Arsenal before his recent departure. He was synonymous with the club, and therefore considered it, rightly or wrongly, his own. Despite funds being available, he chose to be frugal.

From my distant point of view, and from what I have read

on the subject, he chose not to strengthen the squad in 1986/87 after finishing 3rd the previous year, eventually bringing in Stewart Robson who was injury-prone and not a good fit for the team. McAvennie left. Cottee left. McAvennie came back. Too late, we were down again in 1989. This time the board were less sympathetic and chose to let John Lyall go.

He went on to win promotion with Ipswich in 1991/92, proving he could still do it, and, had he been allowed to stay, I am sure he would have done the same for us at the first attempt.

There is a lot of talk these days about the club not belonging to us any more, about the heart and soul being ripped out of the club. For me, John Lyall leaving the club in 1989 signalled the beginning of the end of the West Ham I had always known and loved. His death in 2006 merely confirmed things would never be the same again.

It was appropriate that the first game after his passing should provide the opportunity to reach our first FA Cup final since Lyall had taken us there twenty-six years before. A minute's silence before the game at Villa Park was broken by someone in the crowd who started a chant of 'Johnny Lyall's Claret & Blue Army' – and it spread. Normally, people breaking a respectful silence should be vilified, and it's the reason now why most of the time organisers give up and merely go for a minute's applause, to drown out the fuckwits.

But on this occasion it was a respectful interruption. The esteem in which we held Lyall and the love everyone had for him spilled out, and the chant spread. It spread around the ground until every West Ham fan was singing it, and probably a few Boro fans too. It was a touching moment.

After that, with emotions running high, it was never in doubt that West Ham would win the game. I had been unable to get a ticket and settled for a seat at the New Inn in Idle. After Marlon Harewood had smashed in the winner and the final whistle had blown, the emotion, fuelled no doubt by a few pints, took over, and I bawled my eyes out.

Liverpool had won their semi-final they day before and

would be waiting for us in the final at the Millennium Stadium. As always seems to happen, we had to play them in the league next at Upton Park. Pardew made changes, partly through players being exhausted and having knocks from the efforts at the weekend, and partly, I suspect, because he wanted to keep his cards close to his chest. Elliott Ward made a rare start in place of Danny Gabbidon, Sheringham started in Ashton's place and Jimmy Walker took Shaka's position between the sticks. It wasn't long before Cissé beat him at the near post to put Liverpool 1–0 up.

West Ham made a good fist of it though; Sheringham and Benayoun both went close. In the second half Nigel Reo-Coker survived four offside claims in the same spell to round off a slick move to equalise. But it was to be Liverpool's day, and Cissé grabbed a second to give them the points.

The most significant moment of the game, though, had been the sending off of Hayden Mullins. It should have been a free kick to West Ham, García tugging and nagging at Mullins near the halfway line. Mullins reacted by giving García a shove in the chest, and García went down clutching his face like he'd taken a right hook. Referee Howard Webb saw it as a straight red, which I suppose it was; Mullins should not have raised his hands, but there were mitigating circumstances. For his part, Luis García was also dismissed.

Mullins had become a very important and underrated cog in the West Ham machine; I had to admit I had been wrong about him. He had played all but one of our league games that season and appeared in all our FA Cup games. The red card meant he would be suspended for the final. Both clubs appealed the decision, but the FA saw violent conduct from each of the players and both cards stood.

The first two games of Mullins's suspension were the final two league games of the season. West Ham finished with a flourish, beating West Bromwich Albion 1–0 at the Hawthorns, and famously helping to deprive Tottenham Hotspur a Champions League spot by beating them 2–1 on the final day. The

Tottenham players all had a dose of the trots, courtesy of an apparently dodgy lasagne served at their Canary Wharf hotel. No sympathy here. Carl Fletcher, deputising for Mullins, fired in the opener, and Yossi Benayoun scored what proved to be the winner in the second half.

Whatever happened in the cup final, the season had been an outstanding success. To be in 9th place with 55 points was more than we could have hoped for. The new signings had merged beautifully with the existing staff; Benayoun gave us the guile, and Ashton had given us the presence and cutting edge up front – making us a force to be reckoned with in the Premier League.

I tried to get a ticket for the cup final, but I had more chance of getting a date with Kylie Minogue. My Aunty Barbara (not a real aunt, but everyone has an aunt who's not their real aunt) generously sent me some money and told me to do my best to get a ticket. Not a chance. Despite being reasonably well connected, whoever I asked looked the other way, or said, 'Of course... I just have these other twenty people who asked me first.'

I considered heading down to Cardiff anyway and trying my luck, but I had heard stories of the prices being quoted by touts and decided the best thing would be to watch the game in the company of a good friend. And there was none better than Stuart the QPR fan. I took the train down to Peterborough and watched the game with him and his son Callum, who I had assumed would also be rooting for West Ham. But, as it turned out, because Peter Crouch had a spell at QPR, he wanted Liverpool to win.

The game has been well documented. You do not need me to tell you what happened. All I can describe is the emotions running though me at 2–0 up. Here were plucky West Ham, 2–0 up in the cup final against a Liverpool team who were champions of Europe. My heart was absolutely bursting with pride. We did not look at all out of place. But when Cissé pulled one back and then Gerrard equalised in the second half, I resigned myself to the inevitable.

Then Konchesky's shot (okay, Konchesky's cross) found its way into the top corner and I started to think maybe our name was on the trophy. As the game entered the dying seconds I couldn't take it anymore and my walnut-sized bladder let me down again. I went for a pee and hid in the toilet until I thought it might be safe to come out. As a result, I missed Scaloni kicking the ball out for an injured Liverpool player. I also missed Liverpool throwing the ball back to him, then unsportingly closing him down immediately, causing him to give the ball away deep in our own half. I missed Gerrard's screamer that equalised and took the match to extra time. All I heard was Callum yelping with joy as the goal went in.

I was glad I missed it. It could have been expensive. I think I would have been buying Stuart the QPR fan a new TV, and facing a stretch for punching a six-year-old.

That was it. Okay there were another thirty minutes. Okay Harewood stabbed a tired leg at a late chance, but the boys had already given everything and more. There was nothing left to give for the penalties; the outcome was not in doubt.

It was one of my proudest moments as a West Ham fan. Defeat was expected, but we lost the West Ham Way. We showed the rest of the world what we were capable of. We contributed to one of the greatest FA Cup finals ever. We gave it everything. In fact, we borrowed just so we could give more than we had. But it wasn't enough.

The season had given so much and, justifiably, we were looking forward to the next season, to build on our success. Especially as the reward for earning runners-up spot in the FA Cup was a place in the first round of the UEFA cup.

15

SEXYBACK

Spreadsheets. Can't live with them, can't live without them.
Sure as hell can't delete them.

The summer brought with it the usual bi-annual disappointment that is England's performance in a major tournament. This time, elimination on penalties was at the hands of Portugal, and it was Wayne Rooney's turn to be sent off. I try not to get excited about World Cups – but once they've begun, the disappointment of England's inevitable exit still hurts.

Swedish manager Eriksson had already announced he was to leave after the World Cup, which saved them the bother of sacking him, and left them the sole task of appointing a successor. Despite only having one job, they chose Steve McClaren, and the nation united in performing a simultaneous facepalm.

At least they didn't try to steal our Alan Pardew. His stock had risen greatly over the past twelve months and we quite understandably wanted to hang on to him. Now we had something to build on, and with Europe to look forward to, we would see what he was made of.

The priority was a right-back. Lionel Scaloni had left after his loan spell, and my preferred choice – Luke Young of Charlton – had looked likely to sign, but failed two medicals. Pascal Chimbonda of Wigan was also on the radar, but nothing came to pass. In the end we signed Tyrone Mears from Preston for a fee of £1 million, and Ghanaian John Paintsil was also eventually signed from Hapoel Tel Aviv for a similar fee, on the recommendation of Yossi Benayoun. Paintsil joined the squad on the pre-season tour of Sweden, pending the granting of a work permit, and was eventually signed in August. George McCartney joined from Sunderland for £600,000.

USA international Jonathan Spector also joined from Manchester United for £500,000, and Lee Bowyer returned for a second spell at the club – a move that did not prove entirely popular with many fans, myself included. Up front, we retained the services of Ashton, Zamora and Harewood, despite interest from elsewhere. We also gained Carlton Cole, a promising young striker from Chelsea, for an undisclosed fee believed to be around £2 million.

Goalkeeper Stephen Bywater left, making his loan move to Derby County permanent, and Shaka Hislop went to FC Dallas. So the goalkeeping gap was plugged by Robert Green, who signed from Norwich City for £2 million. Young midfielder Mark Noble went off to gain experience on loan at Ipswich Town. Surprisingly, Carl Fletcher, who had stood in for Hayden Mullins in the FA Cup final just a couple of months before, opted to join Crystal Palace for £400,000. Maybe not so strange if the rumours surrounding Pardew's relationship with Mrs Fletcher were to be believed. Me? I don't believe any rumours like that at all, whatsoever.

Dean Ashton was rewarded for his fine form with an England call-up from Schteeve McClaren, for the friendly against Greece at Old Trafford.

Things were looking up. We had brought good players in… and Lee Bowyer. We had sent some average players out. Our striker had been called up to play for England. We had Palermo to look forward to in the UEFA Cup.

Of course, it had to go tits up.

Dean Ashton broke his ankle in training with England and all the hard preparation work undertaken leading up to the start of the season was effectively undone.

Despite all the new signings, Mears and Bowyer were the only two new faces to start against Iain Dowie's Charlton on the opening day at Upton Park. We fell behind in the first half to a penalty harshly given against Danny Gabbidon for handball, but were not behind for long. Djimi Traoré was sent off for two stupid fouls, the latest player to find out that you make trivial challenges in front of Howard Webb at your peril.

In the second half Lee Bowyer put in a great cross from the right, which Benayoun missed at the near post, but Zamora tucked away at the far. Zamora had scored some of the best goals I had seen from a West Ham player. Against Ipswich in the play-off semi-final for instance, Birmingham away, Arsenal away – the list went on. But that day he scored the shittest goal I have seen in my life. Bowyer crossed from the left. Well let's be honest, Lee, you were trying a shot weren't you? And as the ball skidded across in Zamora's direction he made one of the ugliest shapes ever seen on a football pitch. Iain Dowie in the Charlton dugout looked jealous. He connected with it on his right foot (just), and if a ball can trickle in the air, that's what it did. First one Charlton defender threw himself at it, then the goalkeeper missed it, then a third Charlton player made a ridiculous effort to clear it on the line, merely serving to divert it into his own net. Who cares? It was as valid as Di Canio's volley against Wimbledon. You don't get points for style.

Teddy Sheringham came on as a second-half substitute, making him the oldest outfield player to appear in the Premier League for West Ham, but it was the following substitution which brought the third goal: Carlton Cole announced his arrival by scoring with his second touch, his first being to chest down Bowyer's through ball.

It seemed as though maybe Ashton's injury would not be quite as damaging as we had thought, as we picked up a further point at Watford. Tormentor-in-Chief Marlon King, who had scored against us for Gillingham and Forest in previous seasons, did it again with a scorching shot to put Watford 1–0 up. But Zamora grabbed an equaliser from a terrific Konchesky cross.

Four points from the opening 2 games put us in a positive frame of mind for the trip to Anfield for our first meeting with

Liverpool since the cup final. We were still looking for our first win there, now in forty-six years, but we travelled buoyed by our performance in the cup final, with the leading scorer in the Premier League firing on all cylinders, and with Lee Bowyer actually playing well.

Zamora raised hopes with a cross that moved in the air and sneaked in at the near post, but a screamer from Daniel Agger, and a goal from the telegraph pole in a football kit that was Peter Crouch, gave Liverpool a 2–1 lead at half time.

The best chance of the second half fell to… Lee Bowyer. He missed. As you were.

Still, 4 points from 3 games was good enough for 4th place in the embryonic table for 2006/07 and we had played well; we had most of the new signings still to come in, and two new signings still to arrive that would rock our world.

Argentinians Carlos Tevez and Javier Mascherano were un-veiled at Upton Park on 5 September 2006 at a press conference in which both players looked as surprised as most West Ham fans, and indeed most football fans in general, who quite rightly wondered how a club like West Ham had managed to sign two players like that. I was asking myself the same question. After all, just weeks before we had bought Tyrone Mears, George Mc-Cartney and Carlton Cole. Now we had pulled off the deal of the century. How so?

You know how they say if something looks too good to be true, then it probably is.

The signings coincided with the board announcing they were in preliminary talks about a possible takeover. One of the interested parties was Media Sports Investment (MSI), owned by Kia Joorabchian, who owned the registration of the Argentinian pair.

Joorabchian had founded the company in 2004, forming a partnership with Brazilian side Corinthians, loaning them money in return for a share of future profits. Tevez was signed for Corinthians by MSI for $22m in 2005, but MSI retained rights in the player, making him effectively contracted to them rather than Corinthians. Are you with me? Then I shall continue.

When MSI and Joorabchian found the asking price to buy Arsenal a bit steep, they came to talk to West Ham, and it is almost certain the provision of Tevez and Mascherano was merely done to evidence the fact they were serious suitors – and did not provide any evidence to suggest West Ham had suddenly won the lottery.

The expression on both players' faces suggested they had just had bags taken off their heads. It looked like the cuffs had been taken off and they were blinking at their first glimpse of daylight in weeks. You could see them asking themselves why all the cameras were going off and who the grey-haired bloke standing between them was.

Quite how the rest of the squad would have reacted to their arrival had also not been thought through. I am no psychiatrist, but if a tight and relatively successful group suddenly has two ringers parachuted in, it cannot be good for morale.

And indeed, the signings must have affected their spirits, because we suddenly found it virtually impossible to win a game of football.

Pardew decided to start with both on the bench for the televised game against Aston Villa the following Sunday. Villa took the lead through former West Ham youth team player Liam Ridgewell, but Zamora kept up his hot run of form with an equaliser. Tevez came on as a sub, but could not fashion a winner, although he looked lively. Pardew must have sensed Mascherano was not up for it. He left him on the bench. Mascherano would play only seven times for West Ham with a record of played seven, lost seven. There can be few players even in our recent history to have such a wretched record.

Tevez looked bright, though, and earned a start against Palermo in the first leg of the UEFA Cup tie. He had a couple of good chances, but the tie slipped away from us as Palermo took a 1–0 advantage into the second leg in Sicily two weeks later.

We then went on a disastrous run, losing at home to Newcastle

2–0, and by the same score at Manchester City. I went to the latter game and could not recall a flatter performance. It was a routine defeat. The announcer called our number 32 'Carlos Teveth', trying a fancy Spanish pronunciation; he didn't impress anyone.

We were then dumped out of the UEFA cup 3–0 in Palermo, beaten comprehensively by a team playing in pink. Not only that, they had David Di Michele. That short disastrous run was followed by a slightly longer disastrous run, losing at home to Reading and away at Portsmouth and Tottenham without finding the net. We finally scored against Chesterfield in the League Cup but still lost. At Tottenham, Jermain Defoe did nothing to further endear himself to West Ham fans by biting Javier Mascherano. The referee saw the incident and booked Defoe so the FA took no further action. Bizarre.

We had slipped from 4th after 3 games to 19th after 9 games with just 5 points on the board picked up in the first 4 games.

You can look at Pardew's record at other clubs and see he has an initial effect, generally, then tends to go on long losing streaks. But this was so obviously connected to the disruption and speculation surrounding the unsolicited arrival of the Argentinians that I was feeling a bit sorry for him.

It was backs to the wall when Blackburn Rovers came to Upton Park – normally good value for 3 points and they did not disappoint. It was an intense atmosphere as we had not won a point or scored a goal since the arrival of the Argentinians. Pardew made changes: Tevez and Mascherano, who to be fair, had been out of favour for some time, did not feature at all. In came Sheringham, who broke the seal on 21 minutes with a beautifully directed header from a chipped cross from Benayoun.

Hayden Mullins scored his first Premier League goal to apparently clinch victory, but being West Ham we couldn't resist allowing Blackburn to sneak one back in the last minute just to make things interesting. We held on for a massive victory, which left Mark Hughes looking like he had just won a lemon-sucking competition, and seemed to confirm we didn't really need those pesky Argies.

It was still six years until the London Olympics and the stadium at Stratford had yet to be built, but already the Labour government were squashing any thoughts West Ham might have of taking residence there after the games.

Culture secretary Tessa Jowell poured cold water on any designs the club might have had on a move in an interview in the *Sunday Telegraph*. Sports Minister Richard Caborn had already held talks with West Ham about taking the stadium after the Olympics and was a keen advocate. But Jowell told Simon Hart at the *Sunday Telegraph*:

> I want to be absolutely clear about this. The decision by the Olympic board is that the legacy use will be for athletics.
>
> What is also clear is that when we were going through the first stage of the cost review and looking at the various options on legacy costs, we discovered that football would actually be much more expensive because we are absolutely bound to provide an athletics legacy and running a parallel procurement is very, very expensive.
>
> Not only are we bound by what we were told by the IOC but we are bound by a belief in the importance of there being an athletics legacy. So football was really knocked out at that point.

The article also quotes 'one senior source close to the Games' as saying:

> I don't know why but Caborn seems to be pushing the football option while everyone else is very anti. I don't know why he is so stuck on the football issue.
>
> We are at the design stage for the main stadium now and this is just ludicrous. Caborn is rowing a boat against a stream here.

So that was that then. What did we care? We didn't want to move anyway.

16

SMACK THAT

WEST HAM UNITED 1, SHEFFIELD UNITED 0
PREMIER LEAGUE, 25 NOVEMBER 2006

Love Island. Take Me Out. Blind Date. Big Brother. *Reality TV that
screws with people's emotions in the name of entertainment.*

Having broken the losing streak, it was important to go on a
winning one. And we did: a winning streak of two games.
You would not have bet a lot of money on us beating Arsenal
given recent form, but we did 1–0, with Marlon Harewood
scoring a memorable last-minute goal which sent the fans, and
Pardew, wild. A bit too wild with his 'in yer face' celebrations in
front of Arsène Wenger.

Pardew claimed a masterstroke in tactics post-match, saying
he had set the team up to keep it tight for as long as possible
and packed the bench with strikers (Harewood, Sheringham
and Tevez), meaning Bobby Zamora had to play up front on
his jack and do all the hard work, which he did, manfully, for
an hour. I have no doubt that was his plan. Although it's easy to
be a master tactician after the event. That's exactly how I would
have played it too, Alan.

It emerged that while Joorabchian's talks to take over the club
were hitting problems, a second bidder had emerged. Icelandic
Eggert Magnússon's takeover was being backed by billionaire
businessman Björgólfur Guðmundsson.

At that time Guðmundsson was one of the world's richest
people, supposedly worth $1.2 billion.

He had made his money by various means, but initially

through a brewery which he opened following graduation from university.

He allegedly sold the brewery to Heineken for $300m then returned to Iceland where, by the time of the takeover talks, he had acquired stakes in one of Iceland's main banks, Landsbanki, and another four of Iceland's top businesses.

He was also chairman of pharmaceutical company Actavis, and had interests in Bulgarian and Polish telecommunication companies. It wasn't all good news though. He had a criminal record after being convicted in 1991 of five minor bookkeeping offences and given a twelve-month jail sentence that was suspended for two years, in what many regarded as a politically motivated prosecution.

Magnússon was also a wealthy man in his own right. He sold his bread and biscuit business, Fron, in 2001, and was a director of Straumur, the Icelandic investment bank. He was an influential figure in European football as head of the Icelandic Football Association and a member of the UEFA executive committee.

Between them they had some serious wedge, as they say in banking circles. But like any potential move to Stratford, it wasn't going to happen, so I didn't overly concern myself with it.

I persuaded the unmentionable ex that we should go to Middlesbrough, throwing in a night in a hotel in Durham on the Saturday to sweeten the deal. It was hardly worth the effort as we lost an insipid game at the Riverside 1–0. We lost again, more inevitably at least, at Chelsea by the same score, before West Ham-world was turned upside down.

On Tuesday 21 November 2006 a short statement on the club's website read:

West Ham United is delighted to announce that the takeover bid from a consortium led by Icelandic businessman Eggert Magnusson has been successfully completed this morning.

Following the finalisation of necessary paperwork and formalities between lawyers acting on behalf of the two parties on

Monday evening, a statement was released to the London Stock Exchange today, confirming acceptance from the major shareholders of an £85 million offer.

For a club steeped in such strong traditions this was a big deal. A really big deal. Not just a big deal financially, but emotionally too. The chairman was not a Cearns, a White, a Brown or a Pratt. Well, actually, we would reserve judgement on that.

'Eggy', as he became affectionately known, had kind eyes and seemed to be instantly welcomed, being the acceptable face of international corporate banking slowly taking over football. He talked the talk, but we had yet to see if he could walk the walk.

Initial signs were good, with Sheffield United being put to the sword 1–0 (if that counts as being put to the sword), but that was as comprehensive as it got for West Ham at that time, and Hayden Mullins doubled his Premier League total.

But then came a run of form you would not want when trying to impress your new employers. We lost 2–0 at Everton, Lee Bowyer proving that he is to goal-scoring what Katie Hopkins is to tact and diplomacy. Then the annual home defeat to Wigan was followed by a 4–0 hammering at Bolton. That Sam Allardyce was really starting to get on my tits.

Pardew was sacked on 11 December 2006, just over three years after he had come in. It had certainly been an emotional rollercoaster of a ride with two play-off finals and an FA Cup final to look back on, not to mention a highly successful first season back in the Premier League. But for all that, Pardew always carried the air of an arrogant man, something confirmed by those who had worked with him.

I still couldn't help feeling a little bit sorry for him though. His progress had been thrown by the signing of two players he had not asked for as part of a takeover deal which never took place. I dare say Pardew's luck may have turned eventually anyway, but he deserved to let it happen at its own pace and not have it accelerated the way it was.

Eggy and Björgólfur Guðmundsson or 'Bogy' (as no one called him except me – actually, I don't think anyone even knew he existed, just Eggy, who, fittingly, also looked like an egg) acted swiftly to bring in Alan Curbishley as the new man in charge.

Curbishley needed no introduction to West Ham fans of a certain age of course, having come through the youth ranks as a player. In August 1974 he became the youngest player to be named on the team sheet, as an unused substitute against Everton. He made his full debut in 1975 but was always understudy to Trevor Brooking as a creative midfielder. Frustrated by a lack of first-team opportunities, he left in 1979 for Birmingham City having made 85 appearances and scored 5 goals. I met Curbishley in 1996 while covering Charlton Athletic Veterans' tour to Barcelona. He spoke of his frustration at the time, and seemed to harbour real bitterness at the lack of opportunities presented to him during his time there.

I found that hard accept. Curbishley was a good player. But he wasn't a *great* player like Brooking. It was hardly surprising his chances were limited – I saw no reason for the sour taste. Anyway, it didn't seem to affect his decision to accept the post of manager:

> If you could have said to me when I was 16, joining the club as an apprentice that one day I'd be the manager I would have thought it was impossible. I'm deeply, deeply delighted and obviously looking forward to the challenge. I know everybody says the same thing – but I am. It's just a privilege to be here.

Curbishley brought with him another former Hammer, Mervyn Day, as his assistant, and Charlton legend Keith Peacock as part of his backroom team.

Their first task was to take on Manchester United, who were flying and heading for the title. They had not lost away all season and won 7 of their last 8 matches. West Ham, on the other hand, had not. Curbishley had never won a Premier League match against Manchester United in fourteen attempts. It didn't bode well.

But maybe as an ex-player Curbishley had brought something of the 'West Ham Way' with him. Manchester United battered us, missing gilt-edged chances through Cristiano Ronaldo, Ryan Giggs and Wayne Rooney before Sheringham and Harewood combined on the right with fifteen minutes to go to set up Nigel Reo-Coker to score the winner.

Reo-Coker was actually proving himself to be a bit of a twat around that time. Linked with a move to Arsenal in the summer, there had apparently been official enquiries made, which he alleged were never passed on to him. He seemed to blame Pardew for any potential move breaking down and started behaving like a spoiled brat.

Needless to say, his form suffered too, and some felt he was largely responsible for Pardew getting the sack. But Pards continued to pick him, so you work it out. Whatever the issues, it seemed the change of manager gave Reo-Coker a new lease of life, whether he merited it or not.

It was a great start, an unexpected start, and a 0–0 draw away at Fulham meant we had two welcome clean sheets and 4 points from Curbishley's first 2 games in charge. We closed 2006 at home to Portsmouth and Manchester City. We lost 2–1 to Portsmouth, Teddy Sheringham scoring his last goal for West Ham, and 1–0 to City, to temper the enthusiasm somewhat for the Curbishley regime and draw an end to what had largely been a dreadful first half of the season.

Surely, 2007 would yield better things, starting on New Year's Day with a nice straightforward game away at Reading.

17

A MOMENT LIKE THIS

Nine quid for a burger at the football? Are you having a laugh?

I don't know what happened that New Year's Day at the Madejski. It's all consigned to the farthest reaches of my memory in any event. I would rather forget about it to be honest. I won't go over it again here. It's all too painful. But it didn't help that Yossi Benayoun publicly criticised his team mates after the game, saying they played like drunks and that the defence was awful. Perhaps he was angling for the annual Nigel Reo-Coker 'Mr Popular' award.

West Ham were trying to make the England cricket team feel better after they had lost their Ashes series in Australia 5–0, the first whitewash since the 1920/21 tour.

The initial bounce experienced from Curbishley coming in and the new owners should have made us confident, but instead we stayed in 18th place, trying desperately not to look down. Still, we did have the January transfer window to look forward to – and a new owner with apparently limitless funds.

Javier Mascherano had already seen enough and wanted to hop off to Liverpool. It was hard to form an opinion. It was clear he was a massively talented player, but he just wasn't up for it. FIFA were blocking the move, however, as it would have breached the rule that states you cannot be registered for more than two different clubs in a season. Tevez, on the other hand, always gave 100 per cent even if it wasn't quite coming off for him.

The limitless funds were not spent chasing the likes of Kaká or Rooney though. The first signing of the Icelandic era was… drum roll please… Luís Boa Morte.

We beat Brighton 3–0 in the third round of the FA Cup, fairly routinely, with Cole and Mullins on the scoresheet and Mark Noble grabbing his first goal for West Ham. He looked so pleased I thought he was going to explode.

A couple of days later I panicked slightly on reading the headline 'Magnusson Dies' but it turned out not to be Eggy, but Magnus, the former host of *Mastermind*.

Speculation continued about new signings, but they were not quite the names I was hoping for. Shaun Wright-Phillips was mentioned, not for the first time. This was not inspiring me with much hope. Next up: Nigel Quashie. Nigel Fucking Quashie? Seriously? The same Nigel Quashie relegated with QPR, Nottingham Forest, Southampton and West Bromwich Albion? Was he unlucky or just shit? I know which I thought it was.

Quashie made his debut in the game against Fulham at Upton Park, which was significant as they were near us in the table and 3 points would have been massive. Tevez went off after only ten minutes or so and Radzinski put Fulham in front, but Bobby Zamora equalised before half time. Benayoun seemed to have put his differences with his colleagues to one side to put us in front twice in the second half. Leading 3–2 going into the 90th minute, you know what is coming. It'll end up 3–3 with Bobby Zamora having been sent off. What was beginning to look like a very welcome 3 points against relegation rivals turned into a disastrous draw with more players injured and suspended.

Still the depth of Eggy's pockets had not even begun to be explored. We started to get some idea when Lucas Neill arrived from Blackburn Rovers on a two-and-a-half-year contract. Liverpool were sniffing around him, but he chose to join us. The transfer fee was only £1.5 million and Liverpool had ceded to us, which could mean only one thing: we had offered him stupid wages.

Talks continued, and more players seemed likely to come

before the end of the window. A £4 million bid was turned down by Birmingham City for Matthew Upson, and we were also in for Tottenham's Calum Davenport on a permanent deal after he had made 10 appearances on loan three years earlier in the Championship.

Again, hardly David Beckham. But I was prepared to wait and see.

Things improved slightly at St James's Park where we raced into a 2–0 lead through Cole and Harewood, only for the officials to let us down, allowing a shot from James Milner to stand, despite Scott Parker being in an offside position and clearly in Rob Green's line of vision. Nolberto Solano equalised from the spot after Boa Morte had a brain fart and handled in the area, so, despite dominating, we had to settle for a point. Draws away from home were fine if we were winning at home, but any kind of points were proving hard to come by and, worse, the new signings were not gelling.

Watford dumped us out of the FA Cup, 1–0. A very disappointing performance given we had reached the final only nine short months before. Even more disappointing was seeing Teddy Sheringham make his last appearance in the claret and blue. Despite my reservations about him he had proved me totally wrong. He shows that the first yard in football is in the head. He made 87 appearances (including 38 as a substitute), scoring 30 goals.

Liverpool beat us 2–1 at home, with loan signing from Sevilla Kepa Blanco getting on the scoresheet as the transfer window started to slide towards closing, or 'slamming shut', as they always say. Why can't anyone just close it?

Surprise, surprise, FIFA relaxed the three-club rule to allow Liverpool to take Javier Mascherano off our hands and more rumours abounded, this time an £18 million bid to Charlton for Darren Bent, which was denied by all parties, so it was probably true. Charlton would have been mad to sell at that stage, and they were up to their knees in it, as we were. Why would you sell your best player to a relegation rival?

Tyrone Mears went off to Derby on loan for the rest of the season and finally a bid for Matthew Upson was accepted. He joined for £6 million with a further £1.5 million in add-ons, proving that when it came to the transfer market, Birmingham owners Gold and Sullivan drove a hard bargain.

Upson made his debut at Villa Park in a 1–0 defeat and in the best West Ham tradition was promptly injured. Watford came to town and repeated the cup trick, beating us by the same score. It was looking bleak. We were spending money like water, but the team was not improving and wasn't even showing any signs of doing better. The transfer window had shut. We had done our deals, played our cards. Now all we could do was wait and hope our luck changed.

18

RUBY

The nadir of the season had yet to come. They say the darkest hour is just before dawn, but Dawn was still coming around the corner and she was carrying a massive bucket of shit to empty over our heads, in the form of Charlton Athletic and Tottenham Hotspur.

Charlton had disposed of the services of Iain Dowie in December after a disastrous start to the Premier League season, despite spending more than any Charlton manager in their history. So who did they turn to? Alan Pardew of course. When the two teams met at the Valley on 24 February Charlton were 18th and West Ham in 19th, with just 23 points from 27 games and looking dead certs for relegation.

A good result at Charlton was therefore essential. We got battered 4–0. I remember that day well. I turned the radio off and explained to the unmentionable ex we were as good as relegated. Charlton were now 3 points above us in 18th but, more importantly, we were a whole 9 points behind Wigan in 17th and Sheffield United in 16th. It was going to take a miracle to keep us up.

Sinking further still, the club was charged with a breach of Premier League Rules relating to the transfers of Carlos Tevez and Javi Mascherano.

A statement on the official website on 2 March read:

It is the [Premier League] board's complaint that there were agreements in relation to both these transfers that enabled third parties to acquire the ability materially to influence the club's policies and/or the performance of its teams in League matches and/or the competitions set out in Rule E.10.

The board's view is this constitutes a breach of Rule U.18, which states: 'No Club shall enter into a contract which enables any other party to that contract to acquire the ability materially to influence its policies or the performance of its teams in League Matches or in any of the competitions set out in Rule E.10.'

Furthermore, at the time of the transfer agreements for both Carlos Tevez and Javier Mascherano, and until 24 January 2007, West Ham United failed to disclose the third-party agreements to the Premier League and/or deliberately withheld these agreements from the Premier League.

The board's view is this constitutes a breach of Rule B.13, which states: 'In all matters and transactions relating to the League each club shall behave towards each other club and the League with the utmost good faith.

Bollocks.

The first stirrings of a recovery showed themselves against Tottenham at Upton Park on 4 March. With 10 games to go we started to play. Mark Noble scored his first Premier League goal, drilling the ball low into the Tottenham net after Tevez chested down Konchesky's cross into his path.

Then, finally, Tevez scored and the roof came off Upton Park. He had won the free kick himself just to the edge of the D, and no one else was going to take it. He curled the ball just under the bar and the relief was tangible. Off came the shirt as he dived into the West Stand, and he wasn't seen for about five minutes. It looked like, finally, we had some spark.

But teams in relegation trouble are not used to holding on to leads, and so it proved this time: first Defoe from the spot and then Tainio levelled things up in the second half. There was one more Herculean effort, and Bobby Zamora headed us 3–2 in front with just five minutes to go.

Then complete heartbreak as Berbatov and Stalteri scored. It was one of those moments when the world stood still and nothing else seemed important. Football, as we have discussed, is nothing more than a game, but when you are caught up in the emotion it is all that matters. A point would have been disappointing, but not a disaster under the circumstances. To lose the game from 2–0 and 3–2 up was hard to take and, I felt, the body blow would be impossible to recover from.

We were still 10 points from safety with just 9 games to go. We resigned ourselves to the inevitable.

Accepting that relegation was a certainty seemed to change our fortunes a little. We had shown we could play with freedom against Tottenham, but didn't have the slice of luck we needed to put the game to bed.

Against Blackburn at Ewood Park we had the whole season's luck in one match.

First, Robert Green was lucky to stay on the pitch after sliding recklessly into a challenge outside the box, the referee judging no contact was made. Blackburn went 1–0 up early in the second half through Samba, then Tevez won a penalty that looked more like a slip as he checked back in the box in driving East Lancashire rain. Howard Webb gave it, we took it, Tevez scored it.

Then the most bizarre goal of the season. A corner from the left by Etherington, knocked on by Hayden Mullins. Lee Bower had a swipe at it but didn't connect properly; it came out to Bobby Zamora, who hit it straight at Carlos Tevez who was standing on the goal line. Except, according to Howard Webb, he must have been standing behind the goal line as the goal was given.

Without goal line technology it was hard to see how he or the linesman could have been certain the ball had gone over the line. I wasn't convinced, but I took it. To add insult to injury for Blackburn they had David Bentley sent off for two yellows, the second being a deliberate handball on the edge of our box.

Harsh, but it was Howard Webb – and Mark Hughes opened a new bag of lemons for the press conference.

At last a bit of luck. Those sorts of things usually went against us, not for us. It was the turning point. Suddenly, it felt like we could concentrate of football and not be talking about third-party registrations, Icelandic takeovers, or Anton Ferdinand going AWOL during international break when he claimed he had been visiting his granny.

We still had Arsenal, Chelsea and Manchester United to play in the final eight games, but at last we had a sniff. We knew Watford and Charlton were both poor sides and would likely make up two of the three relegation places. Sheffield United, Wigan and Manchester City were also in the mix. But it was still a long shot for us. We were still 7 points away from safety.

That was the situation on 31 March when Middlesbrough came to Upton Park. By this stage, as fans, we were not confident the corner had been turned, but something must have clicked with the players. An efficient, 2–0 win with Zamora knocking in a poorly cleared Tevez cross, and Tevez himself benefitting from some poor defending: he mopped up after a Lucas Neill cross was served up to him on a plate by Boro's defence.

It was as comprehensive as the score line suggested, with future England boss Gareth Southgate stood on the touchline looking like a disappointed geography teacher rather than a football coach. How could we be below them in the table?

At the end of March what had been a 10-point gap to safety was cut to 5; Wigan hit a run of poor form just as we stepped into gear. Sheffield United hovered above them, just 2 points better off.

We went to the Emirates for the first time still dining out on the fact we had been the last team to win at Highbury. Arsenal had not lost at their new home and were comfortably sat inside the top four when we arrived there on 7 April. Much has been said about the goals of Carlos Tevez keeping us alive to that point, but in this match, it was the Robert Green show. Given the results we had since he had come into the team it would be easy to think the average West Ham fan may not have rated him. But it was clear from day one here we had a goalkeeper who had the potential to be among the West Ham greats – and even to be mentioned in the same breath as Phil Parkes, Luděk Mikloško and, er, those two.

Green made a string of superb saves that afternoon against an Arsenal side who had every right to think they would beat us easily. Bobby Zamora had other ideas, latching on to a long punt from Lucas Neill, stretching out his left peg and looping it over Jens Lehmann in the Arsenal goal.

We had upset them. The onslaught came. Green saved shots from Ljungberg, Gilberto Silva, Adebayor (which defied explanation and the laws of physics) and Fàbregas hitting the post. Then Silva, wary of our keeper's form, put one wide when he should have scored. We had seen it many times before and many times since: a brave rearguard action that eventually results in capitulation and the waving of the white flag. But nothing of the like happened on 7 April 2007, and another 3 points were added to the survival cause.

In such good form I confidently headed down the M1 to Sheffield the following Saturday and just because I was there we got well and truly spanked. Tevez played the full ninety minutes, but I did not hear the Sheffield United board or manager Neil Warnock complain about his eligibility at that stage. Funny that.

Home to Chelsea next, one we had written off, but given what had happened at the Emirates a few days before you just didn't know. Tevez scored a brilliant equaliser after oft-mentioned Shaun Wright-Phillips had given Chelsea the lead. Tevez's goal that night was probably the finest he scored for West Ham, bending it in from the left corner of the box. But its significance was undermined as pretty much straight from the restart Chelsea raced up the other end and went back in front. The Blues scored two more and it would be easy to think that having shown signs of recovery, two setbacks like this would put us back to square one, but the team had grown and developed into a solid unit under Curbishley and, as with the previous season under Pardew, was starting to select itself.

David Moyes's hard-to-beat Everton side were next. It was

important we find our winning touch again if we were to keep survival hopes alive. Zamora scored the winner with a fine shot from twenty-five yards after good work from Benayoun, and the belief was back.

Just as well, as it hadn't escaped anyone's notice that there were only three games left and we were still knee-deep in the soft and smelly. As Wigan away approached on 28 April we remained one off the bottom with 30 points, but only 3 from safety with Wigan and Sheffield United both on 35 (albeit with vastly superior goal differences).

The 'Tevez Affair', as it was to be known, was coming to a head. The Premier League fined West Ham a record-breaking £5.5 million for breaching rules in respect of third-party ownership. West Ham's lawyer, Jim Sturman, admitted the club had broken rule U.18, a regulation relating to third-party influence over the policies of a team, and B.13, which requires all members of the League to act in good faith.

The Premier League's disciplinary commission chairman, Simon Bourne-Arton QC, concluded that while there was no proof the third-party agreements materially influenced club policies, they allowed for the possibility.

He also indicated West Ham's former chief executive, Paul Aldridge, had told Premier League chief executive Richard Scudamore 'a direct lie' over the contracts which detailed the ownership of the Argentine players, and how they were owned by four offshore companies.

Bourne-Arton rejected claims made by the then club lawyer, Scott 'Teflon' Duxbury (by now West Ham's chief operating officer), that he had received assurances from Premier League officials that it was not necessary to disclose such documents. The commission also found the contracts with the four offshore companies were not legally binding.

We were spared a points deduction, but the Premier League flexed its muscles, saying it could terminate the registration. It chose not to, and Carlos was clear to play against Wigan. This was the end of the matter as far as I could see.

A win at Wigan was vital then. Luís Boa Morte lobbed the keeper for the first. Zamora rolled the ball to Benayoun for the second after great work from Tevez and McCartney. Carlos hit the post and Reo-Coker could only hit the rebound straight at the defender on the line. Then, from a Wigan corner, Tevez picked the ball up on the edge of our own area and rolled it into the path of Reo-Coker on the right, who played the ball into an unmarked Boa Morte in the middle. He shaped to shoot but rolled a deft pass to the left for the onrushing Marlon Harewood – on as a substitute – to get the third; his 53rd and final goal for West Ham.

It was a significant result. Now level on points with Wigan, the goal difference deficit, which had been 11 on Saturday morning, was suddenly just five.

As we headed into our final home game of the season, it was a comfort to know that although it was against Bolton, it was not Sam Allardyce's Bolton. He had resigned a couple of weeks before. Our luck was in again. We had to win. With champions Manchester United away on the last day, anything other than a win was unthinkable if survival was to be a reality.

And win we did. Tevez, the newly crowned Hammer of the Year, won a free kick in virtually the same spot as he had done against Spurs, with exactly the same outcome. Goal! Noble and Boa Morte combined in midfield to pick out Tevez in the box. Goal! Tevez lobbed the ball across the area for Mark Noble to volley home. Goal!

3–0 up at half time and the nerves were settled. Bolton, now managed by Sammy 'Off-side' Lee, rolled over and showed us their bellies for the first time in forever.

Out of the bottom three for the first time since 5 December, I had to remember not to get carried away. Sheffield United, one place above us and level on 38 points, were at home to Wigan, 1 place and 3 points behind us – but with a better goal difference. If the inevitable happened at Old Trafford and Wigan beat Sheffield United, we were going down.

19

BEAUTIFUL LIAR

MANCHESTER UNITED 0, WEST HAM UNITED 1
PREMIER LEAGUE, 13 MAY 2007

David Cameron. Drops a bomb then slings his hook, leaving us with
that witch Theresa May in charge. Well, nominally. Thanks a lot Dave.
As Danny Dyer would say: twat.

Wigan came from behind to beat Sheffield United. Had we
lost to Manchester United we would have been down. But
we won. Carlos Tevez scored in the first half, playing a one-two
with Zamora that looped up in the air. In one motion he hit the
ball first time along the ground and under Van der Sar.

As at the Emirates a few weeks earlier we had poked the hor-
net's nest and had to face the consequences. Manchester United
had just been crowned champions and would have wanted to
sign off with a win in front of their home fans. But we had the
bigger incentive.

Immediately the popular press latched on the fact Tevez's
goal had 'saved West Ham'. This was of course utter bollocks
as a 0–0 would have been sufficient to keep us up. There can
be no doubt Tevez's goals and performances from the start of
March were instrumental in hauling us out of trouble. But as I
have argued previously, I am convinced that had he not arrived
at all, we would not have been in such a perilous position to
start with.

In the end we survived with 41 points. Watford, Charlton and
Sheffield United went down and we finished above both Wigan
and Fulham in 15th. A glance at the final table gave no hint of

the turmoil we had been through. We could now relax over the summer and regroup.

Sheffield United had other ideas though. Unhappy at the fact they simply didn't accumulate enough points to stay up, they filed proceedings against the Premier League in a bid to enforce a points deduction, thereby saving themselves. FIFA also indicated it would investigate the Premier League's decision. I thought they should wind their necks in and mind their own business. Let he who is without sin cast the first stone, after all, eh, FIFA?

I have often said that when West Ham do well, my personal life is shit and vice versa. But by 2007 the lines were more blurred. What constituted 'good' and 'bad' for me and for West Ham wasn't always completely clear. I had been doing well working in Leeds at Keypoint. My boss was a progressive type and despite my protestations he persuaded me to learn every aspect of the job, which meant when the first round of redundancies came around I was too useful to get rid of.

I had been urging the managing director to run a pilot scheme testing the water for PPI claims. But he was convinced reclaiming bank charges was the way to go, so we set about advertising and obtaining clients in that area.

The terraced house with the floody basement was becoming too much, so we put it on the market, and as my job seemed fairly secure we stretched ourselves and took out a mortgage of £140,000 to buy a fairly new three-bed semi on a nice, quiet estate in Thackley. No cellar. On the day we exchanged contracts the government announced a review of the bank charges situation and all claims were put on hold. Having just committed myself to the biggest debt of my life I faced redundancy again.

Mum and Dad celebrated their fiftieth wedding anniversary in July and I headed down the M1 to London with the unmentionable ex for their celebration dinner. It was to be a lunchtime meal, sometime around 2 p.m. But, like arriving two hours before football, the unmentionable ex could not understand why I might want to arrive at the venue more than ten minutes before the allotted time. Never mind that I hardly saw my family more than three or four times a year. Never mind that it was my parents' golden wedding anniversary. She dragged her heels and made up daft excuses to wait at service stations so she would not have to arrive too early and make polite conversation.

She thought my family didn't like her. My family thought she didn't like them. In truth neither was the case, she just felt awkward in their company which, in turn, made them feel awkward. It wasn't much fun for anybody. So normally I went down by myself, for Christmas and Easter etc., but this being such a momentous occasion she reluctantly agreed to come, like a child at a wedding in an itchy suit.

We stopped at Thurrock services with only around an hour to spare before we were due to sit down to eat at the restaurant. The venue was at Swanley, just the other side of the bridge, so while disappointed I was not going to be there any earlier, we were at least on course to get there thirty minutes or so before to meet my family for drinks.

Except we didn't. While we were in the services there was a tragic accident on the M25 in which I understand a motorcyclist was killed. The road was closed. We had to crawl along the A13 and use the Blackwall tunnel, which took forever. By the time we arrived, they had not only finished the meal, but gone back to my sister's house for coffee and cake.

My poor old dad was just showing the first signs of dementia and was pacing up and down outside worrying. While it was not the unmentionable ex's fault there was an accident, and while I acknowledge a family's life was destroyed that day, I still blame her for dragging her heels and making us miss the meal. In my mind I never really forgave her.

To add insult to injury, we had only been at my sister's an hour when she was tugging my coat wanting to leave. We had a hotel booked in Hemel Hempstead to break up the return journey. Despite the fact I had been driving all day she wanted to leave straight away. I said nothing because I knew it would cause a scene. My family did not really understand. I was fuming.

None of which has anything to do with West Ham, of course,

but you must have learned by now, my books are not just about West Ham, but about perspectives. About the role West Ham plays in everyone's lives. How you remember things that happened in your life through West Ham games and recall individual matches using memories from your personal life. That's what I remember about the summer after the great escape.

Back in the world of football West Ham set about preparing for the 2007/08 season by making Scott Parker the first signing, paying £7 million to Newcastle for the midfielder who Curbishley knew well from his Charlton days. He was brought in to replace Nigel Reo-Coker, who finally got his wish and left for a 'fresh challenge' at Aston Villa, who paid £8.5 million for him. The fee we paid for him from Wimbledon was never disclosed, but it would have been nowhere near that, and I saw Scott Parker as an upgrade both in ability and attitude.

Marlon Harewood joined Reo-Coker at Villa, Sheringham went on a free transfer to Colchester United, Paul Konchesky to Fulham for £2 million, Roy Carroll was released and Shaun Newton and Tyrone Mears went to Leicester City and Derby County respectively. The biggest loss was Yossi Benayoun, who joined Liverpool for a fee of around £5 million. Benayoun had been the difference in our first season back and was still pulling the strings despite the team not playing well the following year. However, his comments after the defeat at Reading on New Year's Day probably meant the writing was on the wall from that point. He was going to be difficult to replace.

With all the new money coming into the club, by mid-July we still found ourselves with a net spend of just £100,000. It was time to find out just how deep Eggy's pockets were. Craig Bellamy signed from Liverpool for £7.5 million. Kieron Dyer from Newcastle for £6 million. Freddie Ljungberg from Arsenal for a deal valued at around £3 million. Goalkeeper Richard Wright joined on a free transfer from Everton to replace Roy Carroll. French winger Julien Faubert signed for £6 million from Bordeaux and Nolberto Solano, also from Newcastle, on a one-year contract on deadline day.

Although those figures look cheap by today's standards, they compared favourably with the levels of fees being paid by the top clubs at that time. If you took the very, very top players out of the equation, these were the next level down. Liverpool, for example, paid £20 million that summer for Fernando Torres, but brought in the likes of Benayoun for £5 million, Lucas Leiva for £6 million and Martin Skrtel for £6.5 million. We were there or thereabouts in terms of the quality of players being purchased, both with established internationals and with promising younger talent.

With the exception of Solano who was 33, they were all players in their prime: Faubert was 23, Parker 26, Bellamy 28, Dyer 29 and Ljungberg 30. All had plenty of fuel left in the tank.

Add to that the long-awaited return of Dean Ashton and we had a squad to be reckoned with; even if the average age was slightly higher than we might have liked, it seemed it would provide stability while we gathered momentum and funds to buy younger players.

Of course, in true West Ham tradition, most of the new signings were injured by the time we took on Manchester City at Upton Park on the opening day. Faubert ruptured his Achilles in a friendly, and Parker was suffering with knee ligament trouble. Of the new signings only Ljungberg and Bellamy started. City had some cash of their own to splash, with new manager Sven-Göran Eriksson appointed by new owner, the former Prime Minister of Thailand Thaksin Shinawatra.

Sheffield United were becoming a bit of a pain in the arse. They would not go away. After losing their challenge to the Premier League they threatened high court action. Tevez went off to Manchester United, but still there were wranglings over who should receive the transfer fee. The Premier League said the proceeds should go to West Ham, which did not impress Kia Joorabchian. So, basically, everyone sued everyone else, and no one took any responsibility. Terry Brown had gone, and nothing seemed to stick to Scott 'Teflon' Duxbury. It was hard to see how it would end. All that hard work to survive could potentially be for nothing.

City had struggled as we had the season before under Stuart Pearce, but looked a different proposition in the August sunshine as they romped to a 2–0 win. Two of their new signings, Bianchi and Geovanni, scored the goals.

Opening-day defeats, particularly at home, are always a disappointment, but the signs were promising. We had Dean Ashton back, albeit carrying a little extra timber and a dodgy bleached barnet. Kieron Dyer played in the next match away at newly promoted Birmingham City. A Mark Noble penalty was enough to earn victory, which was just as well as the next match was at home to Wigan, a game we always lost.

Wigan duly took the lead, but for once West Ham managed to avoid yet another home defeat to the Latics, thanks to a goal from Lee Bowyer.

Four points from the opening three matches was a fair return, but we had the same from the opening three games of the last two seasons – and they went on to end very differently. We had new signings to come back in. All we needed to do was make sure everyone stayed fit.

20

BLEEDING LOVE

DERBY COUNTY 0, WEST HAM UNITED 5
PREMIER LEAGUE, 10 NOVEMBER 2007

*Meeting people you know vaguely on the tube on the way to work
and having to talk to them. Jesus, it's like having teeth pulled.*

August came to a close after the shock news that former striker
Jeroen Boere had died. Boere played for West Ham 25 times
between 1993 and 1995, scoring 6 goals. The most memorable?
A diving header against Tottenham.

Often at the centre of trouble, Boere was forced to retire from
the professional game at 31 after losing an eye in a stabbing incident in Tokyo. He was only 39 when he died at his home in
Marbella.

The current team was preparing to take on Bristol Rovers at
the Memorial Stadium in the second round of the League Cup.
Richard Wright made his debut in goal and a brace from Craig
Bellamy indicated that we could be in for a treat. He showed
pace, power and accuracy, and a willingness to work hard for
his team-mates.

Not so fortunate was Kieron Dyer, who suffered a broken leg
despite no one actually appearing to tackle him. He would not
play again for another sixteen months.

The game at Reading provided a welcome opportunity to lay
to rest the ghosts of New Year's Day and the 6–0 drubbing. Like
Bolton, Reading had been something of a bogey team over the
years, so to gain sweet revenge with a 3–0 victory was as unexpected as it was welcome. We played some magnificent stuff
that afternoon, Bellamy banging one in from the edge of the

box, and Etherington scoring the other two with such aplomb I was worried he might be drug tested (he hit the strikes so sweetly and firmly, and I had not seen him touch a ball like that since the play-off semi against Ipswich in 2004).

Another 3–0 win followed, this time against Middlesbrough, who were usually good value for 3 points and laughably dressed in a white and gold ensemble which suggested they were half decent. Even Lee Bowyer managed to score against them, and Ashton got another. Luke Young, who had failed two medicals at West Ham, showed the reason was probably a shocking sense of direction, as he put one through his own net.

Ten points from five games, and big changes at board level again, with Eggy standing down from his executive role to concentrate on other areas of club development. A 'fresh challenge' maybe? The club seemed hell bent on moving away from Upton Park. Eggy issued a statement to reassure supporters there was nothing sinister about his move away from an executive role, stating:

> We are set to relocate to a new ground. It's clear that the Olympic Stadium is not for us but we have several other options.
>
> After having had discussions with Ken Livingstone we are now focusing on an area near the proposed Olympic Stadium. I think the new West Ham Stadium will fare well there and would be part of a commercial and housing area.
>
> There is a lot to do – but there is a real optimism at the club.

The other options mentioned, at that stage, included the Parcelforce site by West Ham station. The Icelandics, at least, realised at that early stage that any new Olympic Stadium was not an option worth pursuing.

Sitting in 5th place, it was enough to tempt me up the A1 to see our next match at Newcastle, now managed by our nemesis Big (not fat) Sam Allardyce. Sat up in the gods as had now become the norm at Newcastle, we were also treated to sitting in what seemed to be the middle of a construction site. This turned out to be appropriate, as we witnessed first hand our team being demolished. Mark Viduka scored twice for Newcastle and Charles N'Zogbia ran the show and scored a third. Despite a well-taken goal from Ashton, we lost 1–3 and Big (not fat) Sam had us over yet again.

Scott Parker finally made his debut in the League Cup tie against Plymouth Argyle at Upton Park, a game which should not have been as difficult as it was. Fortunately, Dean Ashton scoring in the final minute of extra time saw us safely through for a fourth-round tie against Coventry City.

Against Arsenal in the next league match, Curbishley brought in Parker for Mullins, Ljungberg for Etherington and Henri Camara, a Senegalese striker signed on loan from Wigan on deadline day, started in place of Carlton Cole, who had been finding the going a little tough. Despite these changes the team seemed incapable of capturing the flowing football we had seen against Reading and Middlesbrough. Ljungberg seemed to forget he wasn't playing for Arsenal. I'm all in favour of players being nice to each other, but he seemed to be taking it to extremes, deliberately finding himself offside. Van Persie scored in the first half and Arsenal never really looked like relinquishing the lead.

At the end of September we remained on 10 points and in 11th position. A trip to Martin O'Neill's Aston Villa came next and we left empty-handed yet again. Boa Morte wasn't empty-handed though, as he was booked for punching in an Etherington cross. Carlton Cole couldn't beat Scott Carson in the Villa goal. If only Carlton had been Croatian; Carson may have been more inclined to let one slip through his hands.

Without a league win for a month, Cole finally found some form: a George McCartney cross bouncing off his head put West Ham 1–0 up against Sunderland. But they were dominating, and when their equaliser came it was no surprise. Green then tipped a Grant Leadbitter shot onto the post, effectively winning the game for us. If Sunderland had taken the lead at that point it would have been curtains. Instead, West Ham raced up the other end (well, it was Boa Morte, so West Ham sauntered up to the other end) and the ball broke to substitute Nolberto Solano, who hit a shot against the post which cannoned back to the committed Craig Gordon and bounced in off his calf. It was a much-needed bit of luck, and Craig Bellamy gave the scoreline some injury time gloss it didn't really deserve.

At Fratton Park Nobby Solano showed his head was only good for putting a hat on, missing two glorious chances. I don't mean mis-directing the ball, I mean missing the ball; the second one was a rebound from Cole's shot that hit the bar. Maybe it was the fucking irritating bell that constantly rings at Pompey. Gabbidon was harshly adjudged to have handled in the area, but Green saved Benjani's spot kick, and the West Ham fans went mad, celebrating like it was a last-minute winner.

In midweek we travelled to Coventry in the cup, Iain Dowie's latest haunt. And I use that word advisedly. We fell behind to a goal from Jay Tabb late on and that looked like the end as we hadn't offered much, but Boa Morte waved his left foot at the ball and it took a horrible deflection for an equaliser. A few minutes later Cole ran for a Boa Morte flick on, shook off his defender and rolled it past the keeper for the winner, and a place in the quarter-finals at home to Everton.

Still 11th in the league we went into November needing to put a run of results together if we were to be thinking seriously about a top-half finish. Bolton came to Upton Park not the force they had been under Allardyce, but with recently appointed former player Gary Megson at the helm. West Ham took the lead with a goal from George McCartney, a right-foot volley from twelve yards that defied his left-back status. The much-needed 3 points were whipped away in injury time however, as Kevin Nolan grabbed an equaliser when we had possession and could have easily have run the clock down. Schoolboy stuff, and surely West Ham had learned their lesson from the cup final? Surely no West Ham team would ever do that again?

There was a reaction at Pride Park though the following Saturday. Derby were awful and would go on to record the Premier

League's lowest ever points total of 11. They had already earned their solitary win of the season against Sam Allardyce's Newcastle. We were not to know in November, though, just how poor Derby were going to be – and they had to be beaten. West Ham recorded their biggest top-flight away win since a 6–1 win at Manchester City in September 1962. Bowyer opened the scoring after Solano had already hit the upright from a free-kick. Solano was instrumental in everything we did; it was his floated ball into the area that Carlton Cole knocked down in the area for Bowyer to finish. Only 1–0 at half time, but in the second half we scored 4 more. Etherington snapped up a chance laid on by Bowyer, then Jonathan Spector thought he had scored, but Derby defender Eddie Lewis trapped the ball between his legs on the line and in an effort to dig it out, merely laid an egg into his own net. Sorry, Jonathan, that goes down as an own goal.

Solano and Cole again combined to allow Bowyer to make it 4 before Solano flighted a delicious free kick into the top corner for 5.

Another Hammers hero left us that month. Graham Paddon played 152 times for West Ham between 1973 and 1976, including appearances in the FA Cup Final in 1975. He scored 15 goals. It was his shot that Fulham keeper Mellor spilled into the path of Alan Taylor for the second goal. He also played in the Cup Winners' Cup Final the following season. Paddon was a dynamic, skilful midfielder who was a firm favourite with the fans.

Croatia, managed by former West Ham player Slaven Bilić, beat England 3–2 at the newly rebuilt Wembley, securing their place in Euro 2008 by dumping England out of the competition. On a soaking wet night, McClaren opted to play untested Villa goalkeeper and Desperate Dan lookalike, Scott Carson, in goal. It proved to be a costly mistake, and he stood on the sidelines watching under a big umbrella, earning the moniker, 'the wally with the brolly'. I called him something else I can't repeat here. I was pleased for Slaven Bilić though, he was proving to be a manager of exceptional quality. Or was it just that he only had to be marginally better than Steve McClaren?

West Ham were playing better but gave away the lead again at home to Spurs and for the second time in a month relied on a Robert Green penalty save in the final minute to salvage a point. A vanilla 1–0 defeat at Stamford Bridge was disappointing, given our away form had been reasonably good up to that point. Then Dean Ashton popped up with a winner on the Sunday Sky game at Ewood Park to give us our fourth away win of the season.

Double disappointment followed against Everton. In the quarter-final of the League Cup, Curbishley decided Robert Green should play in goal ahead of Richard Wright, who had been between the sticks for the first three games. I always think this is harsh. After all, that goalkeeper had been part of the team that got us so far, he should be given the chance to carry us further. It was looking promising when Carlton Cole put us 1–0 up, but we crumbled after Everton equalised and one of the two routes to Wembley that season disappeared in front of our eyes. The following weekend, as often happens, we faced the same team again at the same venue, in the Premier League. Unfortunately, it was pretty much the same outcome, and this time David Moyes's Everton won 2–0.

I went back to London early for Christmas and planned to drive back to Bradford on Christmas Eve. But first on 22 December I watched our fifth away victory of the season at Middlesbrough, as Dean Ashton arrowed in a low, hard shot into the bottom corner and Scotty Parker picked up his first Hammers' goal in the final minute, wriggling past challenges in the box to tuck away neatly. Sitting comfortably in 10th place, the mood was positive going into Christmas.

21

NOW YOU'RE GONE

WEST HAM UNITED 1, LIVERPOOL 0
PREMIER LEAGUE, 30 JANUARY 2008
Balding men with pony tails. Yes, Francis Rossi, I'm looking at you.

On Christmas Eve I started to feel distinctly unwell. I had done my Christmas dash back to London and returned running a horrible temperature. Everything was under control, though, and as we were due to eat at the mother-in-law's on Christmas Day there was nothing to organise. So, I went to bed.

I woke on Christmas morning still with a temperature that would have set the bed alight, had it not already been drenched in sweat. My throat hurt. My head hurt. My ears hurt. I actually liked my mother-in-law, but there was no way I was leaving my pit that Christmas morning. The unmentionable ex could see I was distressed and therefore left me to it while she went and had lunch with her mother, ringing every few hours to check I was still alive. I didn't mind being on my own. I was dosed up on paracetamol, ibuprofen and whatever else I could find in the medicine cabinet, and was quietly hallucinating, too ill to watch TV or listen to the radio. I just wanted to sleep – but the pain building in my ears put paid to that.

Overnight the pain became unbearable and, still sweating like Barry White in a sauna, the build-up of pressure was finally released by a terrifying 'pop' in each ear. Fluid ran out of my ears which I assumed would be some kind of infection. But it was blood.

I was scared. The unmentionable ex bundled me into the car and took me to hospital, where I was diagnosed with a double ear infection (no shit, Sherlock?) and two perforated ear drums. I was given something for the pain and warned my hearing may go for a few days, but that it would come back.

With the pain killers I slept for the rest of the day, missing our 1–1 draw with Reading at Upton Park. When I woke, as promised, my hearing had gone. Completely.

It doesn't matter if a doctor tells you it will come back; to lose one sense completely even on a temporary basis is quite shocking and difficult to cope with. Doctors have, after all, been known to get things wrong. I was worried about work as there was no paid sick pay, but I was able to take some holiday to make sure I was feeling right before I went back to the office, even if I still couldn't hear anything.

While I was convalescing the unmentionable ex slept on the sofa, which was fine for two or three nights, then the patience wore a bit thin and she thought I should make more of an effort to get better, so we swapped places. Fine by me. The bed was still a bit damp anyway.

My recuperation was helped on massively by a third consecutive win over Manchester United. Robert Green saved a Ronaldo penalty and we won 2–1 with goals from Anton Ferdinand and Matthew Upson. For once the loss of hearing was a slight advantage as it meant I didn't have to listen to Garth Crooks talking absolute bollocks on *Final Score*.

We had planned to have an open house on 30 December, a plan which I wrongly assumed had been scrapped due to my profound deafness, but the unmentionable ex had other ideas and it went ahead, so I gormlessly wandered around offering people twiglets and shouting at them.

Gradually my hearing started to come back. It was good enough for me to hear people on the telephone at work. Someone gave me a baseball cap that said, 'I'm deaf, not stupid', which helped stop people getting angry when I asked them to write stuff down for me, or phone me from two desks away.

I was becoming an important cog in the Keypoint machine and soon found the PPI claims pilot I had started off using some of our own members of staff as guinea pigs was starting to bear fruit, and the MD wanted to ramp things up with me running the show. He already had cause to doubt my intelligence because he had asked me to top up the parking meter on his Bentley and tossed me the key. I told you, I was running this show. I interrupted his meeting to announce I had been unable to lock it, at which point he explained it locked itself when you walked away from the car. How was I supposed to know that? This was 2007 for god's sake. No one owned cars like that! It didn't help that I couldn't hear him, although it did give me an excuse to do things my way, because I could claim I hadn't heard what the boss had said. That wasn't washing at home, however, as patience wore very thin, even though I had seen a doctor who told me my hearing would never be quite the same again.

By the time we played Arsenal on New Year's Day at the Emirates, some sense of normality had started to return. Jack Collison made an impressive debut, but as was often the case away against the top sides in that era, we failed to make any significant impact and lost 2–0.

Manchester City's impressive start to the season had come to a grinding halt, but they still managed to force a goalless draw at Upton Park in the third round of the FA Cup. Long-term injury victim Julien Faubert played for the reserves and was set to finally make his debut in the home game against Fulham on 12 January, a mere six months after signing. It is the West Ham Way of course. Who could forget Simon Webster? He signed in July 1993 and was immediately made club captain before being crocked in training, not playing until April 1995, nearly two years later. We spent £525,000 for five sub appearances. Richard Hall similarly arrived in a blaze of glory in July 1996 only to be tackled by a postman in a friendly at Carshalton and didn't make his debut until April 1997. £1.9 million for eight appearances in total. So, when Faubert ruptured his Achilles on arrival and didn't get near the first team until January, I feared the worst. Especially as his substitute appearance against Fulham proved to be one of only eight he made that season before facing another spell out injured. It was starting to look like Webster and Hall had been bargains in comparison.

Inevitably we lost the cup replay at Manchester City and, as with Everton back in December, we then faced the same opposition a few days later at the same venue in a league match. This time the outcome was different, as Carlton managed to score first, before an equaliser from Darius Vassell meant the game ended in a 1–1 draw.

Then Liverpool came to Upton Park for a midweek fixture, which appeared to be heading for 0–0 until, in the final minute of added time, Jamie Carragher made an unnecessary lunge at Freddie Ljungberg and brought him down in the penalty area. A clearer penalty you were unlikely to ever see. Mark Noble dispatched the spot kick to give us a little bit of revenge for the 2006 cup final, nicking something off them in the last minute for a change. It was our first win over Liverpool in the league since November 1999.

A 1–0 defeat followed at Steve Bruce's Wigan Athletic on a bog of a pitch, Kevin Kilbane beating Rob Green with a looping header in the first half. A draw against Birmingham was also disappointing, given that they were deep in relegation trouble and would eventually go down at the end of the season. Freddie Ljungberg scored after 7 minutes, but a clumsy challenge from Lucas Neill that on another day might have gone unpunished gifted Birmingham a penalty. It also gifted them a point that was probably deserved. Hayden Mullins certainly deserved to be sent off for a horrible two-footed lunge on Danny Murphy, but referee Clattenburg sent off Lee Bowyer instead, who made a second, slightly less crap challenge on Roger Johnson straight afterwards. I found that quite amusing. After the game, we were 10th.

Performances were bland. Curbishley had a good bank of players to pick from and we generally played, well, blandly. There was no spark like there had been at the end of the previous campaign, but then we didn't have Carlos Tevez anymore. But we did have Dean Ashton back, and we had exciting players like Ashton, Bellamy, Solano, Etherington, Ljungberg and, er, Boa Morte. But we were still a bit bland. I cannot think of another word to describe the football at that time. Even vanilla gets a bad press these days. Ordinary, boring things are described as vanilla. Vanilla is delicious. Alan Curbishley's football was not vanilla – it was bland.

A dull 1–0 win against Fulham came at Craven Cottage courtesy of a controversial Solano goal; Fulham felt his challenge on goalkeeper Niemi was unfair, but the referee saw nothing wrong with it and we collected 3 points. Forty points achieved, there would be no drama like last season. In fact, it would be insipid.

22

4 MINUTES

TOTTENHAM HOTSPUR 4, WEST HAM UNITED 0
PREMIER LEAGUE, 8 MARCH 2008

Skiing. How is landing on your frozen arse all day considered a holiday? Falling down a mountain with two planks of wood strapped to your feet is not a sport, either.

Chelsea came to Upton Park and beat us 4–0. Managed by Avram Grant, who I thought looked like the lovechild of Neil Diamond and Baron Greenback from *Dangermouse*. He had the last laugh though; he was about to lead Chelsea to a Champions League final. Fat Frank inevitably scored. Joe Cole inevitably scored. Ballack perhaps not-so-inevitably scored, and Chelsea were 3 up in 22 minutes. Fat Frank then had a rush of blood to the head, tangling with Boa Morte and getting a dig in as he rolled over the top of him following a firm challenge. The ref saw it and sent Lampard packing.

Although John Terry made a miraculous goal-line clearance from Carlton Cole's header, namesake Ashley notched his first goal for Chelsea to make it a miserable, bland afternoon, after which we found ourselves, monotonously, back in 10th.

Anfield next, not a venue we would necessarily have chosen after a 4–0 home defeat, especially with Torres in red-hot form. Perhaps predictably, he helped himself to a hat-trick and Gerrard grabbed another and we lost 4–0 again. Again, it was dreary. Again, we were 10th.

At White Hart Lane we faced a Tottenham side more or less on a par with us in the league, but guess what? They beat us 4–0. It wasn't all bad news though, as Boa Morte was sent off for two crazy challenges in the first half which meant he would be suspended, and maybe Curbishley would be forced to wake up and make some changes. We lost three consecutive games 4–0 but somehow remained 10th. I would have taken that over a relegation scrap. But only just. This was almost as painful. It was tedious.

Surely the rot had to stop at home to Blackburn Rovers, our traditional Premier League punch bags. Mark Hughes also generally came to grief as a manager at Upton Park. But the form was so awful it was no surprise when Roque Santa Cruz put Blackburn ahead in the first half. Ashton equalised soon after, then Freddie Sears, a nineteen-year-old youth team product, came on as a substitute with fifteen minutes to go. It was a Tony Cottee moment. Local, home-grown talent comes on, scores and goes on to get 100-plus in a glittering career with the club. As per the script, he latched on to a Dean Ashton back-heel. His first shot was blocked by Friedl, but the rebound fell kindly for him and he stooped gracefully to head in the rebound – just as Tony Cottee had done on New Year's Day 1983 when the ball bounced back off the crossbar against Spurs. We weren't to know Freddy would not score again until New Year's Day 2011. His goal filled us with hope, though, however misplaced, and the 2–1 win meant we were… 10th.

Another youth team graduate, central defender James Tomkins, made his debut at Goodison Park, making it six home-grown players who had featured that season. Curbishley was painfully cautious, but he did at least seem willing to give youth a chance in a measured and sympathetic way. Those six players included the already established Mark Noble, and Anton Ferdinand along with Jack Collison, Kyel Reid, Tomkins and Sears. Tomkins almost scored against Everton, but in the end Dean Ashton netted another belter to grab a point in a game we should have won. Ashton had a free kick miraculously saved by Tim Howard's studs after it took a mean deflection. Freddy Sears had one of those sliding doors moments when through on goal he beat Howard – but not the post. Maybe if that had gone in things would have worked out differently for the young striker. I suspect not, though. Still, a point was better than nothing and it lifted us to 6th (only kidding, we were of course in 10th).

At the Stadium of Light Ljungberg scored his second and final goal for West Ham, but it wasn't enough to prevent a 2–1 defeat and send us back into 10th.

Single-goal defeats at home to Portsmouth and away at Bolton reeked of a team that wanted the season to end so they could start again. Poor old Derby, already relegated, they were put to the sword at Upton Park. Bobby Zamora scored his final goal for West Ham and Carlton Cole tapped in a second for a 2–1 win that left us in 10th. We did not realise at the time it was Zamora's last goal for us, but a special mention has to go to Bobby who gave great service to us in the four years he was at the club. Four years spanning five seasons is about as long as service gets in the modern game. Bobby specialised in the spectacular and the vital. His play-off goals against Ipswich and Preston are milestones in the modern history of the club. In total he made 100 starts, 52 substitute appearances and scored 40 goals.

After that the season rather petered out, with 2–2 draws at home against Newcastle and Aston Villa, and a 4–1 defeat at Old Trafford, most memorable for an acrobatic bicycle kick goal from Dean Ashton. We finished 10th.

Overall, and from a distance, the season had been a great success, but a lot of money had been spent and one might be forgiven for expecting something a little more thrilling. I went to the games sometimes carrying a box of matches with me to prop my eyelids open. Chants of 'Too fucking negative' from the stands must have hurt Curbishley, but West Ham fans are a demanding bunch, and sometimes simply winning is not enough. It has to be done with style.

Still, we had a board with deep pockets, rich shirt sponsors in XL Airways and a safe, if somewhat pallid, pair of hands on the rudder. As long as the Icelandic economy stayed buoyant, there was every reason to be optimistic.

23

I KISSED A GIRL

WEST BROMWICH ALBION 3, WEST HAM UNITED 2
PREMIER LEAGUE, 13 SEPTEMBER 2008
Queuing to pay for petrol behind someone doing their weekly
shop at the garage. Go to the fucking supermarket.

The summer of 2008 was a chance for the club to move forward. Having steadied the ship after the turmoil of 2006/07, and with the signings made in 2007/08, a solid 10th place finish presented an opportunity to press on. Surely, top names in Europe would now want to join, seeing the level of spending that was going on, especially given the fact we had a springboard to push forward into Europe. In Dean Ashton and Craig Bellamy we had two of the best strikers in the Premier League. Robert Green had proved himself to be worthy of an England call, even if that was somewhat slow to materialise, and in Matthew Upson and Scott Parker we had the spine of a very good team (although it later transpired Upson's spine was actually made of papier-mâché).

England were not involved in Euro 2008 largely thanks to Steve McClaren, who was shown the door by the FA, and in came a second foreign manager: Postman Pat with a heavy Italian accent. Maybe he would recognise Robert Green's ability.

It is a strange thing among football fans who follow a club side closely that they always criticise the incumbent England manager for overlooking their players. But once they are selected, and after the initial euphoria dies down there comes the worry. Will they get injured? Will they let the nation down?

Many people say they no longer care about the national

side. I wouldn't go as far as to say that myself, but England's matches do not have the same prestige they used to. There are a number of reasons for this, partly because when I was growing up, England's matches were the only live football you ever saw on TV, apart from the FA Cup final. That made them special. The Home International series, England v. Scotland on a Saturday afternoon on *Grandstand* or *World of Sport* was a thing to behold. Now it's just another game. Just another opportunity for your players to get injured, another opportunity for your players to let your country down.

Having said all that, I still feel it like a dagger through the heart when England get knocked out of a major tournament. I watched the Euro 2008 final from a bar in Santorini, which was possibly the best place to watch Spain beat Germany.

The summer transfer activity showed worrying signs. The previous two windows had seen a lot of players brought in for decent fees. But now it seemed the chairman's pockets were not as deep as we thought. In the letter sent out to season ticket holders for renewal in May 2008, the chairman said:

> Although certainly less eventful than the previous season I have been pleased with our progress and it gives the club a platform from which to progress further …
>
> I share the frustration expressed by Alan [Curbishley] about the scale of our injuries but endorse his view that the squad he has assembled should be given a chance to play together while allowing the exciting young talents emerging from our Academy the chance to establish themselves in the first team squad.
>
> When I first purchased the club in December 2006 I was keen to emphasise my long-term commitment to building the club. It was always my intention to invest further funds in the club to strengthen the first team squad.
>
> To this end the club has invested at [*sic*] net £40m in the squad since the takeover – and I hope that next season we will finally see a settled side with a realistic chance of competing for honours.

To me this had an ever-so slight whiff of bullshit about it. Considering the amount of money spent, 8 points, effectively 2 wins and 2 draws, was not a huge improvement on the quasi-disaster of 2006/07. We had lost three games in a row 4–0 and played football that turned your eyelids inside out with boredom. The final paragraph, to me, said we have spent £40 million, now let's see it settle. In other words: you are not getting any more.

And that was how it seemed to be with the majority of the summer signings being loan deals. The only permanent arrival pre-season was Valon Behrami, a Swiss international of Albanian parentage who we signed from Lazio for £5 million. This was an exciting signing; the prospect of his creativity in midfield with Parker's steel and drive was something I was particularly looking forward to.

Dean Ashton finally won his first England cap, playing the first half of a friendly against Trinidad and Tobago in Port of Spain. I suppose there are worse places to win your first cap.

Ashton's form won him a new, lucrative five-year deal at the club. On the same day this was announced the club also disclosed they had reached an out-of-court settlement with that knob Kia Joorabchian.

An article in *The Times* said Joorabchian had instructed his legal team to withdraw a High Court claim made against West Ham United for fees totalling £7.1 million, which he had insisted he was owed by for his involvement in the Tevez and Mascherano transfers.

Worryingly, part of the deal seemed to involve the slimeball having closer dealings with West Ham transfers in future, to allow him to earn back some of the fees he had initially felt he had been diddled out of. There was only one person doing any diddling as far as I could see.

I didn't want him anywhere near the club. I thought he was trouble. But at least it meant he probably wouldn't bite the hand currently feeding him and testify for Sheffield United in their upcoming case against us. A shitty situation if ever there was one.

Another out-of-court settlement had been reached with Terry Brown who had been suing the club for lost earnings after being kicked off the board by Eggy in February 2007 for his involvement in the Tevez transfer. Not only was an out-of-court settlement reached, but he was invited back onto the board. So both Joorabchian and Brown, the people most culpable in my view for the clusterfuck that was 2006/07, not only got paid, but got new jobs out of it. Only in football, and only at West Ham. I hated both of them. Passionately.

I hated all the politics going on in the background and wanted to ignore it, but this really was significant stuff and it was clear a lack of harmony at board level had an influence throughout the club and affected results. People can say what they like about what happens once you cross that white line not being influenced by the atmosphere at board level. It most definitely is.

I couldn't wait for the season to start and to see how the new signings would blend in with the existing squad. Bobby Zamora and John Paintsil went off to Fulham, Zamora claiming as he left that West Ham needed the money. Whether they did or not it was good business and a round £7.5 million came our way. Freddie Ljungberg also left, despite claiming he was happy to stay. I would have been happy to stay too, on a reported £85,000 a week; it was one of the deals that had seen the end of Eggy. Ljungberg had cost a total of around £11 million, roughly £440,000 per appearance, £5.5 million per goal. Excellent value for money. As Ljungberg seemed reluctant to leave for some reason and, even more surprisingly, no one else wanted to take him on with those wages, the club paid off the final two years of his contract. Ouch. Nobby Solano, who had proved much more effective, was also released. Goalkeeper Richard Wright left the club and was replaced by Jan Laštůvka, on loan from Shakhtar Donetsk.

The campaign began with transfer business far from completed, but it was already clear funds were stretched and there would be more leaving than arriving, and that those who were coming in would be loan signings.

The opening game of the season at Upton Park was against perennial party-poopers Wigan Athletic. This time, though, the only pooping would be in the Wigan dugout, as a lithe and fit-looking Dean Ashton scored twice in the first ten minutes to give West Ham an opening day win, 2–1. Ashton's first was a sight for sore eyes, perfect centre-forward play as the ball was first controlled on the edge of the area, a tight turn and a fierce shot lashed into the top corner. That was typical Dean Ashton, and just what we had been missing. I prayed for his fitness.

Ashton's form was especially important as it seemed Craig Bellamy could possibly be on the move – he was in talks with Manchester City. Anton Ferdinand was also heading off, and in an £8 million deal he moved to Sunderland. The transfer was shrouded in controversy. It felt like there was friction everywhere in the club and it seemed only a matter of time before a spark would set off the whole tinder box. Teflon-coated CEO Scott Duxbury claimed the club accepted the £8 million offer from Sunderland after Ferdinand rejected a new lucrative contract said to be worth £45,000 a week. Ferdinand, however, said it was more that the contract West Ham offered him was withdrawn as soon as it was clear Sunderland were interested at that level. I saw no reason why Ferdinand would lie about it and therefore I knew which version of events I believed.

His transfer left the club with only two fit centre-backs, Calum Davenport and Matthew Upson. This was quite a worrying situation as it seemed the sale of Ferdinand was not endorsed by Curbishley.

The lack of defensive cover was ruthlessly exposed by Manchester City at Eastlands as they cruised home 3–0.

A 4–1 home win over Macclesfield in the League Cup was also overshadowed by further controversy over ticket prices, £25 being charged for band one seats. That, and the 3–0 reverse at City, combined to result in West Ham's ninth lowest attendance in the Premier League era: just 10,055 turned up at Upton Park to witness another struggle, the game going into extra time. Most of the other previous lows had been in unpopular

Full Members' Cup or Anglo-Italian Cup ties. The previous low for a major competition had been 6,981 in the League Cup against Crewe in 1992. A record poor turnout that is unlikely to be beaten, one would hope.

The score was 1–1 at full time, Lee Bowyer equalising Macclesfield's early opener, before Carlton nodded in Ashton's tee-up and, as youth team products Zavon Hines and Kyel Reid both grabbed their first goals for the club, they skewed the score somewhat undeservedly in our favour.

Paul Ince was still an unpopular figure at Upton Park. I'm sure I don't have to explain why, but I would reiterate to all the tabloid papers who might think otherwise that it never had anything to do with the colour of his skin (sorry to disappoint you, tabloid press), but everything to do with him being a narky, conceited, big-headed twat.

Now he was the manager of Blackburn Rovers, the team we always beat at home, so it was nice to sit back and relax in full knowledge that for once, Ince would have his pants pulled down. And pulled down they were, then pulled up and back down again as West Ham strolled to a 4–1 win. The first was a Davenport header from a Faubert corner, the second an own goal from Samba, slicing in an attempted clearance of a Mark Noble shot. Jason Roberts rolled one under Robert Green to make the half time score 2–1. Green then saved a Roberts penalty before Bellamy, whose proposed move had not come off, belted a third into the top corner and Behrami picked the Blackburn full-back's pocket to feed Scott Parker who, in turn, set up Carlton for the fourth.

It was George McCartney's last game for the club. His wife had struggled to settle in London and Sunderland had offered him the chance of a return. The club granted the move, and as Sunderland were offering £4.5 million when he had signed for £600k, it seemed like a no-brainer. However, yet again, they had done so without running the idea past Curbishley. And yet again, after the deal had been done, the player gave a different version of events to the official club line. McCartney later said he had asked for a move for family reasons but Curbishley had said no. McCartney accepted that and was ready to buckle down and work at it.

It was the final straw for Curbs, who threw in the towel. You had to sympathise. He was trying to build a squad and for the third time a player had been sold under his nose, seemingly without his consent. Ljungberg had apparently been the first. Although he did not feature in Curbishley's plans he had apparently not been consulted before his contract had been paid up.

In any other line of work that would be considered constructive dismissal. Whereas this kind of thing is commonplace in football today, it was relatively new to the Premier League in 2008. Players had previously been sold against their will, or against the will of the manager, but they had been in the loop. Curbishley took the view that it was impossible to do his job under those circumstances and walked, but that would not be the end of the matter. Curbishley also had the backing of the majority of fans, with one online poll showing 90 per cent in favour of him staying. But his mind was made up.

Former West Ham defender Slaven Bilić was linked with the job, upsetting the Croatian FA in the process. It seemed the board were nothing more than a clumsy set of oafs who could not piss against a wall without filling their boots. What else is new?

Just when things seemed like they could not get any worse, the shirt sponsors XL Airways went bust without paying their latest instalment on the deal. It didn't help that our chairman was a major shareholder, or that the bank in which he had a 40 per cent share was about to go tits-up in the global economic crisis which seemed to be disproportionately affecting Iceland.

The search for a new manager threw up a dozen or so names, none of which had been Gianfranco Zola. So it was a bit of a shock when he took on the role with former Chelsea colleague Steve Clarke as his number two. It was a worrying time. This would either work beautifully or go horribly wrong. Zola was a genius of a player, but that did not always translate into coaching. At the press conference he appeared looking like Jimmy Krankie in a collar and tie several sizes too big. It looked like he had borrowed it from Sam Allardyce. He spoke genuinely of the honour bestowed on him and his desire to play progressive, attacking football.

For their part, the board said they had not gone with the cheapest option, and now they would back the manager with new funds. Why? Why back the untried inexperienced Zola and not Curbishley? I seriously doubted there would be new funds available, and suspected that in fact, the cheapest option had been taken. With Ferdinand and McCartney gone for a combined £12.5 million, all that came in were three loan signings: David Di Michele, Hérita Ilunga and Walter López. In football parlance: big fucking deal.

Zola had a watching brief for the game against West Bromwich Albion at the Hawthorns, and Kevin Keen took caretaker charge for the match which saw the bizarre spectacle, in modern times, of both teams playing without a shirt sponsor. West Ham had Tippexed over the XL Airways logo, while the Baggies had simply failed to secure a shirt deal.

West Bromwich Albion opened the scoring, but Noble equalised from zero yards after a good header from Di Michele. Lucas Neill then gave West Ham the lead and tapped in from similar range after a knock down from Upson. But without proper leadership the team crumbled under pressure, first conceding a penalty before half time, then an 83rd-minute winner right through the heart of the defence from Chris Brunt. Typically, it was West Bromwich Albion's first win of the season.

The loss was insignificant, however. We didn't know it at the time, but it was Dean Ashton's last game of football. Not just for West Ham – his last game of professional football, full stop. An old ankle injury required surgery, and it became clear that more damage had been done than previously thought when he first got injured training with England in 2006.

Ashton was probably the best pure centre-forward I ever saw in my time watching West Ham. We've had nimble, quick strikers like Cottee, McAvennie and Bryan Robson (that's 'Pop', not the crap one who played for England) and we have had tall, brick-shit-house types like John Hartson, or, err, Dave Swindlehurst. But Ashton had everything. Touch, power, accuracy, good in the air, good on the deck – and his pace wasn't bad either. I still weep when I think what he might have achieved had he stayed fit both for us and for England. He made just 43 starts for West Ham, 19 sub appearances and scored 19 goals.

24

HERO

Hipsters. Big beards make me squirm.

Around 10,000 people signed a petition to have the Bobby Moore fund logo on the first team shirts in the absence of a sponsor, but this was rejected when online betting company SBOBET stepped into the breach. The charity's logo was used, however, on kids' shirts, partly because gambling firms could not be used, but also as a result of the strength of feeling put forward by the petition.

David Di Michele had shown good form in the defeat at West Bromwich Albion and he started in Zola's first game in charge against Newcastle at Upton Park. Within 37 minutes he scored twice, the second a delightful juggle to beat his man in the area before hitting a low shot past Shay Given. Matthew Etherington made it 3–0 shortly after the break. Michael Owen's goal was only a consolation, but it might have been more emphatic had Boa Morte not wasted a one-on-one chance in the dying seconds. 4–1 would not have been an unfair reflection, and we thought maybe this Zola fella might not be such a gamble after all.

At Watford in the League Cup, Walter López made his first and only start for the club. He did go on to make five more substitute appearances, but this was his only appearance in the starting XI. Reserve goalkeeper Jan Laštůvka also made his one and only appearance for West Ham. This pleased me greatly, as I was having terrible trouble spelling and pronouncing his name.

The game ended in a 1–0 defeat, but never mind, work in progress.

In the ongoing battle off the pitch with Sheffield United over the Tevez affair, an independent tribunal ruled against West Ham. It concluded we would have gained at least 3 points fewer if Tevez had not been playing and supported the Blunts' claims they had lost TV revenue as a result. Several Sheffield United players also prepared to sue over lost earnings. Maybe if they had put as much effort in on the pitch as they had done in phoning their lawyers they would not be in this mess.

The Blades were on thin ice anyway. In June 2007 it emerged there may have been something underhand about their sale of Steve Kabba to Watford. Something underhand like... not allowing him to play against them even though it was a permanent deal. That kind of underhand that breaches the same rules West Ham had breached? Anyway, nothing came of it, so they must have been innocent, I suppose?

West Ham made arrangements for an appeal to be heard by the Court of Arbitration for Sport in Switzerland, but the FA announced it would not recognise any decision by that judicial body, so there seemed little point. Fair enough, we had breached the rules. But the FA had deemed it was insufficient to warrant a points deduction. Sheffield United would not lay down and accept that if they had been less shite, they might have stayed up.

Guðmundsson's chairmanship at Landsbanki ended on 7 October when Iceland's equivalent of the Financial Conduct Authority replaced all its directors. *Time* magazine would later single him out as one of the biggest single influences in the collapse. He owned 95 per cent of our football club. Fantastic.

So from the deep pockets of 2008 we now had very short arms. Indeed, the net spend overall during the two years of Icelandic ownership to that point had been a mere £15 million. The previous twenty-four months under the previous 'tight' board had been £24 million. The main difference, it seemed, had been the ridiculous wages that some players had been signed on

– Lucas Neill must have turned down Liverpool for one reason only. Freddie Ljungberg was another, reportedly on £85,000 a week. That was the tip of the iceberg. It was clear that players like Kieron Dyer who had hardly kicked a ball in anger were also drawing serious wages – and we were unable to sell them. Why would a player in that situation want to leave anyway? Unless another club came along prepared to pay a stupid fee to suit the club and stupid wages to suit the player, it wasn't going to happen. And it didn't happen. After all, there was an economic crisis looming.

Storm clouds also gathered on the home front as moving to a posh, shiny three-bed semi did nothing to improve the dynamics of my marriage to the unmentionable ex. One of my primary memories of that time was of both of us sulking at opposite ends of the house and feeling guilty at the time for rather enjoying the peace and quiet. Occasionally it would get so bad that I would stuff a few things into a bag and go and stay at a local hotel. I could not stay with relatives for obvious reasons, or with friends, who might be deemed to be taking sides. It was not a happy time.

On the field things seemed to be brighter as Zola inspired a 2–1 victory over Fulham at Craven Cottage with goals from Etherington and Cole. The reminders of the off-field crisis were still there for all to see, though, as hastily ironed-on squad numbers covered up the XL Airways logo.

Spanish striker Diego Tristán signed out of contract. I wasn't impressed. He was 32 years old, and hadn't set the world alight playing for Mallorca or Livorno since leaving Deportivo de La Coruña where he had scored 87 goals in 177 appearances over six years, and in that time also won 15 caps for Spain, scoring 4 goals. It seemed his best days were well behind him, but with Ashton out, Bellamy out and Carlton, well, being Carlton, we only had Di Michele up front who was showing any sort of form.

Carlton did score against Bolton at Upton Park in the next game, but it ended in a 3–1 defeat. Robert Green had a complete nightmare in goal and Matty Taylor scored a third for Bolton from a free kick which almost broke the net. I would say hats off to them, but it was Bolton, so they can do one. After another row at home I took the car along the M62 eastbound to Hull, as I had never been before. I had never seen us play at the old Boothferry Park, so I wanted to make sure I saw us at what was then their new KC stadium. Hull were newly promoted and had got off to a flyer, having lost only 1 of their opening 7 games, which included 4 wins over the likes of Tottenham and Arsenal. It was just as well, because they only won 1 game after Christmas and stayed up by the skin of their teeth.

Hull were in 3rd on 14 points; we entered the game in 6th on 12 points. Victory would have restored a natural order with us leapfrogging Hull. But the natural order of things was actually for us to lose games we should have won, and we did: 1–0. It was a very disappointing day. We looked short of ideas and far from cutting edge, even with Craig Bellamy back in the starting XI. And I had to return home to a stinking atmosphere.

Two more straightforward defeats followed, at home to Arsenal and away at Manchester United. Clearly these were games we did not necessarily expect to win, but Zola's demeanour approaching those games concerned me, as he appeared to be beaten before a ball was kicked – and did not even seem to be entertaining the idea that we might win. Cole had been sent off in the latter stages against Arsenal, leaving us so short up front we faced the prospect of Boa Morte playing as a makeshift striker at Old Trafford. He wasn't even a makeshift midfielder.

Even worse, the one player who had looked like making a difference, Valon Behrami, picked up an injury at Old Trafford and would be out for three weeks. Bellamy was fit though, but he was a shadow of the player he had been the previous year.

October had been a difficult month, picking up 'nul points' from 4 games, and we slipped from 5th to 11th. But it was some consolation at least that after 10 games Tottenham were bottom of the league with just 6 points. Enter saggy chops stage left.

Most likely in a shocking mood again, I drove up to Middlesbrough to see us earn a welcome point and ease the pressure on Zola, who had managed to install himself as the bookies' favourite to be the next Premier League manager to get the sack. Given the economic situation at the club I thought that was highly unlikely. Hayden Mullins scored an opportunist goal to put us 1–0 up, but Middlesbrough equalised from a free kick from that fine athletic figure of a man, Mido.

It was a measure of what I was going through personally that having argued that I wanted to go to football to be with friends, I was now travelling to games on my own, hating every minute of it, avoiding eye contact with people I knew, and driving straight back home again to a domestic situation I also hated. My only release was at work, which fortunately formed more than one-third of my week. I loved my job, and felt valued and respected. Much more so than at home or at West Ham. So, as colleagues fell by the wayside and the profits started to fall, the firm turned to me to set up and run its PPI claims division.

There was only one drawback. I would be based in Doncaster, an hour's drive away, or longer by train. I broached the subject with the unmentionable ex. She was dead against the idea and wanted me to find another job locally. But I loved my work so much I asked for a meeting with the big boss to explain the situation. He agreed to a 50 per cent pay rise, to allow me to work from home three days a week, and pay for all the costs associated with installing decent broadband at home. He also agreed, at my request, that I could stay in Doncaster overnight one night a week during my two days there. It would be a welcome release.

Needless to say, despite the extra cash and negotiating three days in Bradford this did not go down well at home, but, to her credit, the unmentionable ex at least agreed to give it a go.

I went off to work on a Monday morning clicking my heels knowing I would not be back until Tuesday night. It was fucking great.

Everton came to Upton Park to show what a cruel game football can be. After a goalless first half, West Ham took a deserved lead on 63 minutes when Scott Parker back-heeled the ball into Jack Collison's path and he found a top-drawer finish for his first West Ham goal. It looked to be enough as the game entered its final ten minutes. But then 3 Everton goals in the space of four minutes broke our resolve and our hearts in one fell swoop. It was hard to take.

Another point was added in a 0–0 draw against Portsmouth at Upton Park, but the team seemed to be pushing a heavy rock up a steep hill.

The revised work situation did not improve things at home. If anything, things got worse. Ahead of the Sunderland game I had moved out and taken a room in a converted house next to the pub where I watched Sky games when I was unable to go. I plodded downstairs that Sunday afternoon and watched Behrami score the winning goal and somehow contrive to hit the bar from four yards out after Craig Bellamy had squared for him. After the game the unmentionable ex came over and persuaded me to go back home. It wasn't the first time. I did not want to admit defeat, but patience was wearing thin. I didn't like the person I was becoming. I was not generally a shouty person, but I was finding that I could not help myself a lot of the time. I reasoned that I would have one night at home before heading back to Doncaster for forty-eight hours to think things over and flirt with Beth.

Doncaster was fun because we had such a great team. Everyone mucked in to get the job done, and if that meant the top lawyer at the firm rolling his sleeves up and manning the phones at 8 p.m. on a Monday evening then that was what happened. There were few, if any, egos. We called each other by our surnames out of choice, a habit that stuck, and I hope they still do it now.

Joanne Daniels (or just Daniels to me) and her younger sister Sarah (Daniels junior) were a great laugh, and Daniels picked me up from Doncaster station on a Monday morning to listen patiently to my latest tales of woe from home. With Beth, on the other hand, we just exchanged glances. It was nice, but a bit odd too. I thought she either fancied me or had a squint.

December arrived with a couple of tricky-looking fixtures. At Anfield, though, we came closer than usual to breaking our (by now, frankly embarrassing) winning drought there, against a Liverpool side who were at the top of the league. Bellamy hit the left upright with a fierce drive and Carlton got agonisingly close with a header. For their part, Liverpool only really troubled Green on one occasion with a shot from Yossi Benayoun, which Green did well to turn around the post. Clearly there was no love lost between Benayoun and West Ham: as Green made the save he looked not just disappointed, but like his whole world had caved in around him.

A resurgent Tottenham were next at Upton Park. Saggy Chops had turned them around and from last place when Redknapp took over on 25 October they had climbed into 15th, taking 13 points from the 21 available, including a notable 4–4 draw at Arsenal and home wins over Liverpool and Manchester City. It was inevitable therefore that they would make it 16 from 24 as they beat us 2–0. It was little consolation that they would not win another match until the end of January 2009.

It didn't get any easier as the next match was against Chelsea at Stamford Bridge, but Craig Bellamy managed what he hadn't done at Anfield and squeezed one in at the near post, only for Nicolas Anelka to equalise in the second half, scoring his 100th Premier League goal. It felt like at least half of them had been against us. It had been an emotional return to Stamford Bridge for Zola, he still clearly had a strong connection with the team. It was understandable; he had an amazing career there. But it was still hard to watch him hugging John Terry like he was long-lost family. I'm sure I saw Zola check he still had his wallet afterwards.

Press speculation continued about the future of the club's owners. Reassuring noises came from the boardroom that the owners were not going anywhere, but there was unlikely to be any cash available for the January transfer window. To me, that did not sound reassuring at all. And sure enough, on 17 December 2008 Guðmundsson put the club up for sale, valuing it at around £120–£150 million. Needless to say, he was not injured in any kind of stampede.

25

JUST DANCE

HARTLEPOOL UNITED, 0 WEST HAM UNITED 2
FA CUP FOURTH ROUND, 24 JANUARY 2009
Pushy parents at kids' football matches. It's a game.

Aston Villa mugged us at Upton Park with a preposterous goal from a cross by James Milner that took a deflection off Lucas Neill to balloon over Robert Green into the net.

Christmas had been a much quieter affair than the year before, or rather I assume it was, as I hadn't been able to hear most of the previous one. We had a Christmas Party at work at Doncaster Rovers' Keepmoat Stadium, and as I was staying overnight I knew I could get very, very drunk. I remember Beth being there and that I did indeed get very, very drunk. After that I don't remember anything. I checked afterwards and was told there was nothing to remember.

I didn't go back to London for Christmas, so was out for Boxing Day lunch with the unmentionable ex and her mother when I checked the score at Fratton Park and nearly fell off my chair. Portsmouth 1, West Ham United 4. I switched my phone off and switched it on again to be certain it was not a mistake.

Scorelines can be a little deceptive sometimes, and watching this one back maybe this one was. Portsmouth were struggling under Tony Adams, who looked perpetually baffled. Possibly he was still trying to work out how he had managed to end up as a Premier League manager and whether it was all just a drunken illusion.

Pompey took the lead on 8 minutes and Collison equalised on 20, but then the game turned on two incidents. In stoppage time in the first half Jermain Defoe (remember him?) missed a penalty by dragging it well wide of Green's right-hand post. Early in the second half Bellamy made a good run down the left to feed Collinson who struck a post, but Carlton snapped up the rebound. The second major turning point came when Portsmouth hit the post but retained possession, only for it to be wrestled off them by Collison, who hit a long ball upfield to Craig Bellamy. He then somehow beat two defenders simply by allowing the ball to run on, turning quickly and chasing it. By the time he got into the penalty area he had time to crack open a can of beer and read the paper before smashing the ball in for the third. Bellamy then wrapped up the points, slotting home Ilunga's cross.

Stoke were also beaten two days later, not quite so emphatically, but from 1–0 down we won 2–1, although much of the credit has to go to Stoke striker Ricardo Fuller, who was sent off for fighting with his own team mate Andy Griffin. Cole had just equalised with a very competent, curling strike and the winner came from Diego Tristán. I'm sure Tristán didn't know a huge amount about it and I worried that if he protested too hard that he'd got a touch, he may have been ruled offside. The goal was given to him because he was new.

Then came two rarities in the FA Cup win over Barnsley at Upton Park. First, a goal for Hérita Ilunga. Secondly a rare venture outside for the lesser-spotted Kieron Dyer, who came warily out of his cotton wool cocoon as a replacement for Jack Collison. The game was won 3–0 with additional goals from a Mark Noble penalty (that he had won himself) and a Carlton header converting an Ilunga cross.

The board had not lied to us. There was no hint of anyone coming in during the transfer window, the only talk was of players leaving. Scott Parker, Matthew Upson and Craig Bellamy were all linked with moves but by 8 January the only player to actually leave had been Matthew Etherington, who joined Stoke City for £3 million. A popular figure among the fans, unfairly nicknamed 'Ditherington' by some, Matty was Hammer of the

Year in 2004 and was an exciting winger who also had a good eye for goal. He also had a good eye for the bookies and had well publicised problems which contributed in part to his leaving. I was sorry to see him go as I felt he still had a couple of good years in him. His Hammers record was impressive, and he was one of the few to be with the club for over five years. He made 177 starts, 18 substitute appearances, scoring 18 goals in the process. Although he was a goal provider more than a scorer, he will always be remembered for his goal against Ipswich in the play-off semi-final in 2004. I wished him well.

I had been back in touch with an old friend, Nathan, from my days working in Leeds. He had just bought a big house in Shipley and was looking for lodgers to help share the costs. With that option in the back of my mind, the next major row at home saw me heading to his place rather than to a hotel or B&B. Normally, when I needed to collect fresh supplies, that was the time I got collared and persuaded to stay. This time I'd had it. I was leaving. Nathan drove me home one night and waited in the car for me until I had everything I needed. I cannot ever thank him enough for helping me. Just as a note to all you fellas out there reading this, if you think you have hidden your porn stash where your missus won't find it, think again. I got a text straight after arriving back at Nathan's saying, 'I see you took your porn DVDs then?' Never underestimate. Fortunately, we now have the internet.

I was free, and it felt fantastic. And, although I'd had to leave the car it didn't really matter, as I generally travelled around by train anyway, so I went into work on Saturday mornings if I wasn't going to West Ham as I was now one of the bosses – and there was a lot to do. A few others came in voluntarily too, they were a terrific bunch. I tried to make management aware of how good they were and how it should be recognised but it largely fell on deaf ears, so it was down to me to treat those who had turned up to a few beers in the pub after work.

One of those Saturdays was 10 January 2009. I watched *Final Score* in the bar, which reported that Michael Owen had been given too much space on the edge of the box and Craig Bellamy had tucked away Scott Parker's cheeky little pass, that Carlton put us 2–1 with a brilliant strike, but a young upstart by the name of Andrew Thomas Carroll got an equaliser in what had been a great game of football

We were starting to play well under Zola, despite the distractions at board level. Though I have to admit I had thought he was the cheap and cheerful option, brought in because the board knew there was a big steaming pile of poo coming over the horizon and Zola would not create a fuss like Curbishley had. He also would not complain like Curbishley had when players were sold from under him. But he was quietly getting on with his job, and getting it done with style.

Lee Bowyer went on loan to Birmingham City, but I did not shed any tears. Good player as he had been, I simply didn't like the guy. For me, he was not a West Ham player. One might say it was an irrational hatred. In his two spells at the club he made 60 appearances, scoring 5 goals. In those 60 games he was cautioned 18 times and sent off once. He did not return. See you later, Lee.

Much more upsetting, however, was the sale of Craig Bellamy to Manchester City. This confirmed that we really were in the shit financially, and although we still had Dean Ashton we were not to know that he would not pull on a claret and blue shirt in anger again. Carlton was working manfully up front and Tristán and Di Michele were okay, but they were the wrong side of thirty.

Bellamy has since said that he was happy at West Ham and did not want to leave. Nevertheless, he was sold for £14 million, almost double what was paid for him, so although it made financial sense to sell him, the timing could have been better. But financial sense was what was needed – or it seemed we might go under. No matter what the chairman said, he was in deep trouble and was about to be made bankrupt. We were drowning. Bellamy had been with us eighteen months and amazingly made only 26 appearances in all that time due to various injuries. But a return of 9 goals from those 26 appearances represented excellent value, and he remains one of the most fondly remembered short-term servants the club has ever had.

Fulham came to Upton Park and were beaten 3–1. David Di Michele latched on to a loose backpass for the first, but old boy Konchesky scored a screamer from way out to equalise. This was no cup final-type sliced cross, he really meant that one. What I am sure he didn't mean to do was to give the ball away to Carlton, then hack him down in the area for Noble to convert from the spot. Di Michele then slipped a beautifully weighted pass through to Carlton to wrap it up. Beautiful, free-flowing football in the image of our manager.

Meanwhile, living at Nathan's was great. It was a huge Victorian house on four floors and I had a newly decorated room in the attic with its own bathroom next door. The house had a gym in the basement and Nathan had the full Sky package and a Nintendo Wii in the lounge. He was out quite a lot, and at that time I was the only tenant, so quite often I had the place to myself, as was the case for the Saturday cup tie against Hartlepool which was live on Sky. ASDA was a short walk away, too, so I stocked up on beer, crisps and nuts, and made myself at home in the lounge as we cruised to a 2–0 win with goals from Behrami and Noble. The latter earned a lucky penalty for handball that was clearly outside the box, doubling the lead at half time for an advantage that never looked like slipping.

This was a strange experience. Unbeaten in 6 games and playing well, and life on the upturn as well. Deep down, though, I knew I faced a struggle, and my football team was facing one as well. But it wasn't just a struggle. It was a fight for survival.

26

POKER FACE

WEST HAM UNITED 2, SUNDERLAND 0
PREMIER LEAGUE, 4 APRIL 2009

People who swing their arms as they walk. Unnecessary,
and it makes you look like a dick.

The challenges facing the club were reflected in the transfer activity. No one had come in, but players were leaving what seemed like almost daily. Hayden Mullins was sold to Portsmouth for an undisclosed fee thought to be around £2 million. He had a similar length of service to Etherington, having been Pardew's first signing. I had warmed to Mullins, particularly after he had been forced to miss the 2006 cup final through harsh suspension.

His West Ham career ended having made 183 starts, 30 substitute appearances and scoring 7 goals. Julien Faubert also went out on loan, to Real Madrid of all places. Yes. Real Madrid, the big team in Spain that wins a lot of stuff. I couldn't believe it. It was no surprise to read that Julien could not believe it either. Calum Davenport also moved on loan, to slightly less exotic surroundings, joining Sunderland with an option to buy in the summer.

By the time we played Hull City, however, on 28 January, there had been rumblings of potentially making some signings. Radoslav Kováč, the Czech midfielder, joined on loan from Sparta Prague with a view to a permanent deal at the end of the season. Another loan signing, but at least it was a fresh face to replace those caught up in the exodus. The interesting move, though, was for Savio Nserenko on a permanent deal. Nserenko was born in Kampala, Uganda, in July 1989, so was still only nineteen when he signed for West Ham for a fee believed to be around £9 million, including various add-ons on top of an ambitious four-and-a-half-year deal. Alongside his Ugandan roots he had German citizenship and started his career at 1860 Munich before moving to Brescia in Italy, where he had scored a whole 3 goals in 22 appearances. That did not set my pulse racing, but the clamour around his signing did. This was supposedly one of the hottest talents in European, if not world, football. And we had him.

He did not start against Hull, but came on as a substitute for Behrami and, I have to say, I did not see anything to make me think we had anything special on our hands. I did, however, see Mark Noble miss a penalty in a 2–0 win. It could have been 8–0; Hull really were crap, but we had also hit top form. Savio, as he was known, also made a sub appearance against Arsenal in a 0–0 draw at the Emirates, which extended our unbeaten run to eight games in all competitions, and we went into February 2009 having lost just 2 games out of 12 since the start of December. In doing so we had crept back up to 8th in the table and faced a Manchester United side at Upton Park who came and did a professional job on us, with Ryan Giggs scoring the only goal in a 1–0 defeat.

Escaping my marriage had been one thing, extricating finances was proving to be quite another. We had a mortgage in joint names and a joint bank account into which both our salaries were paid. Fortunately, I had already set up a new current account, as Foghorn Leghorn would say, for just such an emergency. So, I was able to divert my salary away. We bought the house for £180,000 in August 2007. When it came to the valuation for me to remortgage, however, I found to my horror it was now only worth £140,000, due mainly to the economic situation. I have to say that the unmentionable ex was entirely reasonable throughout. She would stay in the house until I bought her out, then I would give her a lump sum and she would move out. Except, of course, the down valuation meant all the equity had gone and I could only borrow £126,000. Tricky.

A bit of creative accounting and good timing applying for personal loans meant I was able to do it. But my god, it was a close-run thing. Coincidentally I had been contacted by Seb, another former Keypoint colleague who was now working as a freelance in London. He was on a good contract and put me in touch with the project manager. I was invited for interview in Reading.

There was only one problem. I was skint. I mean really skint. I had £50 to my name until February payday, as all other funds were tied up in the joint account which had been blocked. I searched online and found a round-about train ride that would get me to Reading via Birmingham, and back to Leeds via London in the same day for £35. I went down for the interview and got the job. I was moving back to London. Back home.

The reason the train ticket was so cheap was no doubt because it arrived back in Leeds at midnight. By that time, I had missed the last connection to Shipley. I could not afford a cab so had no option but to walk the eight miles back home on a February night in pissing rain. I arrived back at Shipley around 3 a.m., expected back in Doncaster by 9 a.m. the next morning, but I didn't care. The mortgage was sorted. A new job was sorted. My sister had offered me temporary accommodation in London. I was free. Exhausted, but free.

I went in to work at Doncaster the next day and handed in my notice. This was the only drawback. I would miss the banter with Daniels and Daniels Junior. I would miss the sense of ownership I had with the work. I would miss Beth and her knowing looks. I would miss Dan, Shaun, Lee, Katie and Richard, and everyone else who had put so much into the project and bought into the concept. I went to say goodbye to the IT team who I had worked closely with in the development of the PPI project and had a hug with Jilly that lasted just a bit longer than it should have. You know when that happens? I was at the door and I looked around and saw her smiling at me, so I went back for another cuddle, which definitely lasted longer than was decent. I actually cried as I left the office for the last time on

Friday 13 February 2009. I was travelling into the unknown. It was exciting and terrifying in equal measure.

I arrived in London on 14 February with whatever I could carry on my back, due to start my new role on the Monday as a contractor in financial services. My first client was the Financial Ombudsman Service.

Luckily, I had arrived in time to ensure I could get to Upton Park for the FA Cup fifth round tie against Middlesbrough. If I had thought the new beginning also meant continuing success on the pitch I was wrong. We went 1–0 down as a Gary O'Neil cross eluded everyone in our box and Stewart Downing stooped at the far post to score with a header. Fuck's sake, West Ham. Stewart Downing, with a header!

Hérita Ilunga rescued the tie in the second half with a header that looked suspiciously offside, but it was better than going out. A replay at the Riverside did not fill me with optimism. Although we had not lost away since losing at Old Trafford on 29 October, we faced Bolton next, and we didn't ever win at Bolton. We didn't even draw at Bolton. We only ever got beaten at Bolton. And that's what happened. Another Matty Taylor free kick and the inevitable Kevin Davies goal undid us, and despite Scott Parker pulling one back in the second half, it wasn't enough to prevent defeat.

The replay at the Riverside also ended in defeat. The game was shown live on ITV and I cannot recall us even breaking into a sweat as first Stewart Downing, then Tuncay, scored the goals that put them into the quarter-finals and us on the bus home.

With only two league matches played in February, both ending in defeat, it was time to buck up our ideas against Manchester City, who had Craig Bellamy in their starting XI (no Sheffield United-type agreements) and the most expensive footballer in England in the form of the Brazilian, Robinho.

But it was a home-grown Hammer, Jack Collison, who scored to nick the points as we picked up our form and played really well against a City side that were shaping up to be big noises in the Premier League. Savio exchanged passes with Carlton on the left and pinged in a shot that Shay Given in goal could only palm out to Collison, who looped it back over him into the net to send us all bonkers. Savio looked the part, having come on for Behrami, who had been stretchered off with an injury that would end his participation for the season. Still, at least it seemed we had capable replacements in Savio and Kováč.

The next match at Wigan produced a goal still talked about when people try to defend Zola's time at the club in hindsight. This was the sweet spot of his tenure. This was the pinnacle of his achievement. People still say 'Yes, but remember that goal we scored under Zola at Wigan?'

It's true that it was an outstanding goal of immense quality in a game marred by two red cards. And it was indeed a thing of beauty and may even find its way into the top ten West Ham United goals ever scored, or at least the top ten of those captured on film or video. Parker played a direct ball through midfield to Di Michele, who back-heeled it to Noble, who played it first time back to Di Michele, who then laid it off for Carlton to curl one into the net from about fifteen yards. It was indeed a masterful piece of football, but Wigan did rather stand and admire it rather than attempt to make any challenges.

Cole then got sent off for two bookable offences, and Lee Cattermole got a straight red for an X-rated challenge on Scott Parker. Carlton's vast improvement in form and consistency had won him an England call-up, and on this evidence, it was well deserved. He went on to make substitute appearances in friendlies against Spain and Slovakia.

And that, my friends, was as good as it got under Gianfranco Zola. The board continued to seek a buyer for the club as Icelandic courts granted an extended moratorium over the winding up of West Ham's parent company Hansa.

The courts announced their decision to allow chairman Guðmundsson until 8 June to demonstrate an ability to repay creditors in order to avoid insolvency and, crucially, to find a buyer for the club.

This task, however, had been proving difficult. Not least

because of the aftermath of the Tevez affair, which was about to be settled by a £30 million payment to Sheffield United. Still, legal representative Scott 'Teflon' Duxbury, who presumably knew all about the 'lie' told by Paul Aldridge to the Premier League in the first place, was allowed to continue in his role. The independent tribunal had also found that Duxbury verbally assured Joorabchian that the third-party agreement still existed (even though he had told the Premier League it had been terminated so Tevez could continue to play). In any other line of business he would surely have been shown the door. That, combined with the economic situation in Iceland, almost cost us our existence.

Savio made his one and only start for West Ham in the next match, a 0–0 draw with West Bromwich Albion. Another draw at Blackburn, now managed by Sam Allardyce, kept the totaliser ticking over. El Hadji Diouf had two goals disallowed. One for offside, one for being a git. Couldn't happen to a nicer bloke. As a sign of things to come I went to the home game against Sunderland with my youngest nephew, Sam, and we discussed the prospect of season tickets in the family area for the following season. My dad was keen, as was my oldest nephew Mark, and his two children. The football we had seen was good enough to make me think it would be a wise investment. We beat Sunderland 2–0 with two future prospects getting the goals, Junior Stanislas with the first and James Tomkins with the second.

At White Hart Lane Spurs had recovered sufficiently to be vying with us for a top eight finish. Our recent record against Tottenham had not been good and we lost again 1–0, but picked up a point at Villa Park in a bizarre match where the Villains played all in white and West Ham played in the sky-blue away strip. The referee had been unhappy with the colour clash and as a result there had been a five-minute delay to the kick-off. Diego Tristán scored his second goal for West Ham to snatch a point late on, leaving West Ham on course for European qualification. It was possible that with Chelsea and Everton contesting the FA Cup final, whoever won would potentially free up 7th place, the position currently occupied by West Ham.

Mark Noble missed another penalty, his second of the season against Chelsea in a 1–0 defeat at home, but Tristán's winner at Stoke meant the net return from the two games was pretty much as expected. But damaging defeats at home to Liverpool (0–3) and away at Everton (1–3) meant that even victory over Middlesbrough on the final day by a 2–1 scoreline was not enough to finish higher than 9th.

If you look at league tables, 9th place and 51 points represented progress, one place and 3 points higher than last season. But the reality was that we were on the brink of a huge step backwards given the financial situation at the club and the lack of investment in players that would inevitably come over the summer. In short, we were fucked.

27

NEVER GOING TO LEAVE YOU

WOLVERHAMPTON WANDERERS 0, WEST HAM UNITED 2
PREMIER LEAGUE, 15 AUGUST 2009
Being called 'mate' or 'buddy' by people I don't know.

West Ham chairman Björgólfur Guðmundsson revealed that he had personal liabilities of over £300 million. That made me feel better about my credit card bill.

It looked like the game was finally up.

Teflon Duxbury, technical director Gianluca Nani, Zola and Steve Clarke were advised their jobs were safe.

West Ham was Guðmundsson's only viable asset; but it seemed that the sale of the club would not even match what he had paid for it, let alone the £300 million plus that he owed. The club's new asset-management owners CB Holdings indicated that they would continue to allow the club to run as normal, but a sale would be sought within three years.

Guðmundsson and vice-chairman Ásgeir Friðgeirsson left the club in June, to be replaced by non-executive club chairman Andrew Bernhardt – a senior director with Straumur Bank, which was the majority shareholder in CB Holdings.

Messy.

No sooner had the final ball of 2008/09 been kicked than players started to leave again. The first departure was reserve goalkeeper Jan Laštůvka when a permanent transfer fee could not be agreed with Shakhtar Donetsk. He told the Czech news agency CTK,

We have discussed it with Zola. He said that he would have liked to have me in his squad next season, but the club cannot afford to pay so much for me. I will not comment on the fee, but it is very high if you consider the fact that I basically didn't play all year.

This was how it was going to be. Di Michele left at the end of his loan spell and Tristán's one-year contract expired. Lucas Neill was out of contract and seemed unlikely to accept the wage cut that would inevitably have to be offered.

Freddie Sears, who had seemed to have such a glittering career ahead of him, had disappointed, and was sent off on loan to Crystal Palace, while another youth team product Kyel Reid signed for Sheffield United.

Promising young American midfielder Sebastian Lletget joined from Santa Clara Sporting, and seventeen-year-old striker Frank Nouble came from Chelsea. In a similar vein, building for the future, nineteen-year-old Swiss full-back Fabio Daprelà signed from Grasshoppers of Zürich.

Julien Faubert returned from what must have felt like an LSD trip in Madrid, where he played two games and managed to piss off the management by missing a day's training because he thought he had the day off and was pictured fast asleep on the bench during a game. Unsurprisingly, he was returned to West Ham with a 'please look after this bear' note around his neck. It did rather endear him to West Ham fans, though. Surely only a West Ham player could go to Real Madrid and fall asleep on the bench?

More loan signings. Luis Jiménez, a Chilean international, arrived from Inter Milan. Kováč had also looked like he was going to be off but was signed on a permanent deal.

So, when the season started mid-August away at Molineux the excitement was barely there at all. The transfer activity had been minimal, with kids signed on permanent deals and the rest coming in on loan. It was hardly surprising given the circumstances, but it did not fill me with optimism for the season to come. Added to that, the new kit looked like a tablecloth and had 'relegation' written all over it.

I spent the opening day of the season with Stuart the QPR
fan in Stamford, where he now resided, having split up with
his wife. We found ourselves in the same boat, so spent a very
pleasant sunny Saturday afternoon playing football in the park
with his son Callum.

This was perhaps the most opportune moment for me to receive a text from the unmentionable ex confirming the divorce
had come through, and that I was a single man again. After
about ten seconds of feeling down about it, I picked myself up,
dragged Stuart off to the pub and we both got very drunk. This
seems to happen a lot when I see him. The next morning I reversed my hire car into his wall. People celebrate in different
ways.

West Ham took advantage of Wolves' Premier League inexpe-
rience, winning 2–0 on the opening day. Mark Noble hit a sweet
strike from the edge of the box and Matthew Upson headed in
number two in the second half. This led me to think that maybe
it wouldn't be such a struggle after all. But I had been watching
football a long time. I knew that we had no money and our
squad was so thin it made Charles Hawtrey look like Christopher Biggins. I knew it was going to be hard. Hérita Ilunga also
suffered a fractured jaw in that game, which ruled him out for
a month and, unfortunately, we had no recognised replacement
other than the untried Daprelà.

I celebrated being single by finding a date online and spending a day at the London Eye and having dinner. It was all going
swimmingly until I got to her house one day and saw the state
of the kitchen. Nope, sorry, I don't do mess. Not mess like that.
I was still exchanging long e-mails with my newfound IT de-
partment friend Jilly, who had hugged me a bit too long as I
left Keypoint, and Beth was in touch through that new-fangled
Facebook thing, telling me that she was in an open marriage
and asking me why I hadn't invited her to join me on my lonely
hotel nights in Doncaster. Great, now she tells me.

I was still having to make regular trips north to sort out the
house, which took some clearing in preparation for renting it

out. I hired a big van, put adverts on Gumtree and gave a load of stuff away. It didn't interest me. I didn't want to keep it. Daniels Junior took the TV and the dining table, as she was setting up home with her boyfriend. I was happy to let it go to such a deserving home.

That final time I sat in the living room on a camping chair with just my laptop for company looking forward to lunch with Jilly on the way home. At least I got a house out of it, I reasoned. And lunch with Jilly. Maybe there would be lingering hugs too.

In the meantime, two things happened just before the Tottenham game to put a little perspective on things. Calum Davenport, still a West Ham player having returned from his loan spell at Sunderland, was involved in a stabbing incident at his home in Bedfordshire. He was stabbed in the leg and lost four pints of blood. His mother was also injured in the attack. One of the assailants was the boyfriend of Davenport's sister. It appeared he may have been defending her, or that the attack was some form of revenge, but Davenport was later charged with, then cleared of, her assault. Whatever the truth, two wrongs don't make a right, and he never played for West Ham again. His career was effectively over. In two spells he played 23 times for us, scoring 1 goal.

The other incident was the loss of Jack Collison's father. Ian Collison was only forty-six when he died in a motorbike accident on the M25 on his way to watch Jack play against Tottenham. Jack knew nothing about it until later that evening, but recalled later in an interview in *The Independent* that he remembered not seeing his dad in the players' lounge after the game, and being unable to get a reply on his phone. He said he knew instantly something was wrong. Jack was only twenty at the time.

I had bought a season ticket in the Sir Trevor Brooking Upper (STBU) along with nephews Mark and Sam, and Mark's kids, Jamie and Jessica. Dad had decided against it for the time being. Our first home game as a group together was against Tottenham. The sun was shining, we had 3 points from the opening game and Carlton smashed one into the top corner from way out. What could possibly go wrong?

Well, quite a lot actually. Soon after scoring an early front runner for goal of the season, Carlton laid the ball not only on a plate, but with knife, fork, spoon and napkin for Jermain Defoe (him again!) to score the equaliser. It was like pulling the plug out of a bouncy castle and watching the confidence drain out of the team. It was only a matter of time – 17 minutes to be precise – before Tottenham got the winner.

A few days later I returned for the cup tie against Millwall, sitting in the Bobby Moore Upper, courtesy of the decision to pen the Millwall fans into the STBU to leave the lower tier empty. They might as well have dangled them from the sky on bits of rope, I didn't want to go anywhere near them.

I think I have made myself fairly clear on this subject, I hate football violence and all that goes with it. The people, the films, the books, the stupid talk about 'manors' and being 'out of order'. For fuck's sake, it's a game. Sure, it's territorial and sure, you take the piss out of each other inside the ground. But actually wanting to come to blows? Seriously? Would you do that at the photocopier to a Millwall fan in the office on Monday morning? I suppose some idiots would. Anyway, I got turfed out of my seat because of those morons. Jack Collison had chosen to play despite losing his father in such tragic circumstances only a few days before. That is real bravery.

As with any game against Millwall the media eye was watching. So not only was it embarrassing that the game went into extra time (Neil Harris had put the Lions 1–0 up after 26 minutes), but as the game progressed it seemed clear that an element in the Chicken Run were doing their utmost to get at the Millwall fans – but they were suspended in the STBU. Easy to be brave when your opponents are encased in concrete ten metres above you. Some spilled out onto the pitch, and with each one, a little bit more of me died inside. What decade were these people from?

Stanislas equalised with three minutes left and obviously,

when you equalise against fierce rivals so close to the end, there will be an outpouring of emotion. Unfortunately that emotion was stupidity, and fans poured on to the pitch from all directions. I didn't know where to look, nor could I decide what was more excruciating, having to equalise so late against Millwall, or seeing fat West Ham fans with carrier bags around their wrists slipping over on the hallowed Upton Park turf.

And there was another half an hour of this crap to endure. Longer, actually, if you take account of the players being taken off the field by the referee after Stanislas put West Ham 2–1 up from the penalty spot, and the further delays endured after Zavon Hines scored a third. All utterly embarrassing, and ultimately a waste of everybody's time and money as we were drawn away to Bolton in the next round so were a dead cert to go out anyway.

At last, a permanent signing to get excited about. Alessandro Diamanti joined on another undisclosed fee, thought to have been around £5.5 million over three years, from Livorno in Italy, the same club Diego Tristán had played for. He had scored 16 goals in Livorno's promotion campaign and was said to be something of a dead ball specialist. His show reel was certainly impressive, and meant this was something to be excited about, especially as Jiménez had not looked to be anything to write home about.

The much-heralded Savio went off to Fiorentina with Portuguese international defender Manuel da Costa coming in the other direction, in what looked like a straight swap. Savio, who had arrived in such a blaze of glory, appeared to struggle with the level of expectation and the price tag heaped on him, and he made just 1 start and 9 substitute appearances, failing to score. I prayed that the fee we had paid for him was nearer the lower figure of the two mentioned: between £500,000 and £9 million depending on what newspaper you read. In another somewhat surprising move, James Collins was sold to Aston Villa for £5 million on deadline day. We hadn't seen that one coming. Out-of-contract Mexican striker Guillermo Franco later signed after deadline day on a one-year contract.

We drew 0–0 at Blackburn, but they were no great shakes, then Wigan beat us 1–0 at the JJB Stadium, which was a measure of the backwards steps we had taken. Liverpool beat us 3–2 at Upton Park, Fernando Torres opening the scoring and Diamanti equalising from the penalty spot after a foul on the lively Zavon Hines. Dirk Kuyt put Liverpool back in front, but Carlton headed another equaliser before half time. Torres was unstoppable at that time though, and it seemed clear that if we scored 6 he would score 7, it was just one of those days. His second goal, and Liverpool's third overall in the second half, ended the contest.

Bolton put paid to our interest in the League Cup, as expected, winning 3–1, and then Manchester City's emerging monsters also saw us off, 3–1, at Eastlands. It was not going well. After winning on the opening day we had failed to win since, other than the Millwall cup tie. We had 4 points and sat in the bottom three going into October. Something was going to have to change.

28

FIGHT FOR THIS LOVE

WEST HAM UNITED 2, ASTON VILLA 1
PREMIER LEAGUE, 4 NOVEMBER 2009
School proms. Halloween as an actual thing. Other Americanisms.

Things did change in October because I met the woman who would go on to be my wife. Elaine was at a *Pet Shop Boys* Concert at the O2 and we kept bumping into each other. Maybe I was bumping into her deliberately, I can't be sure. Anyway, we were dancing and went for a drink afterwards. Petite, beautiful, sweet-natured and… Brazilian. I hadn't seen that last one coming. We exchanged numbers and texted each other every day until I could think of a suitable way to ask her out. She was clearly a music fan, so I asked her to join me at a *Green Day* gig at the same venue in a few weeks. She accepted. I was in love: completely and totally.

Meanwhile, the FA had been busy trying to work out how big a kitchen sink they could throw at West Ham for the crowd trouble against Millwall.

I could see why all this had to be done, but short of doing an IQ test over the telephone before allowing people who at least know how to operate a telephone to purchase a ticket, I didn't see what they could do about it. They may as well have charged the club with: 'Failure to ensure their fans don't think naughty things.'

A point was won (or was it, two were lost?) against Fulham as Carlton put us 1–0 up, heading home a Diamanti free kick, and Fulham had a man sent off before the break. Whatever was said at half time, the team were still digesting it as Fulham went 2–1 up inside the first 12 minutes of the restart, and West Ham had to rely on an injury-time goal from Stanislas to rescue the point they should have had as a minimum.

I travelled to Stoke to see my good friend Clare Kendall, a Londoner I met while working in Manchester for the CIS, but who had made her home in Stoke. Eventually, sick of the commute up and down the M6 every day, she took a job with the Britannia Building Society in Stoke, who shortly afterwards merged with CIS and she ended up back in Manchester. How's your luck?

Clare is a Chelsea fan, but her mate Steve was a big West Ham fan and we went to the game together, witnessing a tepid 2–1 defeat, but while there we also saw what looked like common assault by that thug Robert Huth on Matthew Upson. We all saw it anyway, even if the referee and two linesmen didn't.

I still hadn't got around to buying a car so hired one for the weekend and made the most of it by cutting across country on the way home to watch Stuart the QPR Fan's son Callum play for Lincoln City's youth academy against Chesterfield's equivalent. They looked like they could do a better job than West Ham. Stuart recently reminded me of this occasion, and that I had stood on the touchline next to Chris Waddle. I have no recollection of that whatsoever.

Certainly this current crop of mercenaries and kids were not pulling up any trees, but they did manage to claw back a 0–2 deficit at home to Arsenal to claim a point, but then squandered a 2–0 lead at the Stadium of Light to draw 2–2. It was totally frustrating as Zola went into each press conference shrugging his shoulders and blaming bad luck.

The ownership situation by this time was becoming too complex for me to follow. There was a consortium headed by American financier Jim Bowe called the Intermarket Group who seemed to be putting together a serious bid to buy the club. But details were sketchy. The names of David Sullivan and David Gold continued to be mentioned, as they had recently sold Birmingham City to Malaysian businessman Carson Yeung. It was a well-known fact that David Gold was a West Ham fan. Not so well known, perhaps, was that he was born at 442 Green Street, opposite the Boleyn. Did you know that? He never mentioned it?

More pressingly, after 10 games we were one off the bottom with only 7 points to our name. A win against Aston Villa was vital.

Although the football wasn't much to write home about, I was, at least, enjoying the games with my two nephews. In the STBU you had to be a little bit careful with language, but at the evening games it was often a bit more relaxed if the match was taking place in term time.

Against Aston Villa at Upton Park we laboured our way to a 2–1 victory for only our second win of the season. James Collins was playing for Villa, and it seemed odd to see him turning out for the opposition. A noble penalty and a winner from the zippy Zavon Hines secured the points.

It would have been nice to think that this would provide a base to build on and move forward, but in the next game we reverted to type. Everton had two shots and scored 2 goals.

I hired a car for the drive north to Doncaster, where I had unfinished business following my somewhat rapid departure. I had contacted Daniels to see if the Keypoint gang fancied a few beers and a catch-up. I was staying at the hotel I had used while I worked at Keypoint so invited the huggy Jilly for dinner. By now, despite flirtatious e-mails back and forth, it had become clear that hugging would be the extent of it.

The Friday night was great fun – Daniels was as hilarious as ever, as was Daniels junior. On Saturday I took Jilly out and, despite the aforementioned realisation, still made the forehead-slapping error of inviting her back to my room. She politely declined.

The David Gray concert was looming, but I had almost dismissed Elaine from my thoughts as dates were hard to come by – and anyway I thought she was out of my league. Beautiful, witty and multi-lingual, I didn't think of her as Brazilian when I was with her, she was just Elaine. Pretty soon she was all I could think about.

We drew 3–3 at Hull City after being 2–0 up, then 3–2 down. At least we were scoring a few goals, but we had to stop leaking or we would be in trouble. The following Monday night I met Elaine to see David Gray at the Union Chapel, Islington. I risked an arm around her, I felt like I was fifteen again. She did not push me away.

I had asked my brother-in-law to come and pick us up as I wanted to be sure Elaine got home okay. I had meant for him to come in the family hatchback, not one of the limousines that he drives for a living. All dressed up in his chauffeur uniform, he gave me a look that just said, 'Play along with it, mate.' There was an ice bucket in the back with a bottle of champagne and two glasses. I started to wish the concert had been further from home. I kissed her. She kissed me back. I knew this was it.

Next up, Burnley came to Upton Park having taken just 1 point from 18. Collison, Stanislas and Carlton from the penalty spot put West Ham into a 3–0 lead. Franco and another penalty, this time from Jiménez, put us 5–0 up.

In typical West Ham fashion, though, we conceded 3 goals and fell apart, feeling fortunate in the end to hang on to win 5–3. Had the game lasted another ten minutes we might well have drawn or lost, we were that clueless. I was under no illusions. We went 5–0 because Burnley were poor, not through any brilliance on our part. Once they found their stride they made us look very ordinary.

This was illustrated perfectly by the next game, when playing decent opposition in the form of Manchester United, we lost 4–0 at home. We were absolutely dire.

Elaine invited me to her birthday party the Sunday after another gutless 1–0 defeat at Birmingham. Bob had found me a car, an ex-rep's Peugeot 405. Despite only being six years old it had more miles on the clock than Kieron Dyer's ambulance, but for £600 I couldn't turn it down, and I drove to the party in Brockley to find I was the only English person there. My Portuguese was limited to say the least, and I sat in the corner nursing the one drink I had allowed myself. Her friends were very nice, but they viewed me a little suspiciously. Elaine asked me why I was not joining in. I explained that I was English, and we didn't really do 'joining in' unless we were drunk, on holiday in Spain, or preferably both.

She poured me another drink and told me I could stay. I didn't spend another night at my sister's house for three months.

29

FIREFLIES

WEST HAM UNITED 2, BIRMINGHAM CITY 0
PREMIER LEAGUE, 10 FEBRUARY 2010
Bad punctuation. (Note to Editor: please check this section carefully.)

There's really not a huge amount to say about West Ham's team performances though 2009/10. It was largely what you might expect from a group of players assembled to meet a budget rather than any tactical plan or long-term goal. West Ham's ultimate aim was to be bought by someone rich.

We were still in the bottom three after losing to Birmingham and remained bottom three after losing midweek at Bolton (no surprise there). We also went into Christmas in the bottom three despite picking up a point against Chelsea who were destined to be champions.

A Boxing Day win over hapless Portsmouth did help lift us out of the relegation zone, but Portsmouth were set to be relegated on 19 points having been deducted 9 at the start of the season for going into administration. Even without that deduction, they would still have finished bottom. Their manager, Avram Grant. Honestly, he was a joke, who would have possibly considered employing him? And their main striker, some bloke called Piquionne? Rubbish. They did still manage to get to the FA Cup final that season, but lost to Chelsea.

By this point, Tony Fernandes had entered the running to take over the club. The CEO of AirAsia, he had a track record of taking ailing businesses and turning them around, having converted AirAsia from an airline with just two aircraft, and £25 million in debt, into one of the biggest success stories on the planet. Meanwhile takeover rivals Intermarket suffered a setback when their CEO Jim Bowe passed away unexpectedly.

2009 ended with a 2–0 defeat at White Hart Lane and 2010 started in much the same way, losing a lead to Arsenal in the third round of the FA Cup at Upton Park. It felt like we were just going through the motions at times. Much more of these and we would be wading waist-deep in motions. A point followed at Villa Park and then at Fratton Park, 0–0 and 1–1 respectively, but we remained in 16th place and still in real danger of relegation, which wasn't helping to attract potential suitors.

Fernandes and Intermarket dropped out of the running, which left a straight fight between Sullivan & Gold and the Italian Massimo Celino, owner of Cagliari where Zola had finished his playing career. But it all petered out, and Sullivan & Gold appeared to win the race almost by default.

Whenever there is a change in managership or ownership everyone thinks there will be some sort of bounce. It was more of a dull thud as the first game of the Sullivan & Gold (SuGo) era ended in a 0–0 draw against Blackburn. Bloody Blackburn – who we always beat at home. It was a measure of the way things were going. The team was losing its way and needed some investment before the window closed.

First out was Jiménez, who had been an unmitigated disaster, having scored just 1 goal in 7 starts and 5 sub appearances (and that was a penalty). He looked completely out of his depth, but of course was playing in a team that was not functioning as it should. Nigel Quashie also left after a couple of loan stints at Wolves and Birmingham. His last appearance for West Ham had been in the 4–3 home defeat to Tottenham in March 2007, nearly three years earlier, but the nature of his contract meant he would have been daft to leave voluntarily. Eight appearances and no goals represented a shocking return on a player who should never really have been signed in the first place.

Young Frank Nouble had also been struggling to tie down a place in the team or make any impact when coming on from the bench so was sent off on loan to West Bromwich Albion.

Coming in were Benni McCarthy from Blackburn for £2.5 million, striker Mido on loan from Middlesbrough and Brazilian striker Ilan on a free transfer.

And, err... that was it. SuGo's first transfer window. When McCarthy and Mido took to the pitch it seemed we were in some sort of bizarre hall of mirrors. They were both fat and wobbly. That was not how I remembered them. As they lumbered around on the pitch it was clear they were not going to make one jot of difference and we would have to stay up in spite of them rather than because of them.

Zola crossed swords early on with SuGo, criticising an article that Sullivan had written outlining the need for pay cuts for all the staff at West Ham. Zola did not feel it was helpful. The die had been cast.

One of the cornerstones of SuGo's ownership bid had been to move West Ham from Upton Park to the new Olympic Stadium, despite every man and his dog in the Olympic bidding process telling them that it was not going to happen. Tessa Jowell again stated that the stadium was a Grand Prix athletics venue and would stay as such. She did hint, however, that there would be a bidding process after the Olympics, and they would listen to West Ham's proposals. But in the same way that Megan Fox might listen to a proposal from me, it seemed this was unlikely to be taken seriously.

It seemed SuGo would be a new broom that was much needed, as the Teflon finally wore off and Scott Duxbury was issued with his P.45. Not sacked, apparently, but maybe a constructive dismissal scenario that he felt better not to contest. In a statement on the official website, Duxbury said: 'I am proud of my work at West Ham United but feel the time is right for me to pursue other opportunities.' Ah yes. Fresh challenges too, no doubt. Don't let the door hit your backside on the way out, Scott.

Karren Brady said in an article in *The Telegraph*: 'We thank Scott for his valued contribution and wish him every success in the future.' Then she uncrossed her fingers. It's true though, his contribution was valued – at sod all.

Ilan seemed the only one of the three signings to have any sort of form, in that he looked like a footballer and not a fucking sumo wrestler. He scored at relegation rivals Burnley, but it came too late to prevent a damaging 1–2 defeat.

As we went into the game against Birmingham on 10 February we were a point from safety in 18th place, above Wolves on goal difference and 6 ahead of bottom-placed Portsmouth who had received that 9-point deduction. That's how good we were. Bolton were 1 point above us, Wigan and Burnley 2 points ahead and Hull 3 points ahead – but with a much worse goal difference. Plenty of teams were within reach; we just had to start winning games. Against Birmingham we finally showed some quality. Alessandro Diamanti had been threatening to score from free kicks with his magic wand of a left peg and he finally came good in the first half by smashing an unstoppable shot into the top corner past a flapping Joe Hart. The roof came off the Boleyn. It had been coming. Now the relief was tangible. The players, tellingly, ran to the touchline to hug Zola. Carlton added a second in the second half in one of the most comprehensive performances of the season.

Better was to follow ten days later as Hull were dispatched 3–0 at home. Diamanti's left foot was proving to be a nuisance again as he whipped in really dangerous crosses, and Franco making a welcome return up front was also looking sharp. Valon Behrami scored in the opening 3 minutes. Diamanti drew a second bookable offence from Craig Fagan and Hull were down to ten before Julien Faubert played the pass of the season from within his own half around the Hull full-back up to Carlton, who couldn't miss. A late injury to Anthony Gardner meant Hull were down to nine men when Faubert wrapped things up with a third.

Four clean sheets in a row at home; 27 points and a jump of 5 places in the table in the space of ten days. Diamanti was providing the spark that had been so badly missing, and things were looking up. Perhaps these SuGo fellas weren't so bad.

Expected defeat at Old Trafford was followed by a home

defeat to Bolton on a freezing Saturday afternoon. It looked like to old failings were coming back. No spark, no ideas. Diamanti scored another free kick but it was 88 minutes in by then and Bolton could, and should, have been out of sight.

Away defeats at Chelsea (4–1) and Arsenal (2–0) followed and we were back in the mire again. It was vital to get something from the televised game against Wolves at Upton Park.

In the midst of the poor performances interspersed with the odd flash of brilliance were two contrasting characters. Both first choice, both with very different attitudes. Scott Parker had matured into one of the best combative midfielders in the country. Sure and fair in the tackle, a good passer, with a good eye for goal and a terrific engine, he also had a good record with injuries, which was just as well as we would surely have been in deeper trouble without him. Such were his performances that many observers believed him to be West Ham captain.

In fact, the captain was Matthew Upson, a centre-back of no particular ability who seemed to wander around on the pitch leaving everything to everyone else. Don't get me wrong, Upson was a good player. But not a leader. It was an error of judgement from Zola to make Upson captain and allow him to retain it, especially after the events of 23 March 2010.

James Tomkins was still learning his trade when he scuffed a backpass that fell kindly for Wolves striker Kevin Doyle to give Wolves the lead. Name any West Ham captain prior to Upson, he would have put a consoling arm around Tomkins and told him not to worry about it. But Upson walked away and left him to wish the ground would swallow him up. Without a doubt, in that moment, Tomkins's development was delayed. Team spirit was damaged. The game was effectively already over. Zubar and Jarvis made it 3–0 before Franco pulled one back in added time. Suddenly, just a month after winning back-to-back home games and pulling ourselves up to 13th, we were back in big trouble, only 3 points above the relegation zone.

Stoke City were the next visitors and West Ham took the extraordinary step of trying to stop their long throw expert Rory

Delap by placing advertising hoardings around the touchline. This said a lot about our current predicament, trying to nullify the opponents' weaponry rather than trying to use our own. In any event, Delap simply kicked the hoardings over and launched a throw in for Ricardo Fuller to score the winner.

Now we were only out of the relegation zone on goal difference. It was crunch time.

30

OMG

IKEA. Apart from the restaurant. That bit is okay.

I was jetting off for my first visit to Brazil. This, I was to discover, was the best way to deal with crunch times. Elaine had already gone out a week before me, so I picked the cheapest possible flight that involved changing planes in Milan and Rome before heading off on the 11-hour trek to São Paulo. While I was in mid-air over the South Atlantic, we drew 2–2 at Goodison Park. Everton went 1–0 up and it stayed that way after Mido had a penalty saved.

Da Costa scored with a header from a corner, but Yakubu scored late on for David Moyes's Toffees, who looked like making it a seventh straight defeat. Ilan had other ideas, though, and went full length to get his head on a Faubert cross on 87 minutes. According to all reports, a fully deserved point, and it put daylight between us and Burnley in 18th, although they had a game in hand. The only down side was a tenth booking of the season for Scott Parker, who faced a two-match suspension.

I have never been to South America before, so it was a bit of an eye opener for me. I was introduced to my new in-laws, Elaine's Dad, Senhor Iran, Mum, Antonia, sister, Eliana and brother, Edson, along with all the other extended family and friends. My pidgin Portuguese only got me so far, so I realised I would have to buckle down and learn.

I learned enough to ask Elaine's friend Euler to lend me his iPhone so I could check the score against Sunderland. I had forgotten completely about the four-hour time difference, so I logged on to find the game was already over and we had won 1–0, appropriately with a goal from Brazilian Ilan.

I was back in England in time to see the 3–0 defeat at Anfield. As gutless and uninspired a performance as I had witnessed in my thirty-five years of watching West Ham. It really was in the balance. As we faced Wigan on 24 April with only two games left after that, we had just 31 points from 35 games. We were 3 ahead of Hull in the last relegation spot, but still having played one game more.

With the remaining games Fulham away and Manchester City at home, the Wigan game was a 'must win', and despite our perilous position a win could potentially have seen us mathematically safe.

Captain, sorry, not captain, Scott Parker came back into midfield to help the cause, and I had Dad with me in the Trevor Brooking Upper to lend support and complain, as he always did, that it was all a bit hit and hope. Things did not look good when Wigan took the lead through a Spector own goal headed in from a Ben Watson corner on 4 minutes. The ball was clearly outside the quadrant when it was taken, but that seems to be the norm now, and I wonder why they even bother painting them in the first place. Perhaps we should adopt the same attitude towards the penalty spot. Take it from where you like, mate, it's only a guide.

Ilan was proving to be the signing of the transfer window, but is sadly forgotten by many West Ham fans for his contribution in the arse end of the campaign. Without his goals we would have gone down. Added to his consolation at Burnley, that point-saving header at Goodison and winner against Sunderland, he added a fourth contribution to equalise against Wigan. Just before half time, Kirkland parried Noble's free kick out to Kováč, who nodded in to give us a 2–1 lead.

The second half was a tense affair. Rodallega equalised for Wigan with what looked like his hand, but referee Wiley allowed it to stand after consulting the linesman. Then with 13 minutes to go: cometh the hour, cometh the man. Captain, sorry, not captain, Scott Parker lashed in Franco's knockdown to give us a lead that was not relinquished.

Hull lost 2 home games in a row to Burnley and Sunderland, meaning that with 2 games left we were 6 points ahead with a goal difference 23 better than Hull's.

I met up with former colleagues Mark Milligan and Mark Donald, both Scots I had met in different jobs, but with Scotland being so tiny, they knew each other. We went along to Craven Cottage for the final away game of the 2009/10 season, one that I could not wait to end, and it seemed the players felt that way too, playing out a 2–3 defeat without stretching themselves on a rain-soaked Sunday afternoon.

Burnley's defeat at Birmingham the day before and Hull's draw at Wigan on Monday meant we were somehow safe despite only amassing 34 points at that stage of the season. In the final game, at home to Manchester City, I witnessed the bizarre situation of West Ham being 1–0 up through a Boa Morte goal (that's not the bizarre bit, though it was rare, I admit.) With us safe, and winning the game, Carlos Tevez was playing for the increasingly cash-rich City. The West Ham fans sang 'Let him score!' every time he received the ball. Tevez didn't score though. It was Shaun Wright-Phillips, who always scored against us when playing for Chelsea, who was consistently linked with a move to the Boleyn, and who tackled Dean Ashton in England training and broke his ankle and our hearts in the process. He rose at the far post to head home an Adam Johnson cross for City's equaliser, which ensured a 5th place finish for them and 35 points for the campaign for us. That's 5'4" Shaun Wright Phillips. With a header.

We stayed up on 35 points, but with our 'superior' goal difference, 30 points would have seen us safe. It was a bizarre campaign that defied explanation. How could a team that had played such delightful stuff at times during the previous year struggle so badly this time? Simple really: lack of investment. It was too early to blame SuGo for any shortcomings. They decided

Zola was not the man for the job and fired him shortly after the end of the season. Apparently, it was for breach of contract when he was again critical of Sullivan for saying that every player with the exception of Scott Parker was up for sale. I had mixed feelings about it. Zola seemed to be a lovely chap, but lovely chaps don't often succeed in the world of football management. My heart went out to him when I saw him bringing tea and biscuits out to journalists assembled outside his house when the news broke, and he managed to lock himself out.

On the other hand, not for the last time, Sullivan had spoken before engaging his brain.

31

PLEASE DON'T LET ME GO

STOKE CITY 1, WEST HAM UNITED 1
PREMIER LEAGUE, 18 SEPTEMBER 2010
That sodding brass band that follows
the England football team around.

SuGo set their stall out early on in their tenure. On 18 May
2010 they released a ten-point pledge to the fans stating their
ambitions, their intentions, and making promises.

It may be the close-season but here at West Ham United we are
all busy preparing for 2010/11 and putting in place the next steps
to take this club forward.

Having admittedly had a tough end to the last campaign,
we are determined to build on the many positives we have at
the club and use the summer months to make sure we hit the
ground running next time around.

As the Board of West Ham United our pledge to you is to do
the following:

1. **Appoint the right manager**
   Our efforts are focused on recruiting a high-calibre manager
   with the necessary experience to deliver good football and,
   most importantly, results. A shortlist of candidates has been
   identified and the appointment will be made with enough time
   to prepare for pre-season.

2. **Sign new players**
   For too long, the focus has been on players leaving rather than

arriving. We will strengthen in the right areas to ensure an exciting and balanced squad that is well placed to cope with the rigours of a Premier League season. Our main aim will be to bring in players hungry to do well who share our ambitions and aspirations.

3. **More investment in the Academy**
Tony Carr remains at the heart of the club and his work in developing future first-team players remains essential for the long-term success of this club. We will make sure homegrown talent nurtured in the 'West Ham Way' will always be given the chance to complement established players brought in from elsewhere.

4. **Continue to clear the debt**
We have a responsibility to ensure this club is never again placed in a perilous position. Great strides have been taken to get us on a sound financial footing but there is still a way to go. Difficult decisions have had to be made – and that will continue to be the case – but our bottom line on the bottom line is to ensure the club survives.

5. **Freeze season ticket prices for renewals**
We are delighted we have been able to freeze season ticket prices, save for the VAT increase, but we will not stop there. We are looking at more ways of rewarding those fans who make such a long-term commitment and have excellent offers for younger supporters, who are the lifeblood of this club. Member benefits will also improve.

6. **Build the status and image of the club**
Our standing at home and abroad is rightly built on our proud history and our commitment to young talent. The values of the Academy of Football developed since the days of Bobby Moore define what we are all about. With the world's spotlight set to

shine on this part of London, the time is right to spread the word further.

7. **Make it enjoyable to come and watch**
   We want to bring the fun back. It is a serious business but we know you work hard all week and want to kick back at the weekend and enjoy yourselves. We want you to be excited on a matchday, and not just about the style of football. We are looking at ways to improve our pre-match and half-time entertainment and will welcome suggestions.

8. **Get closer to the community**
   This club does excellent work in the local area already but we want to move even closer to schools and businesses on our doorstep. We can extend our commitment to multi-sports, education and healthy living and show there is more to this club than just first-team football. We take our social responsibility very seriously.

9. **Go for the Olympic Stadium**
   Leaving the Boleyn Ground will be a wrench but the Olympic Stadium is an amazing once-in-a-lifetime opportunity in a financial and football sense. Our potential partnership with Newham Council promises to take this club to a new level, while protecting our history and traditions. To move forward, we have to move – but always with an eye on the past.

10. **Listen to supporters**
    Arguably the most important of all is our commitment to listen to what you have to say. We know we are just the custodians of this club. You who follow us every week, whether near or far, are the true owners. Whether talking to you online or in print, or face to face at fan forums, we will be open, transparent and available.

This ten-point pledge is just the start. We are here for the long term and our goals will evolve as we progress. We are proud to be here and will never stop working for you.

All of us share the same hopes and dreams. It is not just about aiming for cup finals or derby victories but about feeling part of something together and all pulling in the same direction. As the name says, we are very much West Ham. United.

All bold stuff and music to our ears, except the leaving of the Boleyn. The appointment of the right manager and signing the 'right' players would seem to be a given really, but these were the things that had proved so difficult over the last few years. Perhaps there should have been a sub-clause: 2(a) Keeping those players we have fit. Kieron Dyer was still on the books after all.

Okay, so appointing the right manager. Avram Grant. The man who guided Chelsea to a Champions League final in his sleep, as most of us could have, and had just taken Portsmouth down. It was hard to judge at the time. The Portsmouth situation had been difficult. He had come in three months into the season after Paul Hart had been sacked, and Pompey had that 9-point deduction to deal with. It's easy to say anyone could have taken Chelsea to a champions League final, but only Roberto DiMatteo has managed it since. For me, Grant's demeanour did not inspire confidence. He looked like a man on the brink of the sack before he had even started. But he must have been doing something right, right?

Like signing good players, as per point two? Thomas Hitzlsperger, the German international, was a good start. He had always impressed me when playing for Aston Villa, and he had the right nickname – 'Der Hammer' (a reference to his left foot rather than his footballing allegiances). He had signed for Lazio in January but made only four starts so was happy to make the move back to the Premier League.

Hitzlsperger signed before the World Cup started. West Ham's representatives in South Africa had not covered themselves in glory to that point: Benni McCarthy had allegedly been axed from the South Africa squad for taking some women back to his room after a friendly against Colombia, to be fed cake, presumably. He was unlikely to have been fit enough for anything else. Elsewhere, Valon Behrami was sent off playing for Switzerland against Chile.

Robert Green had finally been selected to represent England in a major tournament, in their opening game against the USA. Elaine and I gathered around the TV in Brockley with all the other residents in her shared house, all supporting England, all supporting West Ham's Robert Green on my insistence. Anyway, the game ended 1–1. Let's just leave it there, shall we?

Green could not be blamed for a tepid 0–0 against Algeria in the next match, a game I struggled to keep in touch with as I was at an AC/DC concert in Paris. Not that bothered anyway. The third game against Slovenia I missed because I was in mid-air en route to Fuerteventura. It was the first time I had failed to have a connection with an England World Cup campaign. Despite being unbeaten with 5 points, England finished second in their group to the USA, who got the easier second-round game against Ghana (which they lost) and England had to face Germany in Bloemfontein on 27 June.

As I had seen only one of the group games I made the effort to watch the Germany match, proudly wearing my West Ham shirt to reflect the fact that Matthew Upson was in the starting XI and former Hammers Frank Lampard Jnr, Glen Johnson, Jermain Defoe and David James also started. I watched the game on a big screen in Fuerteventura with Elaine, my nephew Mark and great-nephew Jamie, who, bless him, had his face painted with an England flag. Upson scored and Lampard's strike against the bar bounced down about two feet over the line, but wasn't given. Maybe we deserved no better after such a dismal display at the group stages.

So anyway, pledge number five, freezing season ticket prices for renewals. Well, yes technically, except it was announced in June that Band One prices for individual matches in the newly invented 'Category AA' were going up to £69. Was this football or a night at the opera?

Oh, and pledge number nine… the Olympic Stadium move? It was revealed that the site had been used to dump radioactive waste in the 1950s and 1960s. So far, so good.

Back to pledge two and the signing of the right players. Pablo Barrera, a Mexican winger signed after a £12 million bid for a young Brazilian winger called Neymar had been rejected for some reason. Tal Ben Haim, the Israeli full-back who was previously at Bolton and Portsmouth, also signed, and a young New Zealander by the name of Winston Reid who had starred in their World Cup Campaign, scoring in a 1–1 draw against Slovakia and starring in a 1–1 draw with Italy. Frédéric Piquionne was signed from Olympique Lyonnais for £1 million.

We were being linked with big names. Yakubu. Chimbonda. David Beckham. Yes, David Beckham. David Gold told Radio London we were trying to persuade him to sign but the chances were less than 50/50. So why mention it at all? Miralem Sulejmani, a bright Serbian winger at Ajax, agreed to come, but a work permit could not be secured. Big signings were being talked about, yes, but small signings were being made. Only time would tell if pledge two was realistic.

Pre-season we looked in good shape – of seven friendly matches played West Ham were unbeaten, winning 6 and drawing 1. In true West Ham tradition, marquee signing Hitzlsperger got injured on international duty with Germany and would miss the start of the season. Despite that, the positive pre-season meant we went to Villa Park on the opening day expecting to compete and come away with at least a point. We did not expect to be spanked 3–0.

But not to worry. Vice-chairman Karren Brady confidently predicted a top eight finish, so we would beat Bolton at home for sure. I had persuaded Dad to take a season ticket with me in the STBU and so there were five of us in a row, covering four generations. It was great. It almost made up for the pain of losing 3–1 to Bolton. Carlton missed a penalty at 0–1. Maybe things would have been different had that gone in, but we were poor. The result against Villa did not appear to be a blip.

Alessandro Diamanti went back to Italy, signing for newly promoted Brescia, and Swiss full-back Fabio Daprelà joined him. Diamanti lived up to his name. He glittered like a diamond. But he was not quite the real thing.

We played Oxford United in the League Cup at Upton Park and struggled. It was painful to watch. I was working with another West Ham fan, Colin Williams, who came to the game with me, and we watched in slack-jawed disbelief as West Ham failed to make an impact against League Two Oxford who had only just returned to the Football League. Scott Parker dragged us up by the bootstraps and scored a late winner. To add insult to injury, I was on the train going back to Elaine's house in Brockley. I had dozed off on the train and wasn't sure where I was, so stuck my head out of the door to see what station I was at, only for the doors to close on either side of my head. I got back to Elaine and she burst out laughing at the black stripes down each side of my bonce. It was so refreshing to be with someone who laughed at me for getting my head stuck in a train door and did not notice that I was home well after midnight.

Defeat at Manchester United 3–0 was another tame performance that did not indicate anything was likely to change soon. Upson remained uninspiring as captain, Parker remained the driving force, Green was busy. Grant stood on the touchline with his arms folded looking like he was about to burst into a chorus of 'I am... I said.'

Victor Obinna, a Nigerian who had played in the World Cup, signed on loan from Inter Milan, following in the footsteps of, er, Luis Jiménez.

Around this time I had been working with Biteback on a third edition of *An Irrational Hatred of Luton* due to popular demand. The third edition, sporting a brand-new livery, typesetting and photographs, came out in August 2010, and boss Iain Dale arranged for a signing session at the Newham Bookshop before the Chelsea game on 11 September. Elaine joined me sitting outside the shop with Iain and a satisfying stream of people came up asking me to sign books. As had been the case with all signing sessions, a number of people asked me if the was 'any violence' in it. When I responded in the negative they wrinkled their noses and walked off. It didn't bother me. As you will already have gathered from earlier sections of this book I abhor violence of any sort, especially in the name of my football club. And I have no time for the perpetrators. But I can understand why people find it exciting I suppose. Like that dog that chases the car, I am sure that when actually presented with the opportunity most would run like the fucking clappers.

We had tickets up in the West Upper for some reason I can no longer recall, and we waved at the rest of the family in the cheap seats as West Ham cheerfully submitted to Chelsea, who took a 3–0 lead. Scott Parker again provided the only moment of class from West Ham's perspective as he cushioned a lob over Petr Cech in the Chelsea goal.

Bottom of the table with a goal difference of −10 after only 4 games, we faced Stoke City next at the Britannia Stadium, a team who had themselves only just earned their first win after losing their opening three matches.

The game coincided with the Jewish day of Atonement, Yom Kippur, and Avram Grant had received previous clearance to be absent as a result. First team coaches Paul Groves and Kevin Keen took his place in the dugout as a Scott Parker goal just before half time was enough to earn our first point of the season.

I had been invited to write for Iain Dale's West Ham website 'West Ham Till I Die' and was finding the immediate feedback of writing a blog quite hard to take. For once people were not always complimentary. In fact, at times they were downright rude.

I was my own worst enemy after the Stoke game though. Given that we had picked up our first point without Grant, I somewhat flippantly entitled the blog 'I wish it could be Yom Kippur Every Day', by which I meant if it was, Grant would not be out of the dugout and we might get more points.

But the article was pounced upon by people who got hold of the wrong end of the stick and started to beat me over the head with it. I was accused of comparing Yom Kippur with Christmas, of disrespecting the most solemn and holy of days, of misunderstanding the whole thing.

Let me make this quite clear. I was in no way comparing Yom Kippur with Christmas. It was simply a bad joke and I apologised immediately. I certainly had no idea of the offence it would cause, otherwise I would not have even thought about publishing it. Iain Dale published my apology and took the article down. I also stopped writing for the blog as I felt that if people were going to misunderstand me so comprehensively it might be better not to give them further opportunities. It was an early taster for me of the power of social media to create misunderstanding, and also an early confirmation that offence is taken – not given. I had absolutely no intention to offend.

I showed the article to a Jewish friend, Elane. She laughed. She said it was funny, but then she knew my humour. Then she said: 'Oh Rob, you really don't understand at all do you.'

I had been using the internet since 1999 and twelve years later I was still struggling to come to terms with the fact that every man and his dog could now see your work and pass critical comment, whether valid or not.

In 2003 when *The Legacy of Barry Green* was published, some bloke called Gerard reviewed it on Knees Up Mother Brown and was less than complimentary, saying that the book did not live up to the subtitle, 'How West Ham went from East End Pride to Nationwide.' But he had read the book in isolation and not in the context of the previous two. And, as often happens on the internet, someone expresses an opinion and a stream of brainless sheep add comments because they are up the arse, or want to be, of the originator. One referred to my story about giving up smoking and called the unmentionable ex my 'Fagash Lil of a girlfriend'. I think unless you have ever been on the end of something like that you probably have never stopped to think about the impact it has on people. I certainly always think twice before being too critical online. At Simon Smith's behest I went online and took part in a live discussion with some of the main critics, but as often happens, people who snipe about you behind your back are as nice as pie to your face.

In 2009 shortly after returning to London I saw a post on the 'Over Land and Sea' (OLAS) Facebook page and I mentioned that I had 35 copies of *The Legacy of Barry Green* in my garage. Someone responded saying something along the lines of 'I'm not surprised, it was self-indulgent crap.'

I was flabbergasted by this lazy and undeserved insult. For someone who didn't know me to say something like that. I got upset when Gary Firmager, OLAS editor, did not say anything in my defence. I e-mailed him about it and got no reply. I took it personally. I stopped whatever writing I had continued to contribute to OLAS. Looking back on it now it was a massive over-reaction on my part. I'm ready for any criticism that will undoubtedly come my way when this book hits the stands. But to anyone who wishes to scoff I would say just this: judge me after you have had your fourth book published.

I didn't have a feud with Gary; I simply didn't talk to him anymore. He made no attempt to pacify me, but that is not the sort of thing that Gary does. He has a thicker skin than me. We had been good for each other. He had given me a voice. I have given him years of free copy. I approached Gary in 2016 just before we left the Boleyn and we embraced, and if I am not mistaken both shed a little tear. I'm not convinced Gary even knew what it was all about. I, on the other hand, seemed to be spending my whole life apologising.

32

LOVE YOU MORE

WEST HAM UNITED 4, MANCHESTER UNITED 0
LEAGUE CUP FIFTH ROUND, 30 NOVEMBER 2010

Men who insist on taking their tops off the moment the sun comes out.
Please stay out of the supermarket. And my line of vision.

There is as much to say about Avram Grant's season in charge at West Ham as there was to say about Zola's last. Not much. But at least there were occasional flashes of brilliance in 2010/11 to remember fondly, including the run in the League Cup that started in such unsure fashion against Oxford. It continued in much more confident vein at the Stadium of Light, where goals from Victor Obinna and Frédéric Piquionne secured a 2–1 win and passage to a fourth-round tie at home to Stoke City. Significantly, it was our first away win in any competition since winning at Wolves on the opening day of 2009/10.

One noticeable absence from the SuGo's ten-point pledge was any promise not to open gobs and embarrass us in public, criticise players in the national press or undermine the position of the coaching staff. In the *News of the World* Sullivan suggested that some foreign players might not have been giving 100 per cent:

> We've got a few foreign players who wanted to leave but we didn't receive any offers… I think they couldn't be bothered but now the deadline has passed they realise the only way out is to play for the club and to play well and I think they will make a contribution. They realise now that they are here until at least

January so they will get their heads down and work for the benefit of the club. They had their heads in the air before that.

Yes, nice one, Dave.

Things were progressing with Elaine, and as I had pretty much moved into her shared house in Brockley, we decided we needed more privacy and we rented a flat in Bromley, on the site of the old hospital a few yards from Bromley South railway station. Mum and Dad had recently moved back up to the area from Hastings to be nearer us, and with my sisters in West Wickham and Crayford it was reassuring and comforting to have everyone close by.

The only day we could move was the Saturday of the home game against Tottenham. Given our form, I did not think I was likely to miss much, but we earned our first victory of the season 1-0 though a Piquionne goal. Drat, I bloody well missed it. My dad saw it though – my nephew took him and he thoroughly enjoyed it. His dementia by now was such that he did not recall previous games in sufficient detail to put him off going again. It was all a bit 'hit and hope' though.

Despite the door opening a crack, and two more points coming courtesy of draws at home to Fulham and away at Wolves, we remained bottom of the table.

Another loss came in October. Malcolm Allison, one of the key members of the 'Academy' of the 1950s, and the man Bobby Moore credited with teaching him everything he knew, died at the age of 83.

The class of 2011 continued to struggle without anyone with Allison's vision on the pitch or in the dugout. Baron Greenback stood, arms folded on the touchline, looking like he was about to burst into a few bars of 'Beautiful Noise' as we lost at home to Newcastle 2-1 and against Arsenal at the Emirates 1-0.

In between we beat Stoke City 3-1 after extra time. With the game being too late in the evening for Dad and the two kids, I took Colin from work and another colleague, Stokie Steve Kane, to see the match. We were a little delayed getting in and missed

Stoke's opener, much to Steve's annoyance, which grew through the evening as Scott Parker scored in the 84th minute to take the tie to extra time, and extra-time goals from da Costa and Obinna took us through to the last eight.

The league was a different story. Three more successive draws, 2–2 away at Birmingham, at home to West Bromwich Albion and 0–0 at home to newly promoted Blackpool, left us rooted at the foot of the table. We had 9 points from 13 games, level on points with Wolves and 4 behind Birmingham City and 5 away from Wigan and safety. So, after the customary 3–0 defeat at Anfield, the home match against the Latics was declared by SuGo as 'Must Win' and the game to 'Save Our Season'. You can say it was unwarranted pressure, but Sullivan might argue that it worked as we won the game 3–1. Our second league win of the season on 27 November. To me that spelled one thing – and even with the 'Save Our Season' game won or lost – Relegation.

Still, we might have a shiny new stadium to play Championship football in. The bids had been submitted to be tenants of the Olympic Stadium after the games in 2012. Despite all the protestations of Tessa Jowell and Ken Livingstone, and despite all the misgivings of the Icelandics, it seemed that with sufficient thrust, pigs might fly.

West Ham were favourites to land the Olympic Stadium according to the deputy chairman of the 2012 games committee. Sir Keith Mills, ironically also a director of Tottenham Hotspur, said in The *Daily Telegraph*:

> West Ham's proposals are to leave the running track in place and if it stacks up economically I am sure the OPLC will award it to them. If it doesn't stack up they have an alternative in Tottenham with an athletics legacy elsewhere.'
>
> We promised in our bid to leave an athletics legacy. The IOC president has made it clear that it is more important not to leave a white elephant in London than whether that legacy is in the stadium or elsewhere in London.

The OPLC's job is to ensure there is a legacy and to ensure there are no white elephants.

Yes, but a running track? We took on Manchester United in the League Cup quarter-final expecting an avalanche on a snowy November night at the Boleyn. No Olympic Stadium was ever going to recreate the atmosphere inside Upton Park that night as West Ham produced their customary if increasingly rare shock result against top sides. With the quicksand of the Premier League temporarily removed, we played freely and beautifully and two first-half goals from an unexpected source put an unexpected complexion on the game at half time. Jonathan Spector had been a bit part player since joining in 2006 but these were his fifteen minutes. This was his moment. This is how we will choose to remember him. Remember him launching himself at an Obinna cross and making just the right contact to take the ball away from United keeper Kuszczak and into the net. Remember him sweeping a loose ball in from six yards for the second. Forget all the rest. Remember him for that. Carlton scored twice more in the second half. We had plenty of other reasons to remember Carlton, but this was up there, along with a post-match interview in which he had so much steam coming off the top of his head someone called the fire brigade.

It has always been frustrating supporting West Ham. Even in happy, successful times there were inexplicable defeats that cost us dear. But the flip side of that is that even in the darkest hours there are moments of brilliance that make it bearable. 4–1 against Liverpool in 1988. 1–0 at Highbury in 1989. 1–0 against Manchester United in 1992. 4–3 against Spurs in 1997. You get the picture. The 4–0 win over Manchester United in 2010 will go down as one of the best – and strangest – results in our history.

33

WHEN WE COLLIDE

WEST HAM UNITED 2, BIRMINGHAM CITY 1
LEAGUE CUP SEMI-FINAL (FIRST LEG), 11 JANUARY 2011
*Big fake eyelashes, drawn-on eyebrows, Botox faces and collagen lips.
You should not be able to see any part of someone's face
when you are standing behind them.*

Normal service resumed with a 1–0 defeat at Sunderland at the weekend. We had been temporarily lifted off the foot of the table by a heavy defeat for Wolves on the Saturday, but we clearly missed 20th place and by 6 p.m. we were back in our now-accustomed position.

Opinion on the proposed move to the Olympic stadium was divided. There were rumours of protest groups being formed. Many fans felt that the SuGo ten-point pledge was meaningless, particularly the part about listening to the fans. Many fans didn't want to move. No one listened. The move was happening whether we liked it or not, and whether we protested or not it was part of the plan.

A 3–1 defeat at home to Manchester City was no big surprise, but disappointing nevertheless, especially given that we had managed to raise ourselves so well for the cup match against United. City were a different prospect, though, and they disposed of us clinically, the only bright spot being a goal for young James Tomkins. I took Dad to the game, but it was becoming increasingly difficult. We had to drive because Dad could not cope with public transport, and had to park a good 25-minute walk (at his pace) away from the ground. He did not qualify for a disabled badge and I could not drop him at the gates and come back for him when there were just the two of us. Often, by the time we got to the turnstile he was breathless, and we had to wait a while for him to recover before climbing the stairs to the upper tier. That often meant missing the first five minutes. Despite wearing plenty of clothes he got cold and was sometimes asking to leave just after half time. I had to go with him, of course. Don't get me wrong, I am not complaining. I would quite happily have not gone to the game at all to spend time with my dad. But I got the sense he was only coming along to please me.

I looked into getting a parking space at the stadium but there was a waiting list as long as your arm and then it was about £30 a game. Not really viable. The best option was to try to go with more than just the two of us so I could drop him by the gates and someone else could look after him until I could return. But that rarely happened. We started to arrive earlier so we could park nearer, but gradually match day restrictions on parking around the ground got tighter.

Dad would always ask for a hot dog and a glass of wine, then give me half of the hot dog because he couldn't finish it. He never needed any help with the wine. We had no idea how ill he was at that stage.

Around this time I got involved with the unofficial West Ham podcast *STOP! Hammer Time*, which was part of the Playback media stable who produced podcasts for many of the top clubs, and Chelsea. Former stadium announcer Jeremy Nicholas had written the foreword for the recent reprint of *An Irrational Hatred of Luton* and was appearing as a guest. He suggested that I come along too. I had done radio before, but never a podcast, and was intrigued. I met host Phil Whelans, a comedian with a number of impressive writing credits including *Spitting Image* and his own radio sitcom *My First Planet*, which starred Nicholas Lyndhurst. I also met another regular contributor to the podcast: Jim Grant, a secondary school teacher and friend of Phil from childhood. They had grown up together in Bromley, watching West Ham all the way, so we had our geographical roots in common.

Phil's comedy script-writing background made the West Ham podcast unique in that he would create spoof e-mails from players and directors, or fake Wikipedia entries for players, which were very funny. He also invited guests who were usually a lot more famous and interesting than me, but I had my toe in the door now and wasn't going to let it go. I loved it.

As an English teacher, Jim had a penchant for poetry. I posted a picture on the STOP! Hammer Time Facebook page. It was a photo by Steve Bacon from 1983 of Alan Devonshire hurdling a desperate lunge from a Birmingham City defender during the opening game of the 1983/84 season, a game we won 4–0. I love that picture so much. Jim loved it too, and wrote a poem about it, 'Seventh Heavenshire':

> I'll admit I shed a tear
> when I saw that shot of Devonshire
> sparrow-legged but eagle-eyed,
> evading the clumsy slide
> of some defender brute:
> it was beaut-
> iful.
> And suddenly
> I'm in that distant thenshire,
> that never-to-come-againshire,
> when Devonshire
> dazzled at Elland Road
> and the light flowed
> out of him as he feints and wheels,
> electric-eels
> his way past clumsy Everton boots
> and shoots –
> no, stabs –
> stiletto-like
> through keeper's legs.
> Ah, Devonshire!
> Moustachioed musketeer!

Our swash-buckling Dartagnanshire –
you sent me to seventh heavenshire
so many times!
The last in '89
when relegation beckoned
but Liverpool hadn't reckoned
with your relish for the fight.
That night
it was your swansong,
but blimey you were on-song:
with your long hair
to everyone there
it was clear
you were our laughing cavalier,
Oh Devonshire!
Yet there was something poignant
in those last few silky runs and flicks;
though still imposing,
the lid alas was closing
on your magic box of tricks.
But you're still there,
caught photographically in mid-air
In that still-remembered whenshire,
that never-to-be-forgotten thenshire
Our Alan. Devonshire.

The quality of the writing and Phil and Jim's general input are appreciated by the podcast's thousands of listeners. We are indeed privileged to have two such talented guys looking after it. Long may it continue.

Meanwhile, Baron Greenback was in danger of losing his job. There was press speculation that his position was under threat as he took the squad to Ewood Park and a Junior Stanislas goal rescued a point in a 1–1 draw. A little bit of form then popped up from nowhere. We won on Boxing Day at Craven Cottage 3–1, then drew two days later at home to Everton and beat relegation rivals Wolves 2–0 at Upton Park on New Year's Day. Being a bank holiday, I had been able to park on a yellow line near the stadium so Dad was happy. Short walk, hot dog, wine, no hit and hope.

Freddie Sears scored his first goal since his debut (which felt like decades ago). There seemed to be some reason for optimism as the team went up to St James's Park to face Alan Pardew's Newcastle. It was doubly disappointing to suffer a 5–0 reverse, for one thing because we had been showing signs of recovery which now seemed to be blown out of the window, and for another, because it gave Alan Pardew the chance to gloat.

'Captain' Matthew Upson had indicated he would not be renewing his contract when it expired at the end of the season, yet in a baffling decision Baron Greenback kept him as 'Captain' when it was clear for all to see he didn't really give a shit about West Ham. Personally I would not only have stripped him of the captaincy, but given him a six-month spell in the stiffs as well.

We did have some cup matches to look forward to, at least. Three days after beating Barnsley 2–0 in the third round of the FA Cup we had the first leg of our League Cup semi-final against Birmingham City at Upton Park. There had been some controversy over the ticketing process for the game as the previous rounds had all been priced at a tenner for season ticket holders, but it was seen fit to raise the price to a minimum of £21 for band four season ticket holders and to a whopping £52 for band one general sale. The policy appeared to have backfired. The game was live on terrestrial TV and came just three days after another game that people had forked out for. Two days before kick-off there were still 5,000 seats unsold, so the decision was taken to open the turnstiles on the night. In the end 34,754 came in to watch West Ham take a slender lead to the second leg, courtesy of a Mark Noble goal and a Carlton shinner that would not find a place anywhere soon in his top ten.

Victor Obinna stupidly got himself sent off for tangling with Seb Larsson, so in the end a 2–1 lead was as much as we could have asked for. Surely we were on our way to Wembley to play the winners of the Arsenal v. Ipswich semi-final, in which Ipswich held a similarly slender 1–0 lead.

The transfer window was open, and it seemed that SuGo were not convinced that Baron Greenback was the man to take the fight forward, and there was a rumoured approach made to Martin O'Neill to take over on a short-term contract to get us out of trouble.

You can say what you like about Grant and O'Neill, but both are honourable men. It was a shame to see them both being messed about. When West Ham lost 3–0 at home to Arsenal on 15 January, Grant appeared to be saying his goodbyes, throwing a scarf into the crowd after the game.

The only problem was our new board were not particularly men, or women for that matter, of principle. Karren Brady, for example, denied using her column in *The Sun* to influence the decision not to sign Steve Sidwell. When asked about it Grant broke his normal diplomatic protocol, saying:

'Read my newspaper column next week and perhaps I will have my say.' It was unlike Grant to make any sort of comment like that. Clearly he was unhappy with interference. Brady could not escape controversy as a story broke in the *Daily Mirror* suggesting that she had sent texts to all the playing staff after the Arsenal defeat asking what they thought of Grant and whether they thought he should go. The club denied the allegations.

The story about O'Neill was leaked and reported by the BBC as a done deal, and O'Neill got cold feet and distanced himself. The board said they were 100 per cent behind Grant, which was clearly not the case. If they didn't fancy Grant, sack him. Don't go tapping up other options first. This was not how business should be conducted by chairmen who want their managers to trust them. As Tommy Docherty had once said:

'I don't want my chairman behind me, I want him in front of me where I can see him.'

Speaking of people who could not be trusted, let us not forget Tessa Jowell. Now I don't want to speak ill of the recently departed, but I refer you to previous chapters 15 and 28 in which Jowell consistently poured cold water on the horny dog that was West Ham.

Now the tune was somewhat different. She said in an article in *The Guardian:*

> When we won the Olympics we made a clear promise to the international community and the people of this country that the stadium would have athletics at its core.
>
> This wasn't a promise we made to win the bid but a clear statement of intent about the future of sport in our country.
>
> The Olympic Park Legacy Company will make its decision about the legacy tenant for the stadium in just over a week's time and there are now only two bids on the table. Only one of these, the joint bid from West Ham and Newham Council, fulfils the promises we made and the criteria we set out when we were in government.
>
> The commercial strength of West Ham's bid is not just based on its ability to get large crowds to football matches, although that is an important part. It is for the use of the stadium all year round in many different guises, with regular athletics fixtures, showcases for rugby, cricket and American football as well as regular entertainment events.
>
> As the bid is partnered with Newham Council, we can be assured that there will be real community involvement. They will have school community education projects, all sorts of community mass participation events. They have partnered with Live Nation, the world's largest live entertainment company, and Westfield, the world's largest listed retail property group.
>
> This isn't West Ham on their own; you've got some very serious players who will add to the revenues [*sic*] streams.

For those opposed to the move, Jowell and Ken Livingstone had been the ray of hope that the door would be firmly shut on such an idea. But now, faced with the unpopular prospect of an expensive white elephant, the words from a few years earlier had been forgotten. Certainly the bid from West Ham had been expertly crafted by SuGo and Brady, so much so that some polls showed the majority of fans were actually in favour of the move. Throw in a £40 million loan from Newham Council, and you had all the makings of a controversy that was unlikely to go away for the foreseeable future.

In terms of the transfer window, SuGo seemed to have made a rod for their own back by being less than wholehearted in their support for Grant. So, do they now give him funds or not? The reality was somewhere in between as new faces did come in, but the majority were again on loan. Wayne Bridge came in on loan from Manchester City. Senegalese striker Demba Ba was supposed to come on loan from Hoffenheim. Having failed a medical at Stoke, a permanent three-year deal was eventually agreed on a pay-as-you-play agreement which suited all parties. Gary O'Neil came in on a permanent deal from Middlesbrough. In the opposite direction Valon Behrami left for Fiorentina on a contract valued around £2 million. In another loan deal, Éire international Robbie Keane was signed for a loan fee of £1 million and reported wages of £65,000 a week.

The second leg of the League Cup semi-final started well with Carlton putting us 1–0 up on the night (3–1 on aggregate), and even the most cautious of West Ham fans was reaching for the underground map the check the exact location of Wembley Stadium. But as Avram stood with arms folded on the touchline, about to break into a chorus of 'I'm a believer', West Ham stopped playing. Birmingham scored twice to take the tie to extra time. There looked like there was only going to be one winner. And there was. Thanks for nothing West Ham. Thanks for promising the earth but delivering a dirty great big fuck all once again.

34

PRICE TAG

Buying gig tickets. Booking fee. Admin fee. Handling fee. Really?

We shook off the disappointment of failing to get to Wembley at the final hurdle, by pursuing the second route, beating Nottingham Forest 3–2 at Upton Park in the fourth round of the FA Cup. Victor Obinna bagged a hat-trick.

At Bloomfield Road Robbie Keane paid off part of his loan fee with his first goal for the club on his debut. Obinna scored the other two to put us in 18th place, only goal difference away from safety, although Birmingham in 17th had played 2 games fewer. Clearly it was vital not to lose 1–0 to a goal from a six-foot-seven-inch beanpole after missing a host of good chances when we played Birmingham in the league at Upton Park on 6 February. Never mind.

On Friday 11 February, the Olympic Park Development Committee confirmed West Ham as its preferred bidder to occupy the stadium after the 2012 games. It seemed unreal. It was nice to have beaten Tottenham – but at the same time it seemed so far off, and not like it would actually happen.

Having been just goal difference from safety after the win at Blackpool, suddenly we were bottom again with 24 points, 2 from safety, but having played a game more than West Bromwich Albion in 17th. A win at The Hawthorns would have put us above them. For that to happen it would have been useful not to have been completely outplayed and 3–0 down at half time.

Captain, sorry, not captain, Scott Parker is said to have taken matters into his own hands at half time. Grant was no doubt standing, looking on with arms folded, about to break into a chorus of 'Cracklin' Rosie'. Parker is alleged to have given such a stirring half time team talk that West Ham came out a different side. Ba had a shot cleared off the line after being tipped onto the post by West Bromwich Albion's goalkeeper Myhill. Gary O'Neil hit the bar. Ba eventually scored with our third chance, five minutes into the second half, and West Bromwich Albion, under caretaker head coach Michael Appleton (ahead of new boss Roy Hodgson's official start), looked every bit as vulnerable as we had in the first half. Carlton scored a second with a brave diving header. Piquionne came on and hit the bar, before Ba volleyed a deserved equaliser with just seven minutes to go.

Surely this dramatic recovery would be a turning point? Surely the commitment shown by the players in coming back from 0–3, even if it had been at Parker's behest and not that of the captain or the manager, gave an indication of what could be achieved if this set of players applied themselves. Surely?

Now, remember that in June 2010 West Ham signed German international Thomas Hitzlsperger, who promptly got injured representing his country and was likely to be out for a month as a result? Yes, that Thomas Hitzlsperger. He made his debut on 21 February 2011, eight months after signing. The impact was immediate. West Ham claimed a quarter-final place 5–1 against Burnley with Hitz, who scored a trademark left foot hammer blow to open the scoring. Carlton grabbed a brace and Winston Reid scored his first West Ham goal. Freddy Sears completed the rout before Jay Rodriguez claimed a consolation.

Hitz was influential in the next two games. Liverpool came to Upton Park in 6th place and were clear favourites. But West Ham blew them away. Scott Parker got the first, picking up a neat pass from Hitz to hit a superb long range shot past Reina. Ba was playing as part of an unlikely front three with O'Neil and Piquionne and scored a second with a graceful swallow dive to bullet an O'Neil cross into the net.

Former Hammer Glen Johnson pulled one back, tapping in

a Luis Suárez cross, but West Ham were not to be denied and Carlton beat Reina at his near post to complete the scoring in stoppage time to put West Ham yet again within goal difference of safety.

Hitz was on fire. Ba looked the business. Parker was up for it. Green was on form. We had match-winners all over the pitch now. It was looking good. Even Baron Greenback afforded himself a smile before humming a few bars of 'Song Sung Blue'.

Elaine came with me to the next game at home to Stoke City which was also won 3–0. Within five minutes of the start she branded the Potters a bunch of bullies. Not far off the truth as Pulis's side did their best to kick us off the pitch. But goals from da Costa, Ba and Hitz gave us a comprehensive win.

But that was as good as it got. As inexplicable as the upturn in form had been, it suddenly fell through the floor again with only 2 points taken from the final 27 available.

Let me repeat that: 2 points from the final 27. That is frankly unbelievable given that we had taken 11 from the previous 18. How could a team crash and burn like that? What on earth happened in that dressing room to spark such a nose-dive in form? After beating Stoke in the league we lost narrowly and unfortunately to the same opposition in the FA Cup quarter-final, then took a battling point at White Hart Lane. But then, as they say in applied physics, it all went to shit.

Though we went 2–0 up against Manchester United at Upton Park through two Noble penalties, we lost 4–2. Bolton away was a customary 3–0 defeat. Aston Villa at home looked like it might provide something as Robbie Keane put us ahead, but the dagger through the heart was a last-minute winner from Gabby Agbonlahor. As far as I was concerned we were down at that point, as the next two matches were both away at Chelsea and Manchester City and both were surrendered without too much of a fight, 3–0 and 2–1 respectively. Blackburn Rovers provided the final point of the season before the coup de grace was applied by Wigan Athletic at the JJB Stadium on Sunday 15 May.

At 2–0 up through two Demba Ba headers we looked to be

coasting to victory at half time. But losing streaks are hard to stop. Once Wigan had scored through a Charles N'Zogbia free kick, the heads visibly dropped and Conor Sammon scored an equaliser eleven minutes later. A draw still would not have been enough, but Wigan wrapped up the win in injury time as a plane hired by Millwall fans flew overhead towing the banner that read: 'Avram Grant: Millwall Legend'.

In a typically unclassy, and frankly embarrassing, move, after a defeat that condemned West Ham to a season in the Championship, Grant was allegedly summoned to the Wigan boardroom by Sullivan and fired on the spot. Quite why Grant was allowed to continue after his position had become untenable in January was beyond me. Scott Parker clearly could have done a better job with both arms tied behind his back and a bag over his head.

Firing Grant was one thing; not allowing him on the team coach to travel back to London was farcical. Several players allegedly had to protest in order to allow Grant access to the coach.

The final game of the season was presided over by poor old Kevin Keen, the go-to West Ham caretaker manager at that time. Sunderland had a good team which finished 10th, and the 3 points they picked up by rolling us over 3–0 went towards that. West Ham fans, always capable of gallows humour, largely ignored the game and danced the world's longest conga around the Boleyn, to blank out the dross they would otherwise have been obliged to witness.

The season ended with West Ham on 33 points – just 2 fewer than the previous season, but this time it was 7 points from safety; not helped by the fact that there was no Portsmouth with a 9-point deduction to assist. We won just 7 games all season, masked largely by the 8 cup victories. But any team winning only 7 games in a season does not deserve to stay up, and although we had played well in spells during the campaign, you could not argue against relegation being the only appropriate outcome.

The only thing more of a certainty than Scott Parker winning

Hammer of the year was that there would be trouble at the awards ceremony. When you allow fans to mingle with players who have failed to perform, charge them £300+VAT each for the privilege, and throw copious amounts of alcohol (and probably other things) into the mix as well, the result is, as David Sullivan might have said, Armageddon.

35

SHE MAKES ME WANNA

WEST HAM UNITED 0, CARDIFF CITY 1
FOOTBALL LEAGUE CHAMPIONSHIP, 7 AUGUST 2011
People who insist on using their phone as their Oyster card
then forget to unlock the bloody thing at the barrier.

It didn't take too long to come to terms with relegation as we had plenty of warning. About two years in fact.

The baffling appointment of Avram Grant had backfired spectacularly, and the attempt to get shot of him in January had been botched to such a degree that it was going to prove difficult to find a manager to replace him that had any kind of scruples whatsoever.

It would have to be someone equally as desperate as the board. As such, the position was dismissed by people like Steve McClaren, Paolo Di Canio, Alan Curbishley and Gus Poyet.

What we needed was someone who really didn't give a shit what anyone thought. Someone who was prepared to work with anyone if the price was right. Someone who thrived on unpopularity. Someone who was never wrong. Someone like... Sam Allardyce.

Allardyce was installed as West Ham's fourteenth manager on 1 June 2011. As fans we were divided. Here was a man we had systematically detested as the high priest of anti-football for many years. And now he was here, at West Ham, where pragmatism was not always the most distinctive feature of a club with a reputation for playing flowing attacking football with a soft, tickleable underbelly.

Personally, I had grown tired of reading newspaper articles

claiming that West Ham had now added some steel to their artistry. I'd seen that going on since 1974 when Keith Robson joined, and nothing had really changed. We were still a soft touch. Now Allardyce was here maybe the boot would be on the other foot. Maybe we would fall over to win free kicks. Maybe we would deliberately waste time when 1–0 up with five minutes to go. Maybe we would launch it long to catch the opposition unawares. I was tired of seeing our good nature taken advantage of for so long. Maybe now things would change.

That said, we needed Allardyce to 'get' the club. All successful managers at the Boleyn had understood the history and the culture of West Ham United FC and, even if they had not been able to fulfil the criteria in the way we would have liked, at least they understood it.

Allardyce didn't get it from day one. He could not get his head around the concept of playing entertaining football that would not necessarily, percentage-wise, guarantee results. As we were to find out, his statistical, probability-based approach to negative, dull football didn't guarantee results either, so I know which I would have preferred.

Big Sam, as he was known (not fat Sam – I never called him that because he is big, and that is not the same as fat), did not get off on the best of footings in this respect, by immediately disregarding the 'West Ham Way.'

If I am honest, I am also not entirely sure what the 'West Ham Way' is, but it is most definitely a thing, I can assure you. It's about our heritage, playing the right way, sportsmanship, winning though superior skill and endeavour, and losing with grace. In other words, everything that Allardyce's teams up to that point had not been able to demonstrate. So I suppose it was no big surprise that trying to get Allardyce to understand the West Ham Way was like trying to get Donald Trump to understand humility and modesty. It just wasn't going to happen.

Transfer activity was always going to be a major talking point during the summer and, having lost Premier League status, we needed to rebuild quickly with a view to bouncing back at the first attempt. No fewer than twenty-one players left in the summer transfer window, which is a quite incredible clear-out even for a relegated side. A further twelve players came in. I will try to summarise here the comings and goings.

Among the big names leaving, the biggest was Scott Parker. I hated to see him go, but he was near the end of his career and had been called into the England squad. He needed to be at a Premier League club. It was just a shame it had to be Tottenham. Parker had carried the team by himself at times and rightly been recognised as captain by fans and the press, if not by the manager. He played in the first four games of the Championship season before leaving for Tottenham on deadline day for £5 million. As far as I was concerned he went with my best wishes and thanks for four years of sterling service: 123 appearances, 6 as substitute, and 12 goals.

Matthew Upson, on the other hand, could just fuck off. Masquerading as captain for two years he seemed to let everything pass him by, showing no leadership qualities at all. He announced in January that he would not be staying, and when the management showed no signs of dropping him or stripping him of the captaincy he had the temerity to retain it without, it seemed, a second thought. Having arrived in the January 2007 transfer window, he was one of the longer-serving players with 144 appearances (one as substitute) and 4 goals. He left on a free transfer to Stoke City and it stuck in my throat a little that when the number six shirt was withdrawn in honour of Bobby Moore he was the incumbent. I would not miss him.

Kieron Dyer had arrived before the start of the 2007/08 season but been plagued by injury since breaking his leg in his third game. Clearly his body was not built for Premier League football. I'm not sure what it was built for. A game of Jenga maybe. Whatever it was built for, and whoever it was built by, he should ask for a refund. He left having made 17 starts, 18 appearances as a sub, and failing to find the net. He went to QPR on a free transfer, starting the first game of 2011/12 at Loftus Road against Bolton, but was stretchered off after three minutes.

Seriously, you could not make it up. He played seven minutes of that season for QPR but still managed to earn a one-year extension. I didn't know whether to be angry with him or give him a cuddle. That might have fractured six of his ribs, though.

Danny Gabbidon was the longest-serving player to leave, having played throughout our most recent Premier League stint. I was sorry to see him go, he rarely let us down. He made 105 appearances in total, and 8 as substitute.

Jonathan Spector went off on a free transfer to Birmingham City, having the distinction of having scored 50 per cent of his goals for West Ham against Manchester United. That will be two then. A decent squad player, illustrated by a whopping 40 substitute appearances in addition to his 75 starts and 4 goals, he never really seemed to fit in at Upton Park.

Radoslav Kováč had been on loan to Spartak Moscow since January and made a permanent move to FC Basel of Switzerland after 50 appearances. Manuel da Costa went to Lokomotiv Moscow.

I was not the biggest fan of Luís Boa Morte, so I was delighted when he finally slung his hook and went off to Larissa in Greece. 75 appearances, 34 as sub and a lowly 2 goals.

Many of the players that arrived in 2010/11 did not last more than a year. Lars Jacobsen went back to Denmark to FC Copenhagen, which was a shame because I had always thought him a decent full-back.

Pablo Barrera went off on a season-long loan to Real Zaragoza, and Hitz had his contract terminated so he headed back to Germany to Wolfsburg. That was also a shame, but it was maybe unrealistic to expect a player of his quality to play Championship football. The big disappointment was Demba Ba going to Newcastle when he still had two and a half years left on his contract. He was a player who allegedly had knees that might explode at any point and was on a pay-as-you-play deal. What would he care if that game was away at Barnsley on a Wednesday night? Well, it seemed to bother him a lot, as he couldn't wait to get through the door.

After that it was mainly kids going off on loan, but two deals I struggled to understand were Zavon Hines and Junior Stanislas going to Championship rivals Burnley. I had thought them decent players who deserved the chance to show what they could do at Championship level – for us, not for a rival.

Coming in we had twelve players on undisclosed fees, free transfers or loans. Of these, Kevin Nolan was probably the most significant. A faithful lieutenant of Allardyce at Bolton, he was signed by Joe Kinnear for Newcastle in 2009 after Allardyce had left. But clearly the bond was still there from their Bolton days, as he agreed to drop down a division to team up with his former boss once again for an undisclosed fee.

Coming in on free transfers were Abdoulaye Faye from Stoke City, Joey O'Brien from Bolton, John Carew from Aston Villa and Papa Bouba Diop from AEK Athens. Loan signings included George McCartney, returning to us from Sunderland, David Bentley from Tottenham, Henri Lansbury from Arsenal, and Paraguayan striker Brian Montenegro from Uruguayan club Deportivo Maldonado.

Joining on undisclosed fees (i.e. either embarrassingly small, or so big the fans would not accept it if they were aware of it) were Matty Taylor from Bolton, Sam Baldock from MK Dons and full-back Guy Demel from Hamburg.

Demel had been on the radar for some time and I remember Iain Dowie on Sky Sports saying if West Ham pulled off his signature it would be a real coup. We would see. Baldock was an exciting young striker who had been scoring freely for MK Dons. The rest were a bit, well, meh, if I'm honest.

Eiður Guðjohnsen and Ricardo Fuller clearly felt the same way. Allardyce allegedly pulled the plug on a deal to sign Guðjohnsen after he had passed a medical as he had serious doubts over the Icelandic's desire to play for the club. I felt Icelandics had done enough damage already, and we could cope without him. Fuller allegedly failed a medical because his knees were held together with string and glue. His agent, however, came out with some story about him not wanting to relocate his family. A year later he joined Charlton. You work it out. I wasn't sorry that either of them failed to sign.

The proof of the pudding would be in the eating. Pre-season had been mixed with two defeats in Switzerland to Young Boys of Bern and Basel, wins at Copenhagen and Dagenham & Redbridge, a draw at Wycombe Wanderers, culminating in a 2–0 win against Real Zaragoza at Upton Park on 30 July. But pre-season, as we knew, was never a reliable indicator. It was about to start for real. The comeback started here.

Neil McDonald was appointed as Allardyce's right-hand man. He had been a no-nonsense midfielder in his day with Newcastle.

On the stadium front Tottenham continued to whinge on about the fact that we had been selected as the preferred tenant in February and were doing their utmost to waste time and money by seeking a judicial review of the decision. It emerged they were prepared to stop at nothing to achieve their aims too, as police were called in to investigate allegations they had hacked the telephones of staff at the OPLC in order to gain an advantage. The matter ended in criminal proceedings.

Lee Stewart and two other private investigators, Howard Hill and Richard Forrest, were fined a combined total of £123,250 for unlawfully obtaining confidential information on Olympics officials and West Ham executives, including SuGo and Brady.

Although the investigators had been working for Tottenham, unfortunately there was no evidence Spurs knew of or instigated the criminal activity.

Dionne Knight was one of those affected. An executive at the OPLC, her young daughter had been targeted by the investigators. Knight disclosed that she was in a relationship with West Ham director Ian Tomkins. Inaccurate stories had appeared in the press about her receiving payments from Tomkins. The muck and bullets flew. Tottenham seized on anything and everything, with Barry Hearn and Leyton Orient hanging on their coat tails.

Personally, I could not have given a stuff if we did not succeed with the bid for the Olympic Stadium, but this publicity was unwelcome, and I cringed every time I saw the subject on the TV or in the newspapers.

It seemed that no sooner had the 2010/11 season finished, we were under way again in early August, the Championship kicking off a week before the Premier League. All the comings and goings had yet to be finalised, but even so, the team that took on Cardiff City at Upton Park on 7 August only featured three new faces. The starting line-up was:

Green, Ilunga, O'Brien, Reid, Tomkins, Taylor, Parker, Noble (Collison), Nolan, Piquionne (Cole), Sears (Barrera).

Dad and I watched the game from the West Upper, having again been moved from our seats to accommodate the visitors, whose reputation preceded them. It was all very well, but Dad found the going very tough getting up the extra stairs in the Alpari Stand, or the West Stand, as we were not supposed to call it.

It was a sunny day with occasional heavy showers, one of which Dad and I got caught in as we left the game on ninety minutes so he could get out before the rush, only for us to hear the roar of the Cardiff knuckle-draggers as they scored in injury time to grab a victory they really did not deserve.

So this was how it was going to be. Soaking wet with a long walk back to the car, losing our opening game in the second division, and playing neither like our usual West Ham selves, nor a ruthlessly efficient Allardyce team. The future looked uncertain.

A week later we travelled to Doncaster and Kevin Nolan made a payment off his fee, whatever it was, getting the winner in a 1–0 victory. He latched onto an impossible-to-defend floated-cross field pass from Jack Collison. At Vicarage Road James Tomkins rose highest to a corner, putting us 1–0 up in the third minute and Joey O'Brien added a second just before half time after a long mazy run that Watford seemed reluctant to try and stop. Watford manager Sean Dyche must have been going mental. Second-half goals came from Carlton, who finished off a well worked, if not completely under control move, as well as Scott Parker. His parting gift in injury time was a typical pass into the net from 18 yards to seal a 4–0 win that gave us back-to-back away wins for the first time in nearly four years – and also some momentum to take into the home match against Leeds United, who would surely be promotion rivals.

A great game against Leeds United at Upton Park ended 2–2 with their winger Max Gradel absolutely destroying us, despite not actually scoring either of the Leeds goals. In spite of his great form we looked to be heading for a third straight win when Patrick Kisnorbo's own goal made it 2–1 in the second half.

Cole got in front of his marker and struck a sweet, if un-conventional volley from a Taylor corner for 1–0. Leeds fans sang 'we are the morons', which I later found out was a swipe at chairman Ken Bates who had labelled moaning Leeds fans as such. Pretty accurate though, it has to be said.

Gradel missed a penalty after Matty Taylor handled, but Leeds really looked the better side and on the hour Andy Keogh and Robert Snodgrass combined well for Snodgrass to put in a low cross for McCormack to score.

Three minutes later Faubert crossed from the right and Kisnorbo, in attempting to clear the ball, succeeded only in thumping it past Lonergan and into his own net. It was one of the more spectacular own goals. I knew that would not be the end of it though – Leeds had been by far the superior side. Right on full time Jonny Howson's shot came back off the crossbar and Clayton claimed a point that Leeds deserved.

Perhaps I had been wrong about Allardyce. Perhaps he understood the West Ham Way only too well, as giving away injury time winners and equalisers was part of what we had been about for years. He had boasted that one of his West Ham teams would never give away a 2–0 lead, as Grant and Zola's sides had both managed to do with alarming regularity. Part of me wanted it to happen just to show him that making such bold claims in itself was not the West Ham Way.

In another defeat-from-the-jaws-of-victory incident, unbe-lievably, Tottenham were granted judicial review of the decision to award the tenancy of the Olympic Stadium to West Ham. In partnership with Leyton Orient chairman Barry Hearn they had successfully argued that a £40 million loan from Newham Council constituted state aid and was therefore deemed illegal. Spurs chairman Daniel Levy then had the temerity to ask West Ham to drop the charges against Tottenham's private dicks for procuring information illegally. Not a fucking chance, matey.

We had visitors during August. Elaine's friend from São Paulo, Euler, his sister Cynthia and her boyfriend, Emilio, were staying with us in Bromley at the same time that the League Cup match against Aldershot was due to take place, so I bought tickets for all of us to go. This was going to be an experience for them. I wasn't sure what kind of experience, but it would be an experience. Bear in mind that the average Brazilian football fan likes to bounce up and down on a wooden bench, beer in one hand and a flare in the other, so I was not convinced they would be impressed.

It was a beautiful late summer evening. The sky turned a deep shade of claret and blue over the West Stand as the sun set, we had seats in the Bobby Moore Upper and pretty much had the area around us to ourselves.

Aldershot were similarly unmolested after Junior Stanislas gave us the lead in his final game before signing for Burnley. Aldershot of League Two won the game 2–1, and we couldn't really argue. My Brazilian guests all nodded politely and said they had enjoyed it, but it really was a pile of pants. We would have to wait until September for a first home victory of a cam-paign that was supposed to be a walk in the park.

If only away form could be replicated at home, we would be fine. August closed with a terrific 4–1 win at Nottingham Forest, managed by the Wally with the Brolly. West Ham had the appe-tite, racing into a 3–0 lead in the first thirty-two minutes. The first was an own goal from Luke Chambers. This was our second consecutive own goal in the league, and both were products of quality crosses that were hard to defend. Nolan added a bullet header from four yards, Cole also scored with a header, but that was less of a bullet and more of a wet sponge. Forest pulled one back, but it was 4–1 soon after the break as Winston Reid scored, hooking the ball in after beating the advancing Forest defence. This was impressive. Away from home we were playing good stuff, we had a 100 per cent record, but home form had yielded just 1 point from 6 and a disappointing cup defeat. We ended August with 10 points from 5 games and sat in 5th place, behind early leaders Brighton and Southampton, Derby in 3rd and Middlesbrough in 4th. The opening day defeat against Cardiff was already looking costly – there would be very little room for error.

36

NO REGRETS

CRYSTAL PALACE 2, WEST HAM UNITED 2
FOOTBALL LEAGUE CHAMPIONSHIP, 1 OCTOBER 2011
Mark Lawrenson's predictions. In fact, just Mark Lawrenson.

The home win we craved finally came on 10 September against Portsmouth. But although we again scored 4 goals it was less than convincing. Portsmouth took the lead early on before a powerful yet beautifully flighted free kick from Matty Taylor brought us level. Having seen him do this to us when playing for Bolton I hoped we would see a lot more of it.

But it was the only one. On-loan midfielder Henri Lansbury put us 2–1 up in the second half to round off a good move down the right after the cross was put in by Mark Noble. David Norris equalised and for the third home game running we looked disjointed and second best. Then the bit of fortune we needed appeared. Liam Lawrence was sent off for Portsmouth and we were awarded a penalty for handball which Noble dispatched for 3–2. Taylor then floated in another unplayable cross for Carlton to loop in the fourth. Portsmouth grabbed a late third after Piquionne had been sent off for raising his hands off the ball, and Tal Ben Haim went down in the box, victim of an invisible sniper. It was a win that we needed but it was less than convincing, if that is even possible after scoring 4 goals at home. As Dad said, tugging my arm at the end, 'All a bit hit and hope.'

Millwall ended the 100 per cent away record with a 0–0 draw at the New Den, but had you offered me that result before the game I would have taken it. A clean sheet was most welcome. Considering how much Allardyce loved a clean sheet we seemed to be finding them hard to come by. But we achieved one against Millwall, and had a goal disallowed which would have given us an undeserved victory against a team managed by Kenny Jackett, the only football manager named after a potato.

Peterborough United came to Upton Park and again we struggled, but the hallowed clean sheet meant that a first half Noble penalty was enough to earn the 3 points.

Allardyce's tactic seemed to be a big lone striker up front supported by two quicker, more mobile midfielders, in what he called a 4–3–3 formation, but often the support was so late coming it was effectively a 4–5–1. I could see the idea: he wanted 4–3–3 in possession and 4–5–1 without the ball. It was going to take a bit of time and some rotating of personnel to get the balance right.

It turns out we still hadn't got it quite right when Ipswich came to Upton Park and mugged us 1–0 with an 89th-minute goal. To add insult to injury it came from two-time former Hammer Lee Bowyer. Southampton and Derby had 19 points from 8 and 9 games respectively. We had 17 from 9 and sat in 4th. More so than the Premier League the Championship was a marathon not a sprint, but it was important not to fall too far behind and leave a mountain to climb. After all, we were expected to bounce straight back.

Social media was a double-edged sword. It gave a mouthpiece to people who would otherwise only write with crayons. But it also put people in touch and provided valuable public services. I had been particularly happy to find my old primary school teacher Frank Harper on Facebook, and we arranged to meet up for a drink and a bite to eat before the game against Crystal Palace at Selhurst Park.

It was great to catch up with Mr Harper and to have the opportunity to thank him for being so influential during my formative years. Sadly, he was now in a wheelchair, having suffered poor health in recent years, but his daughter accompanied him and we chatted about school days. It was very revealing. When you are a kid you think teachers are always in control and should be respected at all times. Well, I did anyway. I certainly respected Mr Harper. Then he told me about the day he left early to get to Villa Park to watch Palace in a cup match and left us in the charge of the teacher in the next classroom, who kept popping in to make sure we weren't killing each other with scissors. When I think back we really were quite a well-behaved lot. Compared to the teachers, anyway. Frank, for I can call him that now, gave me a lift to the game (as a blue badge holder he could park right by the turnstile) and we bade each other farewell before I went to meet my nephew and my dad.

It was Dad's birthday so me and my nephew Mark decided to treat him to a rare away game at his old stomping ground of Selhurst Park. It was a very hot day for the first of October. Dad had a run-in with a steward who tried to stop him taking his bottle of water into the stadium. Mark pointed out that Dad had turned seventy-eight that day and reminded the steward about the queues for drinks, indicating that if Dad wasn't allowed in with it he would stick it where it would prove very inconvenient.

Manuel Almunia came in as an emergency goalkeeper on loan from Arsenal following an injury to Robert Green. Palace looked the better team and took the lead through Darren Ambrose. Nolan grabbed an equaliser from typical range. Glenn Murray restored Palace's lead in the second half with a smart shot, and it looked enough to take all 3 points and our unbeaten away record, but John Carew on as a sub as the big man in the 4–5–1 nicked a headed goal from a superbly flighted McCartney cross. In the end, Dad, Mark, Mr Harper and I all went home happy.

Shock news came on 11 October as it emerged that the whole bidding process for the use of the Olympic stadium was to be effectively scrapped and started again. Tottenham and Leyton Orient's bitching had served its purpose and the process would be even further drawn out. I had to admit, it did not seem fair that West Ham should have been awarded the use of the stadium with the aid of public money and on the apparent say-so of a bed-headed ignoramus (certainly in the field of sport), in the unkempt shape of Boris Johnson. So maybe it would be fairer if the whole process started again. I wasn't happy at the amount of public money being spent, though. It made me uncomfortable. Why couldn't we just stay put? Regardless of what you thought about the deal, Barry Hearn was starting to get on my tits. I could see no reason why he was so concerned about the process, other than because Leyton Orient might miss out on a piece of the action. His raison d'être seemed to be to put a spoke in the wheel, and he was doing a pretty good job.

Blackpool were promotion rivals and we did not expect, given our home form, to beat them 4–0. John Carew retained his place at the point of the formation after his performance at Palace and he opened the scoring on 12 minutes by nodding in another superb cross – this time from Faubert. Sam Baldock, who we had pleaded with Allardyce to play, scored twice, first making the most of being played onside to beat the keeper one-on-one and the second nipping in to take advantage of some hesitant defending. Collison added a fourth and for once the score line in a home game was convincing.

The next game – midweek against Southampton – was going to be pivotal. After eleven games we had crept up into 2nd position, 2 points behind Southampton. We were unbeaten away; Southampton were unbeaten at home. Something had to give. It was us, of course. Instead of us going a point clear at the top, a 1–0 defeat put the Saints 5 points clear. Although it was by no means a disaster, we had to be looking to win the league, and this was a massive kick in the nads.

We had still only lost three games from 12, but the football was bitty at times. Southampton were playing superb stuff under Nigel Adkins and looked nailed-on certainties for promotion, having only just come up from League One the year before. It narrowed down our chances.

We needed to bounce back a few miles along the coast at Brighton the following Monday. Kevin Nolan showed why he was the captain. And proper captain material at that: hustling, encouraging, cajoling, consoling. Hassling defenders, running on to loose balls, dispatching swerving shots past despairing goalkeepers. I was starting to like him a lot.

Sam Baldock was a central figure again in the win over Leicester at Upton Park on 29 October. In a bizarre role reversal, the giant Carew put in a cross and the diminutive Baldock scored with a header. Mark Noble then played a super cross-field ball which Joey O'Brien cut back into the path of Julien Faubert, who placed his shot superbly for 2–0. Leicester pulled one back before a proper route-one goal, a long clearance downfield from Robert Green, flicked on by Piquionne on the edge of the box for Baldock to volley in for 3–1. I didn't hear anyone complaining about long balls at that moment.

Leicester grabbed the goal of the game with a thumping volley by Andy King from the edge of the box. But it was not enough. West Ham cemented second spot with 27 points from fourteen games, 3 points behind Southampton and 3 ahead of the chasing pack of Crystal Palace, Middlesbrough, Derby and Hull.

37

WE FOUND LOVE

Allardyce showed some signs that he might be listening to the fans when it was rumoured that he was considering signing El Hadji Diouf, possibly one of the most unpleasant individuals in football. I wanted him nowhere near my club, and it seemed I was not alone. Allardyce took the hint and did not proceed with the signing, though I am certain that, if asked, he will say his decision was for footballing reasons.

We won at 6th-placed Hull, the excellent away form continuing, which was just as well because at home we had not been able to beat Bristol City and had to be satisfied with a 0–0 draw. The win at Hull came courtesy of goals from Baldock with a sharp volley from close range after a Carlton knockdown. Cole again was the provider, feeding Collison for the second.

It was getting to the point where away games were more welcome than home matches. Whether the players were feeling the weight of expectation at home, whether it was more difficult to set up tactically, or whether it was sheer nerves, it was hard to say. Personally I felt it was tactics. We had a good squad of attacking players, why not stick with what we were doing away and go 4–4–2 at home? It was frustrating to watch, especially as Sam Baldock had found some form, and alongside Carlton up front at home he would surely have been a threat.

But I have always said I know little of football tactics. Allardyce was the man being paid to do the job. I had no doubt he knew what he was doing. But it was painful to watch at times.

We had been told the running track being retained at the Olympic stadium would not be an issue as there would be state of the art retractable seating installed. This worry was covered by Karren Brady in her column in *The Sun* on 12 November where she wrote:

> Members in the London Assembly are sceptical about viewing football in the new Olympic Stadium ... I've heard the comment dozens of times before. But whereas the public don't have access to plans for the 2014 occupation by a football club — hopefully West Ham — members do.
>
> And if they had taken the time to look they would have seen that the design engineers have a solution by placing fans in retractable seats right up to the touchlines, if required, to provide a fantastic football solution whilst maintaining the track perfectly for athletics.
>
> That wasn't possible in stadiums like the old Wembley but technology and the world moves on.

David Gold also confirmed on his Twitter page that 'There will be some form of retractable seating.'

Well, if that was to be the case, I did not have too much of a problem with the idea. I had seen all those international matches and European games played in former Olympic stadia. I did not fancy having to bridge that running track. It would not be easy to persuade West Ham fans, who had grown up being able to touch the players as they ran past the chicken run, that anything other than seating covering the running track would be acceptable.

We had to concentrate on being a Premier League club first, though, and the next fixture was away at the Ricoh Arena against Coventry, where we had last played out a 2–1 win coming from behind in the League Cup in 2007. History repeated itself, even to the point of the equaliser being a somewhat fortunate deflected effort, before Piquionne contrived to score an even more fortunate goal for the winner.

Opposition among West Ham fans to the stadium move was gathering pace. Before the game against Derby, 20,000 leaflets were distributed by a protest group WHU's View calling for an official referendum among fans for their opinion.

Derby took the lead in the 34th minute but Carlton equalised just before half time. Kevin Nolan then scored his first Upton Park goal with a well-taken volley from the edge of the box, keeping it low and showing great technique. A Noble penalty made it 3–1 and put us back to within 2 points of leaders Southampton.

Piquionne scored away at Middlesbrough in a virtually deserted Riverside stadium; just 18,457 were there to see Carlton wrap up the points for our seventh away win after Piquionne had initially put us in front in the 9th minute. We were still 2 points away from Southampton at the top, but more importantly, 6 points clear of Cardiff in 3rd. While it would be nice to win the league, promotion was the aim, and if it had to be 2nd place then so be it. It was looking like it would happen, so I took the risk of booking a trip to Brazil for four weeks in May 2012, when Elaine and I would marry. Just don't fuck it up, West Ham.

No sooner had I booked the tickets than we lost two in a row. I accept full responsibility. We lost 2–1 at home to Burnley then by a whopping 3–0 at Reading. I had cursed us. Joey O'Brien was on as a 5th-minute substitute for Guy Demel, but only lasted a further fifty-five minutes before receiving a second yellow. Reading went ahead shortly after and then in a moment of pure madness, Jack Collison saw red after Jimmy Kébé mocked him by appearing to adjust his socks while in possession of the ball. Collison didn't like that and went through him like a train. It was inexcusable, but had I been in Collison's boots I think I would have done the same.

Dan Potts, son of West Ham legend Steve, made his debut at home to Barnsley and acquitted himself well in the 1–0 win. At Christmas we still sat in 2nd place and within touching distance of the top of the table. But despite the number of players coming in, we still suffered the same West Ham malaise of injuries and suspensions which had necessitated the debut for Potts Jr against Barnsley. On Boxing Day, we drew 1–1 with Birmingham before going down 2–1 at Pride Park against Derby on New Year's Eve. Because the kick-off was fairly early I had thought it was on TV, so went to collect Dad to bring him over to watch it with me at our flat. By the time we got back I realised that not only was the game not on TV, but I'd got the kick-off time wrong and it was over.

Luckily, Dad was able to watch live action with me as the first game of 2012 was on the New Year bank holiday, which meant I could park on a yellow line a short walk from the ground – making life a lot easier. Instead it was West Ham who puffed and wheezed their way to a 1–0 win over Coventry to keep the promotion push alive.

38

DOMINO

WEST HAM UNITED 2, NOTTINGHAM FOREST 1
FOOTBALL LEAGUE CHAMPIONSHIP, 21 JANUARY 2012
Married couples who have 'Date Nights'.

It seemed clear Allardyce was not in the slightest bit interested in cup competitions to distract from the main task in hand. Personally, I have never seen how cups can be a distraction. Anything that means you are winning has to be positive. Deliberately playing a weakened team designed to lose is an insult to the fans of both sides. But that wasn't something Allardyce was ever particularly bothered about, and we went out of the FA Cup against Sheffield Wednesday at Hillsborough in predictable fashion. It was a shame, because when we have a team mid-table and are in a position to undertake a cup run, we always seem to draw Manchester United away in the early rounds and go out anyway. A team in form could have had a real crack at it.

Going out of the cup early is all well and good it if is later justified by good results in the league. We beat Portsmouth at Fratton Park 1–0 with a Mark Noble penalty, then Nottingham Forest 2–1 at Upton Park with two Mark Noble penalties. It was difficult to watch, but it seemed the ends would justify the means as that win over Nottingham Forest put us top of the table (thanks also to Southampton's home defeat to Leicester). Allardyce's decision to dismiss the cups appeared to me justified, as did my decision to book a trip to Brazil for May.

The transfer window saw a few new faces come in to pep up the promotion drive. Nicky Maynard was signed from Bristol City, defender George John from FC Dallas, Barnsley's top scorer, Portuguese Ricardo Vaz Tê signed and young Manchester United youth prospect Ravel Morrison signed for an undisclosed fee thought to be in the region of £1 million. Morrison had talent, no doubt about that, but it was mostly a talent for getting himself into trouble. No sooner had he joined than he was being forced to defend a homophobic tweet. It seemed maybe Alex Ferguson was happy to offload the lad, knowing he would never be able to make it at the very top level. Vaz Tê, on the other hand, looked like someone who could cut it very comfortably at this level, and Maynard also had a proven track record. George John was allocated squad number 25, but did not make a first-team appearance during his two-month loan spell.

Ipswich thumped us 5–1 at Portman Road, but somehow we clung onto top spot, and we were top of the table when Millwall came to Upton Park on 4 February.

I was turfed out of my seat again. Dad decided discretion was the better part of valour and, having had the climb up the West Stand for the Cardiff match, felt that being at home with a glass of whiskey was the best choice. I was tempted to join him, but I do love a game against Millwall, and we owed them more than one, especially after struggling against them that night in the League Cup when we were embarrassed both on and off the park.

The portents were not good when Kevin Nolan was sent off for a two-footed challenge, but on the stroke of half time Joey O'Brien flicked on a Mark Noble free kick and Carlton was there to nod us 1–0 up. It was no more than we deserved on the balance of play. It was a full-blooded derby with challenges flying in, not all of them legal, but the referee had to let them go or there would be no one left on the pitch. Millwall equalised on 66 minutes through the appropriately named Liam Trotter, but I was more concerned about what was going on in my usual seat in the Trevor Brooking Upper, and I made a mental note to buy some antibacterial wipes and an Air wick for the next home game.

West Ham were not to be denied, though, and finished with

a flourish. Three minutes later Millwall goalkeeper Forde was flattened by Julien Faubert and the ball spilled out to Winston Reid, who volleyed it home from just inside the box. Again, it wasn't pretty, but we ground out a result. We were also facing another suspension, this time of our captain and one of our most influential players. But we beat Millwall, so I didn't really mind. They had a youngster called Harry Kane, Tottenham's own Harry Kane on the bench that day, too.

Southampton came to Upton Park and stole a point. A foul by Billy Sharp on Mark Noble resulted in a penalty, but in the ensuing mêlée Matty Taylor raised his hands and Sharp went down like the proverbial sack of spuds. I doubt very much if Taylor actually touched him. It was a bad-tempered game that Southampton grew into and Green had to make a string of fine saves to keep West Ham ahead. But Southampton's man advantage finally told, and Jos Hooiveld, who had scored the winner at St Mary's earlier in the season, stabbed home the equaliser on 75 minutes.

We had a man sent off for a third game in a row at Blackpool. James Tomkins squeezed between two defenders for the opener, and within four minutes Nicky Maynard opened his West Ham account with the second. Kevin Phillips pulled one back for Blackpool before half time in a decidedly open game. In the second half Blackpool's Roman Bednář chased a through ball and Robert Green came racing out of goal and clattered into him. The referee saw him as the last defender and sent him off, which seemed harsh as Faye was covering. With no substitute keeper on the bench Allardyce withdrew Julien Faubert and put Henri Lansbury in goal. As far as I could see he might as well have put Angela Lansbury in goal, because we were screwed.

But Lansbury (Henri, not Angela) was inspired and shut out any further Blackpool efforts as Gary O'Neil and Vaz Tê scored two more to make the final score 4–1 to The Hammers. It was bizarre, because normally in such situations Allardyce was very defensive, but on this occasion, he seemed to take the view that attack was the best form of defence – and it worked. I wished he had done that more often. It was just as well for the referee that we carried on to win the game, as Robert Green had the red card reduced to yellow on appeal.

It had not gone unnoticed that despite the ten-point pledge, which included moving to the Olympic stadium and listening to fans, no one at board level had thought to put the two together and ask the fans what they thought about the move. WHU's View continued to press for this, but the problem as I saw it was that results would be skewed. If you distribute 20,000 leaflets, half will go in the bin. The other half will be filled in only by those with a strong opinion, which meant there was a silent majority that the board interpreted as a majority in favour. David 'I used to live at 442 Green Street' Gold's estimates ranged from between 70 per cent and 90 per cent in favour, depending on which radio show he was on. How anyone could suggest 70 per cent of West Ham fans were in favour of leaving the freehold of Upton Park and gamble on renting an enormous fruit bowl for the remote possibility of Champions League football was ludicrous. It was like paying for a lottery ticket by losing your right arm.

Home form continued to be the Achilles' heel as we drew 0–0 with Crystal Palace, a result that saw us slip back down to second behind Southampton, who had won at Watford. A 2–0 win at Cardiff secured some revenge for the opening day defeat, but then a disastrous run of five consecutive draws put paid to any hope we may have had of the title, and realistically, of automatic promotion. Although draws kept the points ticking over, it was no good when Southampton and Reading were winning every week. By the time we had drawn 1–1 with Watford, Doncaster and Middlesbrough at home, and by the same score against Leeds at Elland Road and 2–2 with Burnley at Turf Moor, we had slipped to 3rd on 69 points, a whopping 9 points off Southampton in top spot and 4 behind Reading in 2nd who had put together a remarkable run of form to come from nowhere into the promotion race.

Around this time there was a young Australian lad in the

youth team by the name of Dylan Tombides. In 2011 while he was representing Australia, a random drugs test identified that he had testicular cancer, but in April 2012 he returned to training after surgery and chemotherapy. He was remarkably upbeat considering it was yet to be confirmed that he was in the clear, but his doctors had told him he could return to training. He told whufc.com:

> I had a blood test the other day and that was my third since my operation. I need to get ten all-clears and that will officially tell me that I am clear of the disease.
>
> The doctors have told me that if I am likely to recur, it will be in the first year, and if I don't then I should be cured for life. I've got another eight or so blood tests and other CT scans to go then hopefully I'll get the all-clear.

We all had everything crossed for young Dylan.

Allardyce faced an uphill task from the day he was appointed to win over the hearts of the West Ham fans. At this point he had my respect, but not my heart. They say respect has to be earned, but I had been brought up to respect first, and withdraw it later if necessary. Comments about the West Ham Way had not helped, but now our polite request for a more attacking set-up was met with suggestions that we were 'deluded.'

At Peterborough however, we played well, and earned a first win in 7 games, a Vaz Tê header and a long-range effort from Gary O'Neil secured a 2–0 win. It was much needed with the next game at home to Reading. Still 4 points ahead, a win would have put us within touching distance, and Allardyce went for a more balls-out approach with Vaz Tê playing a much more advanced role. It looked to be paying dividends just before the break, as West Ham dominated and led through Carlton's smart turn and shot in the first ten minutes. But Reading dealt a knockout blow just before half time, scoring twice, and then earned a third soon after half time. Vaz Tê got his Mohican onto Matty Taylor's corner for 3–2, but the Reading steam roller was well and truly on its way down the hill to the title, and despite Hunt playing the ball in an offside position their fourth goal was awarded, putting 7 points between West Ham and automatic promotion with only six games left.

Allardyce was tight lipped afterwards but you could see he was itching to say 'See? That's what attacking gets you – sod all!' Well, not attacking also got us five draws in a row, Sam. Play the percentages. Roll the dice occasionally.

Reading were out of sight, our only hope was that Southampton might falter, and they did, but not enough. In fact, Southampton took only 10 points from their last 18 available; we took 14 including a 4–0 win away at Barnsley on Good Friday and a 6–0 thumping of Brighton on 14 April. Allardyce seemed to have accepted that we needed to be a little more expansive in our play, and by the time we played Hull City at Upton Park on the final day of the season, it was still – mathematically at least – possible to get automatic promotion. There were a number of combinations that would have allowed that, but they all involved Southampton losing at home to already relegated Coventry City, and that was about as likely as Big Sam admitting he was wrong.

Southampton won 4–0 so our 2–1 win over Hull was academic. It was to be the play-offs.

39

R.I.P.

BLACKPOOL 1, WEST HAM UNITED 2
FOOTBALL LEAGUE CHAMPIONSHIP PLAY-OFF FINAL, 19 MAY 2012
Stupid interview questions. 'Give me an example of
when you have had to show initiative.' Fuck off.

Now, hands up who has been concentrating?

Well, if you had been paying attention you would know that I had booked tickets to go to Brazil to get married to Elaine in May. It was the kind of thing where you could not really turn around and say, 'Darling, do you think we could put it back a few weeks?'

Having cruised past Cardiff City 5–0 over the two legs of the semi-final, we faced a Blackpool side who had beaten Birmingham City in their own semi-final tie. A Blackpool side we had beaten 8–1 on aggregate over our 2 league matches and who finished 2 places and 11 points behind us.

We knew from experience the play-offs could throw up the odd shock: we had been promoted ourselves from 6th place in 2005, after all. But it's really about form. And we had the form. Including the play-off semi-finals, we had won 6 and drawn 2 of the 8 games we had played after the Reading defeat. Perhaps the knowledge that automatic promotion was out of the question had triggered some sort of release valve. We scored 23 goals in those eight games too. We were a joy to watch. Under Sam Allardyce! Imagine.

So, it was with heavy heart that I went on the Wembley website the day before setting off to Brazil to buy tickets for the play-off final, knowing I would not be going. My nephews were going, and my ticket went to Steve Harris, a colleague at Barclays (not the guitarist from Iron Maiden).

On the day of the final itself I was four hours ahead of proceedings at Foz do Iguaçu, the enormous waterfalls on the border of Brazil, Argentina and Paraguay. While you lot were stuffing your faces with hot dogs and swilling beer like it was going out of fashion, I was in a restaurant overlooking the dramatic waterfalls, eating traditional Brazilian feijoada with my beautiful wife-to-be.

I had no signal on my phone. When we returned to the car park we decided to push the boat out and take a helicopter trip over the falls. When I went into the booking office the TV was showing the start of the Champions League final between Chelsea and Bayern Munich. In my best Portuguese, which still wasn't very good, I asked him if he knew the result of West Ham v. Blackpool. Blank look. I motioned to his laptop and asked if I could use it for five minutes. The news I wanted was confirmed. We took the helicopter ride over the waterfalls, though in truth, the helicopter probably wasn't needed. I could have flown all by myself. I'm sure you don't need me to recount the details of that dramatic day at Wembley.

Although we gained promotion, which had been the aim from day one, we had been rather fortunate given the scabby form we had shown at the Boleyn, winning the fewest games at home of any of the top six. Even Ipswich in 15th won the same number of home games as us. It was our away form, a record breaking 13 wins and 6 draws, that had carried us through. It was the best away record in the division; better even than champions Reading, by 3 points. It left us wondering what might have been had we shown a bit more intent at home. In the end we missed out on automatic promotion by only 2 points. But the main thing was, we were promoted.

Robert Green had signalled well before the end of the season that he was unlikely to stay beyond the expiration of his five-year contract. Despite a very attractive offer being made to him by SuGo, or so we are told, Green decided the grass was, well, greener, elsewhere. He went to QPR and largely sat on the bench watching Brazilian international Júlio César play in goal. Well done, Robert.

It was Phil Parkes himself who recounted a story about Green at a live *STOP! Hammer Time* podcast in May 2015. He said Robert Green had been sick of constantly being reminded that Parkes was the best goalkeeper West Ham ever had. When he moved to QPR the first thing he saw as he walked into the stadium reception was a giant poster on the wall of... Phil Parkes.

On the subject of goalkeepers, Stephen Henderson had joined on an emergency loan from Portsmouth in March and was an unused substitute in the play-off final. His signature was secured in May and he became the first signing of the summer transfer window. Good pub quiz question, that. Steady keeper as he was, he was not likely to be Green's direct replacement, as we would need a goalkeeper with more Premier League experience. This turned out to be former nemesis at Bolton Jussi Jääskeläinen; the short-sleeve-wearing, time-wasting Finnish goalkeeper we had always craved. He joined on a free transfer. Marek Štěch also left by mutual consent, and later in the summer Swiss goalkeeper Raphael Spiegel joined from Grasshoppers of Zürich for an undisclosed fee.

Six players were released. Of them, the highest profile was Julien Faubert. I liked Julien. He was a bit rubbish most of the time, but every now and then came up with something breathtaking. He was a West Ham player, alright. His farcical loan period at Real Madrid summed him up, bless him. He had a frustrating habit of trying to cross the ball from the area between the halfway line and the 18-yard box, and I was never sure if that was just something he did, or if it was on manager's instructions. It worked now and again, but I always felt he would have been more effective crossing from the goal-line. We said au revoir after exactly 100 starts, 21 sub appearances and 2 goals. Yes, 2 goals.

Also leaving, less emotionally, were John Carew (9 starts, 12 sub appearances, 2 goals), Abdoulaye Faye (25 starts, 4 sub appearances), Papa Bouba Diop (14 starts, 2 sub appearances, 1 goal), Frank Nouble (6 starts, 13 sub appearances, 1 goal) and Olly Lee, (nil, nil and nil.)

George McCartney's loan was made permanent, and another man returning for a second spell was James Collins. The Ginger Pele made a welcome comeback.

But the biggest-name signings were yet to come. Mohamed Diamé came from Wigan and Modibo Maïga from French club Sochaux-Montbéliard. Alou Diarra was probably the most exciting of the summer arrivals: a defensive midfielder with 44 France caps to his name, he had to be half decent, didn't he? No, as it turns out.

The season opened on a blisteringly hot day, on 18 August. I remember getting on the train at Bromley South and seeing the temperature outside as 32 degrees. Football in that weather is fine if you are just watching. It's also fine if you can have a few beers in the Black Lion at Plaistow beforehand, as I did with Steve Harris before going to watch West Ham dominate early proceedings against Villa and take a 1–0 lead through Kevin Nolan. The goal was slightly controversial as Vaz Tê had been flagged offside before the linesman changed his mind. It was controversial in the Villa camp anyway. It was important to win on the opening day, particularly for a newly promoted side to get confidence going. The real bonus for me that day was that Mo Diamé looked like a real beast, a complete handful.

Confidence for the trip away to Swansea in the next game was heightened by the signing of winger Matt Jarvis from Wolves for a club record fee, which was officially undisclosed, but believed to be in the region of £10 million. Allardyce had shown during the promotion campaign the value of a well-flighted cross, but as a team we had demonstrated that this was not always easy to achieve. Sam looked at the stats, saw that Jarvis made more crosses than anyone else, and told SuGo to get him. As they had made it clear he was the number one target, the price went up each day so in the end, we got a distinctly average player, who did put in a lot of crosses – but they were all distinctly average.

We did not turn up against Swansea. An under-hit back-pass from Collins left Jääskeläinen stranded and Rangel had a relatively simple task to open the scoring. Michu and Danny Graham added two more and a 3–0 scoreline did not flatter Swansea at all.

Nicky Maynard and Maïga both scored midweek to propel West Ham into the third round of the League cup against Crewe. Stephen Henderson made his debut in goal, and the wonderfully named youth team player Matthias Fanimo also made his debut as a substitute, along with John Moncur's son George.

It was all very well having a man in the team who made more crosses than anyone else, but you also needed the quality to do something with them. Andy Carroll would, on paper at least, appear to be the solution to that problem. He joined on loan from Liverpool, quickly followed, rather surprisingly, by a certain Yossi Benayoun. It was a surprise because he had left under something of a cloud, having given a verbal agreement to extend his initial two-year deal and reneging on that once Liverpool showed an interest. He had since moved to Chelsea, who were keen to offload him for a season to assist with their financial fair play requirements. I had no problem having him back. I thought he was a terrific player. And this time there was no contract to renege on.

Carroll made his debut against Fulham, but ironically the man supposed to supply his crosses had picked up a knock in training and had to sit on the sidelines and watch us destroy Fulham in the first half. Nolan opened the scoring in the first minute. Carroll was the focal point: winning everything. Reid and Matty Taylor added goals before half time and the game was effectively over. Carroll fell awkwardly later on and was taken off. So, as Jarvis was fit again for the game at Norwich, Carroll would be out for a month.

Back in the Premier League against Norwich, featuring Tottenham's own, on loan Harry Kane, we did well to get a 0–0 draw, picking up a first away point of the season. West Ham were second best throughout the game but battled hard and a point was well deserved. We then struggled at home to Sunderland, who took the lead through Stephen Fletcher and it took a very late Kevin Nolan strike to rescue a point.

It was all change again for the League Cup tie against Wigan. They would go on that season to be the first team ever to win the FA Cup while also being relegated. Normal service for home games against Wigan was resumed as we got well beaten 4–1. Dylan Tombides made an emotional debut, coming on as a substitute for Gary O'Neil. It was a remarkable story and it looked like young Dylan had won his battle against cancer. We did not make too much of a fuss at the time as we were certain his appearance would be the first of many.

40

DON'T YOU WORRY CHILD

WEST HAM UNITED 4, SOUTHAMPTON 1
PREMIER LEAGUE, 20 OCTOBER 2012
Wasps. Mosquitos. Gnats. Buzzy things.

I met up with Stuart the QPR fan at Loftus Road. We always ate at the Queen Adelaide pub around the corner from the ground and caught up, usually with his dad, David, and friend Paul. Nice bloke, Paul. In fact, most QPR fans are nice. Oh, there was that time Paul said it would be funny if West Ham got relegated, but I barely remember that, if at all. In fact, it was forgotten almost immediately.

I was using Callum's season ticket so had to sit on my hands as West Ham won 2–1 to claim their first away victory of the season with goals from Matt Jarvis and Vaz Tê. Eight yellow cards for West Ham that night in what I don't recall being a particularly dirty match. How you can get eight bookings and not have a player sent off is one for the probability statisticians. (I had to look it up – it was a Premier League record that stood until May 2016 when Tottenham had nine players booked at Stamford Bridge.) I was yet to be convinced about Matt Jarvis. I was certainly sceptical about the price we had paid for him. He seemed a little timid. Mind you, the plan was to play him and Carroll together, and so far, that hadn't happened. Carroll came on as a sub against QPR, and we had won eight points without them playing together, so think what we might achieve when it finally happened?

Jarvis and Carroll started together for the first time against Arsenal at Upton Park on 6 October. We got murdered 3–1. Mo

Diamé had opened the scoring with a world-class finish, but Arsenal cut us to ribbons at times. Giroud equalised before half time, then they just moved up through the gears and scored twice more through Walcott and Cazorla.

It was all very well having a player who made the most crosses – but they had to have some sort of purpose. I mean, I could put a cross in – but it wouldn't reach a teammate. This clearly wasn't going to work. Both started again against Southampton, and Carroll worked hard in his central role – making a nuisance of himself – but I don't think Jarvis got one cross in at all, let alone one in the direction of Carroll's head. After a goalless first half, Noble floated in a speculative free kick, which everybody left alone, except James Collins, who tried to get a toe on it, missed, but it went in anyway. Nolan added a second, tapping in a cross from Benayoun, then Southampton pulled one back through Lallana, but it was our day. José Fonte punched the ball in the penalty area while concentrating too hard on Carroll, and Maïga wrapped up the scoring, digging out a lovely finish with his left foot to wrap up a 4–1 win. Still no crosses from Jarvis though.

That win put us in 6th place in the table after eight games with 14 points on the board already. This Premier League business was a piece of piss! But just when we started to think that, the Premier League turned around to bite us on the bum, and we lost 2–1 at Wigan. Jarvis and Carroll played together again – Carroll again looking a handful, but Jarvis's only meaningful contribution was a cross met by the head of James Tomkins, who crashed the ball against the bar. Tomkins did score eventually, from a McCartney cross, but it wasn't enough to avoid defeat to a Wigan side achieving their first home win of the season. Not won for ages? Striker not scored for twenty games? Not won a penalty for two years? You know who you need to play.

At home we looked great. Away from home a lot less so. In a bizarre twist of Championship form, we seemed able to support the lone striker much better at home whereas away from home, the front man was so isolated he may as well not have been there. So he would drop back to get more involved, then not be able to take advantage when we did have possession. Allardyce's obsession with clean sheets was understandable, but we hadn't had one for 6 matches, so maybe he needed to try something else.

Against Manchester City at Upton Park we played well, against a team destined to be crowned champions in May. Nolan had a goal harshly ruled out for offside, and the City team, despite boasting a front three of Balotelli, Tevez and Džeko could not find a way through.

Away at Newcastle Nolan nicked a winner to keep the momentum going, but a Monday night game against Stoke City could only produce another draw. Overall, though, the first half of the season was progressing well. We lost 3–1 at Tottenham, with Andy Carroll scoring his first West Ham goal, then lost again 1–0 at Old Trafford to slip down to 10th in the table. Southampton and Reading, both of whom had looked so irresistible in the previous season's promotion campaign, were both struggling, and we were making the better start of the three.

Life could not have been much better. West Ham were playing well, I had just got married to the woman I loved, we had a comfortable two-bedroom flat in Bromley, I had a well-paid job which I enjoyed, I was close to my family. All we had to do now was sort out Elaine's visa, which meant she would have to return to Brazil for a few weeks to finalise the application. That would be easy. We could not know at that stage that ahead lay six months of worry, trouble, and heartache.

41

TROUBLEMAKER

WEST HAM UNITED, 3 CHELSEA 1
PREMIER LEAGUE, 1 DECEMBER 2012
Theresa May. What a cow. Bit rational that one,
but still putting it out there.

Andy Carroll was ruled out for eight weeks with a knee injury. Of course, at the time we had no idea this was going to be the norm. Chelsea boss Rafa Benítez had yet to experience victory and was not universally popular with Chelsea fans, still smarting from the dismissal of Roberto Di Matteo, who had led them to Champions League glory just a few months before.

Chelsea started on top and looked good value for their 1–0 lead at half time, but we'd had a goal harshly ruled out, and there was still belief. It took until the 63rd minute, though, to draw level. A typical Matt Jarvis cross (i.e. looping up off a defender's leg) found Carlton's head after he had climbed all over Ivanović. Maybe the referee was evening up the disallowed goal. That gave us the momentum, and Carlton, having the game of his life, laid the ball off for Mo Diamé, also having his best game in a Hammers shirt, to drill the ball in a few minutes from time. Maïga added a third in stoppage time for a sweet, sweet, victory.

I took Elaine to Heathrow the next day. The plan was that she would submit her visa application which we had meticulously put together over a number of weeks in São Paulo when she arrived. We knew it would take a couple of months for her visa to be granted by the British Embassy in Rio de Janeiro, so the sooner she got the application in the better. I was due to fly out on 17 December, spend Christmas and New Year with

249

Elaine and her family in Rio Claro, then I would come home on 6 January 2013, and Elaine's visa should have been granted in the first or second week of February at the latest. That was the plan, anyway. I waved her off at Heathrow safe in the knowledge I would see her in a couple of weeks.

In the meantime, the Olympic Stadium saga finally reached a conclusion (or so we thought) on 5 December as we were granted preferred bidder status. I didn't take too much notice as we had been here before.

Boris Johnson, who had inexplicably been elected Mayor of London, confirmed that the club had beaten off competition from the three other bidders to be nominated as the London Legacy Development Corporation (LLDC)'s choice as chosen candidate to take on the 99-year lease.

Karren Brady, equally inexplicably West Ham's vice-chair, said the board were 'committed to delivering our promises'. Oh hindsight, such a wonderful thing. She went on to say:

For the last three years it has been my firm, unwavering belief that the Stadium can truly become a multi-use destination of which east London and the nation as a whole can be proud.

I have never lost sight of our vision to play our part, along with the Stadium's major stakeholders, in ensuring it grows into a global asset. It is the 'jewel in the crown' of the Park, watched by the world.

Our vision for the Stadium has always been about standing up for the promises made for London back in Singapore in 2005. We are committed to delivering our promises as set out in our bid.

The hard work really does start here and work is already well underway to ensure that we really bring our community, which includes 500,000 supporters in east London and Essex alone, with us.

We are already working with key strategic partners to ensure that unemployed east Londoners in key target groups will have access to sustainable employment in the Olympic Park via the 700-plus job opportunities that West Ham's tenancy will create. We guarantee millions of visitors and customers, which will galvanise the Park and act as the catalyst to spark a thriving economy in this part of east London.

I would like to thank the loyal, passionate and patient West Ham supporters who have given their time to share their opinions on our proposed move and, despite the considerable constraints and confidentially agreements we were required to enter into, I can assure them that their feedback was instrumental in shaping the Board's approach to our bid.

I guarantee they will not be disappointed when our full vision for a Stadium that is world-class in terms of supporter experience, sightlines and facilities is revealed. [Still waiting.] We will seek to share full details as soon as we are able to do so.

The nation should be proud. They are paying for most of it. SuGo also issued a statement:

We believe that this move, together with the realisation of other key goals that the Board set out to achieve from the outset, will play a huge part in helping to realise our ambitious vision to move the Club to the next level on behalf of our fantastic and deserving fans.

Our absolute priority is to take them with us, as well as enticing those supporters that have previously eluded us due to barriers such as affordability and accessibility.

We are ambitious for our great club and aim to set the benchmark for visiting away and neutral football supporters from across the globe to come and enjoy the iconic Stadium and be part of our Premier League club experience.

I took this all with a huge pinch of salt. Brady had no idea about how great our club was. She had no idea about much of what the club was about. They had not consulted us, more like insulted us. It felt like we were being dismantled piece by piece by hooligans more violent and abhorrent than anything the ICF could have thrown at us in their heyday. It felt like the club I loved was dying.

We were going to leave the Boleyn. We had Sam Allardyce as manager. We had a porn baron and a knickers salesman as joint owners. Fucking hell, it couldn't get much worse.

Thankfully, results on the pitch were making it bearable. The Chelsea win would go down in history as one of our best performances in the Premier League era. Against Liverpool on 9 December we held our own, but ultimately Fernando Torres was the difference as they won 3–2.

We played West Bromwich Albion at the Hawthorns the day before I flew out to Brazil, and I watched on Sky as I packed my suitcase. We were fortunate, as I recall.

Shortly after arriving in São Paulo we went off to have a few days at the beach at Guarujá near Santos. It felt very strange to be sitting on the beach with a beer on 22 December in 25 degrees of heat. Strange, but nice. It helped to soften the blow of losing 2–1 to Everton at home. After a barbecue for Christmas dinner (a quite bizarre experience), the dodgy internet connection relayed 1–0 defeat to Reading at the Madejski without disclosing too much detail, and a live stream allowed me to watch virtually all of our 2–1 home win over Norwich City on New Year's Day.

The transfer window opened, and the most notable arrival was Joe Cole who returned home from Liverpool on a free transfer. Seeing Joey in claret and blue was a sight for sore eyes indeed. While there can be no doubt he had a successful career, I always felt he never quite fulfilled the expectations that had been piled on him as a youngster. I was still glad to have him back though. Moroccan striker Marouane Chamakh joined on loan from Arsenal, Brazilian striker Wellington Paulista from Cruzeiro on loan and Austrian full-back Emanuel Pogatetz came on loan from Wolfsburg. Yossi Benayoun also returned from whence he came without making any real impact, Alou Diarra went on loan to Rennes until the end of the season and Frédéric Piquionne departed to Portland Timbers in the USA on a free transfer.

Again with bags packed, I was able to watch our third-round

cup tie against Manchester United on ESPN Brasil with Elaine's dad, Senhor Iran. The bonding process with my father-in-law was helped enormously by watching football together. I quickly learned the Portuguese words for offside, free kick, throw-in, corner and cheating bastard.

We had only just come to terms with the fact that Allardyce did not take the cups seriously when we suddenly appeared to be making a ridiculous amount of effort to progress. James Collins scored twice, both goals headers from Joe Cole crosses, and both players enjoying their second spells at the club. Allardyce had boasted that he would never let his West Ham team lose a two-goal lead, but he never said anything about a hard-fought one-goal lead. In injury time van Persie broke our hearts with an equaliser that meant a replay – and almost certain elimination.

I returned home alone. It was an odd feeling. Since I had met Elaine we had only spent a few nights apart, now I had the best part of six weeks at home without her before her visa was likely to be rubber stamped.

People are confused by this. They seemed to be of the view that as she was married to me, a British citizen, she was automatically entitled to stay in the UK. Not a bit of it. First of all, as a spouse, or 'sponsor' as the Home Office so romantically put it, I had to prove that I earned more than £16,000 per annum and that we were in a genuine relationship. Both of which should be fairly easy to prove, as long as you *do* earn more than £16,000, and as long as you *are* in a genuine relationship. Simple, you would think. Except that I was self-employed, so one person's idea of your salary is very different to another's.

And even then, if the visa is approved, there was no recourse to public funds. So, despite being a UK taxpayer for twelve years, she was not entitled to any benefits should she ever need them. This is something casual racists often forget.

Anyway, it was going to be a formality getting the visa approved so, grudgingly, we accepted the wait.

Less grudgingly, West Ham handed over 3 points to Sunderland at the Stadium of Light in a shocking away display that had no redeeming features. The cup replay at Old Trafford was similarly flat, with Rooney scoring in the first minute and us showing no ambition or desire to progress. I met Stuart the QPR fan at a pub and Paul 'Wouldn't it be funny if West Ham got Relegated' Abey. Stuart sat up in the STBU with me. There were shades of 1993 when he sat with me in the East Upper watching QPR win 4–0, as he had to sit on his hands as Loïc Rémy put QPR 1–0 up. West Ham dominated, though, and were unlucky not to win. Joe Cole scored on 68 minutes and the game finished 1–1.

We had a free fourth-round weekend and ESPN were doing a feature on the Manchester United v. West Ham tie in 2001 when Di Canio scored the winner and Fabian Barthez was left hailing a taxi. ESPN asked if anyone had been to the game. I put my hand up like Barthez. Next thing I knew I had a cameraman in my front room and Dan Snowden of ESPN asking me to rifle through my football memorabilia shoe box to find the ticket. The feature appeared on ESPN just before Manchester United's fourth-round tie against Fulham.

Away form continued to suck. 5–1 at Arsenal and 3–1 at Fulham. Seemingly we had no ideas, although Andy Carroll did manage to show his face against Fulham, though not to any crosses from Matt Jarvis.

I met Dr Sik for lunch in town before Andy Carroll did manage his second West Ham goal to earn a 1–0 win against Swansea at Upton Park; Carroll lost his marker to head the winner from a Mark Noble corner.

Then the call came. Elaine rang me at work and told me her visa had been declined. My world caved in around me.

You know those moments when you see or hear something so shocking it makes all the blood drain from your head and all you can hear is a high-pitched whistle? There had been a brief silence on the telephone. I had thought she might have been joking. She wasn't. I made my excuses at work and booked an emergency meeting with a specialist immigration lawyer.

Apparently, the visa application had been turned down

because the VAT certificate I had supplied for my company was a copy and not an original, and my company accounts were not audited.

Company accounts do not have to be audited by law unless your company turns over more than £2 million per annum – something home office rules did not take account of. And an original VAT certificate? Seriously? They were going to separate a married couple over that? I could have provided the original within ten minutes if they had picked up the telephone, but they chose to decline the application. Computer says no.

I had two choices. Appeal, or start again. Actually, there was a third choice: move to Brazil.

The immigration specialist suggested we start again as an appeal could take a year, whereas if we paid to fast track a new application it might only be two more months. So, after forking out a grand to the specialist, another grand to the Home Office for a second application and yet another grand to get my arse back over to São Paulo with a fresh set of paperwork, we could start again.

The despair I felt on hearing the news quickly dissipated and was replaced with pure anger. I understood that sham marriages had to be stopped. But this wasn't a sham. We were in love. As a British citizen I felt aggrieved that my government felt my wife had no right to be with me in my country.

42

WHAT ABOUT US

WEST HAM UNITED 3, WEST BROMWICH ALBION 1
PREMIER LEAGUE, 30 MARCH 2013

Food served on a plank of wood and chips in a bucket.

I was due back in São Paulo in the first week of March for only a few days to submit the new application, and the paperwork involved pretty much filled my second suitcase. We had an appointment at the consulate in São Paulo at 9 a.m. If we missed it, we would have to wait for another slot which could be in two weeks. Yet the taxi driver who took us there, despite being told the urgency of arriving before nine, seemed to think we wanted a guided tour of the city. Constantly reminding him, my Portuguese improved dramatically, and he seemed to finally understand. Elaine is a very calm person generally, but when she got out of the car she let him have a volley of abuse the like of which I had never seen before. It would have lasted longer, but it was 8.59 a.m.

With the second application safely submitted, and having said my goodbyes again, I contemplated my return home. This time, though, I had no idea how long I would be on my own.

Away form continued in a similar vein with a 2–1 defeat at Villa Park. Emanuel Pogatetz had an absolute nightmare and we were grateful for the fact he was only on loan.

Tottenham came to Upton Park and took an early lead before one from Andy Carroll from the penalty spot and another from Joe Cole put us 2–1 in front. But Tottenham had an ugly duckling in the shape of Gareth Bale. Gareth Bale, who had been linked with a loan move away because he was failing to settle, had suddenly blossomed into one of the best players in the Premier League. He was absolutely awesome. It hurts to say so.

I was beginning to think that moving to Brazil might be a good idea as we won 1–0 at Stoke while I was away, then lost a dull game at Stamford Bridge 2–0 on my return. The visa application was submitted, I had seven days with my wife (no thanks to the Home Office), and then returned to an empty flat. All I could do was sit and wait for news from the UK Border Agency and spend hours on Skype on a daily basis.

On 22 March West Ham were approved as the tenants for the Olympic Stadium. It meant final confirmation that we would be leaving the Boleyn Ground. The reality of it still did not sink in right away. Like being told you have two years to live – you think something will turn up. We hoped for something to come along to mean it wouldn't happen. Someone would rescue us.

In a statement issued by SuGo they said:

It's fantastic for everyone at West Ham United that at last all the Club's hard work over the past three years has paid off.

Since we came to West Ham in 2010 we have had a vision to really take the club forward so West Ham United can compete on the pitch at the highest level.

Today's decision offers us a real platform to do this and we are fully committed to making it a real success.

We understand the responsibilities that come with calling the nation's iconic Olympic Stadium, which will be converted into a world-class football stadium, our new home. It is an honour we will take on with pride.

Barely electable Mayor Boris Johnson said:

This is a truly momentous milestone for London's spectacular Olympic Stadium ensuring its credible and sustainable future.

With a series of world class entertainment and sporting fixtures already in the bag for Queen Elizabeth Olympic Park this iconic site is set to be the glittering centrepiece of ambitious regeneration plans for east London, which will capitalise on the Olympic investment into this area for the long term benefit of this city.

I remained sceptical. After all, Conservative MPs and their representatives and lackeys, the likes of Brady and Johnson, were not my favourite people at the time. My MP was a Tory, Bob Neill, who was not in the slightest bit interested in my plight, and flatly refused me a slot in his surgery because he said it was not an emergency. There is a word for people like him. 'Cunt.'

Towing the party line was one thing; flatly ignoring a constituent in trouble is another. Still, with a majority of 20,000-plus he could afford to make one of his interns spend time making reassuring noises on the phone to me for an hour while also flatly refusing to help. And in an interesting parallel, it seemed that we are also being walked over by the board. A few short years earlier we had been told that a move to the Olympic Stadium was not going to happen. Now, due to incessant pressure from SuGo and Brady, a deal had been struck. Don't tell me for one moment that the Tory Old Boys' network didn't have something to do with it. Especially with Coe being involved as well. Much as I hated Tottenham and Barry Hearn, I also half hoped they succeeded. But at the same time, I did feel that a move could be beneficial. If all the things we had been promised came to be, that is.

Spring was cold. Very cold. Cold enough to stop Dad coming to games because it was not good for his chest to walk all that way in freezing weather. When the West Brom game came around on 30 March, it was still snowing. As I left the house I grabbed my season ticket, not realising I had Dad's and not mine. As I entered the turnstile the orange light came on and the steward stopped me and asked me to look at my ticket. I showed him. Dad had the same name as me. He asked me my name. 'Robert Banks' I replied. He looked at me.

'Have you got any ID?' I showed him my driving licence. He looked at me, he looked at my driving licence, then at my dad's season ticket. I twigged what had gone wrong.

'Oh, I've picked up my dad's ticket by mistake. He's not here.' But the tosser made me go round to the ticket office and pay for an upgrade. I wasn't impressed. I was even less impressed when the ticket office sent a snotty letter to Dad warning him not to let other people use his season ticket.

I was, however, impressed by West Ham that day as we won 3–1 with 2 goals from Carroll, the first a thumping header from an O'Neil corner. O'Neil then added a second with a swerving drive, and Carroll a third with a volley from Collins's long ball. The Baggies pulled one back through Dorrans and provided the comedy moment of the afternoon as Mulumbu got himself sent off. Angry at not being awarded a free kick, he picked the ball up and drop-kicked it against O'Neil's back. Take your pick as to what he was sent off for – handball, dissent, ungentlemanly conduct, it had the lot.

Post-match I found myself in the warmth of the Black Lion, with podcasters Phil Whelans and Jim Grant, but also with various other people I had met through the podcast Facebook page. Pre- and post-match drinks were becoming the norm, and on this occasion, I have to admit, I got a bit drunk. The visa situation was getting me down. The fact that no one seemed to want to help was getting me down. I was just down full stop. The recurring theme through my life has always been that when life is shit, West Ham were there to pick me up. Now, rather than West Ham United Football Club, as an entity, it was more than ever about the people who I associated with. As I have always believed, it is important to get to games early to socialise with friends. The football is incidental.

Away at Anfield we somehow managed a clean sheet, but the wait for that elusive victory at Liverpool still continued.

Speaking of Liverpool, I had the honour of being best man for Stuart the QPR fan at his forthcoming marriage to the lovely Lisa. He had asked me back in December and I accepted, not realising the shitstorm that was coming. The way things were going, it looked like Elaine might not even be back in the country for the wedding, which was scheduled for 8 June.

QPR were playing at Goodison Park on 13 April so I arranged the stag around that. We travelled up to Liverpool on the Friday night, met up with those close friends handpicked by Stuart, including Paul 'Wouldn't it be funny if West Ham went down' Abey and Michael 'I could have died' McManus. We took in a comedy club on the Friday night, then the Everton v. QPR game on Saturday afternoon followed by a Beatles tribute band in the Cavern Club on the Saturday night. Liverpool was electric on a Saturday night. Everyone was so friendly. We retired before it had a chance to change.

While I was watching QPR get torn a new one at Goodison, the Hammers managed another point away at Southampton: 1–1 with a goal from Andy Carroll, sending a damp away following home happy. It was to be our last away point of a disappointing campaign away from home. Overall, things had gone well, but a haul of only 11 goals away from Upton Park made it a hard watch for the travelling faithful after such a feast the year before.

There had been no such problems at home though. We drew 2–2 again with Manchester United, as Mo Diamé scored the second with a beautiful low curling drive, then beat doomed Wigan Athletic 2–0 with goals in each half from Nolan and Jarvis.

We were comfortably in 10th place by the time Manchester City saw us off 2–1 at the Etihad. I managed to squeeze in another week in São Paulo to visit Elaine, who had started a course at university to occupy herself and provide something of a safety net should the unthinkable happen and she should not be allowed to return. We had an emotional parting at Guarulhos airport, as in reality we did not know when we would see each other again. A decision on her visa was imminent, but there was no guarantee the news would be positive.

While I was away we drew 0–0 with Newcastle at Upton Park and lost 2–0 at Everton, before the final game of the season. It was nice to get some revenge over the already relegated Reading and we had done by far the best of the three promoted clubs, with Reading finishing 19th with just 28 points (have some of that Jimmy Kébé – pull your socks up in front of us now, you twat.) Being West Ham though, we liked to make life hard, giving away a 2–0 lead (something Big Sam had always said would never happen) but then went on to score twice more to win the game 4–2. Kevin Nolan scored a hat-trick and the other from Vaz Tê.

We finished the season in 10th place on 46 points, a remarkable achievement for a newly promoted team. I didn't know at the time, but the Reading game would be the last game Dad attended. As far as he was concerned he was going to come again in 2013/14. But the ticket office had other ideas.

43

WE CAN'T STOP

WEST HAM UNITED 2, CARDIFF CITY 0
PREMIER LEAGUE, 17 AUGUST 2013
Neymar's hair.

My nephews Mark and Sam had decided not to renew their season tickets so there was just me and Dad left with our seats in the STBU. The fare served at home matches had been reasonable; Dad decided he would give it another season. I applied for us both to renew in the family section but got a rather curt reply, stating that as there were no children in our party we would have to relocate.

Excuse me? No children in the party? My dad would be turning 80 in October, and was, at times, needier than the average child. Plus, he didn't kick anyone in the back for the full ninety minutes like the irritating little fuckers behind us had done for the last two years. A firm stare and a word with the parents could sometimes stop this happening for all of about five minutes.

I did not want to sit my dad anywhere else in the stadium. Quite apart from the expense, there was the issue of stairs if we wanted good view. I was advised there were no tickets available in areas with a disabled lift. One Saturday afternoon in late May as I was driving to Stuart the QPR fan's house in Stamford, I received a call from the ticket office. We spoke at length about the reasons why I felt me and my dad should be able to renew our tickets, but the bottom line was the rules are the rules, and there was no one under sixteen in the party. I hadn't wanted to do it, I only ever use it as a last resort, but I even played the

'Do you know who I am?' card. I asked if he was aware of my connection with the club.

'Of course.' He said. 'You wrote a cult classic.'

'So that cuts no ice?'

'Afraid not.'

I should add that at all times during the call, the gentleman I spoke with was courteous and polite, as, I think, was I. He wasn't to know what turmoil was going on behind the scenes and how my every waking moment was filled with worry – and most of my sleeping hours too. I was also still fuming about the letter they had sent Dad warning him over the use of his season ticket, but he agreed to write to Dad with an apology. It never came.

The following Monday I casually mentioned my situation to Iain Dale. Within ten minutes I had a call back from the ticket office. 'We've decided, on reflection, you can renew in the family area after all.'

I was so flabbergasted I asked for some time to speak to Dad and check what he wanted to do. His response was classic. He told me that if it had taken so long for them to decide, they could stick it. I e-mailed the ticket office and said 'On reflection, my dad has decided not to renew after all. And so have I.'

It was bold for me to do this, but I had to think about the future. I would still probably be able to get tickets for games I wanted to go to. It was a wrench; I had held a season ticket every year I had lived in London since 1986. But apart from anything else, I wanted to show some solidarity with my dad.

Besides, I had more pressing issues to worry about. I didn't know if I would need the cash I was going to spend on a season ticket for another trip to Brazil. I also had Stuart and Lisa's wedding to think about; that best man's speech was not writing itself, and they had asked me to play the guitar during the signing of the register. I hadn't picked up my guitar in weeks.

I had been trying to look after myself in Elaine's absence, eat well and exercise. I was working near Tower Bridge and had started running home from there a couple of days a week, listening to 5 Live news and sport as I did so.

On the afternoon of 22 May 2013, I ran home with tears in my eyes as I listened to the news of the murder of Fusilier Lee Rigby in Woolwich. It was so shocking I had to stop for breath a few times on the route, which I don't normally have to. My legs felt weak. My brain could not comprehend that something so vile and vicious could happen in broad daylight on the streets of London. I grew up through the eye of the storm of the IRA bombings. I had seen a lot of cowardly acts, and I knew that governments and armies can commit atrocities of their own, and these acts of terrorism did not spring from nowhere. But this was so shocking and so terrifying, I had to stop my run.

At that moment my phone rang. It was Elaine calling from Brazil. Her visa had been approved and it was being sent to her from the British Embassy in Rio. As soon as she received it she could come home. A day of mixed emotions? The expression could have been created for how I felt right then. I ran straight to the nearest pub. I felt I deserved it.

Elaine arrived home on 6 June 2013, having left on 2 December 2012. A lot of people laugh and joke about this and ask, 'I bet you enjoyed the peace and quiet, didn't you? Eh? Eh?'

When people said that to me I kept a straight face, looked them in the eye and said, 'No. No, I didn't fucking enjoy it. I love my wife. It's been agony.' Stupid twats.

We had little time to settle, Elaine was back in the country just two days before Stuart and Lisa's wedding, so we travelled up on the Friday night, dined with them, all the parents and Lisa's daughters, Florence and Olivia. The day itself was a welcome release from the worries of the previous six months. We were celebrating two people I love very much getting married, but inwardly I was celebrating getting my own wife back, and flicking a silent 'V' to the Home Office.

I had been at Barclays longer than their internal policy of two years allowed for contractors. They wanted me to stay. I wanted to stay. But I wasn't allowed. Ridiculous. The rules said two years maximum, then you had to be away for three months before coming back. It was agreed that I would go and work on another contract run by an external company for three months or until it finished, whichever was the longer. I was due to start on Monday 24 June. On Friday 21 June I got the call saying I wasn't needed. Mayhem ensued. I managed to find a job working for the Financial Services Compensation Scheme (FSCS) in Epsom, but I hated every minute of it. I drove to the office every morning. In my second week a Sky TV van rammed into the back of my beloved £600 car at traffic lights and wrote it off. I felt isolated and unhappy. Thank god Elaine had come home.

But enough of this self-indulgent crap. What was happening on the West Ham front? We signed Romanian Răzvan Raţ, and perhaps more importantly, we had agreed a £15 million fee with Liverpool for the permanent transfer of Andy Carroll. Not surprisingly, Carroll had picked up a heel injury in the last game of the season against Reading and would not play again until January.

I was very sad to read that the club would not be offering Carlton Cole a new contract. I loved Carlton. When he was on form he was a powerful runner and a decent header of the ball. Fortunately, Iain Dale must have had a word with someone because by the end of October he had re-signed on a short-term contract. Goalkeeper Adrián San Miguel del Castillo signed from Real Betis. Fortunately, he was more commonly known as just Adrián. I could cope with that.

The other big-name arrival in the summer was Stewart Downing. Forgive me if this did not set me alight with anticipation. Whenever I had seen him play for Middlesbrough, Aston Villa, Liverpool or England he looked like a one-trick pony who was so left-sided his right side was withering away. I found him painful to watch at times and now he was a West Ham player. England international or not, I was as underwhelmed as I had been by the signing of Matt Jarvis the year before. Croatian Mladen Petrić also came aboard, and youngster Danny Whitehead was signed from Stockport County. Downing, Carroll and Whitehead were officially undisclosed fees, the rest being signed on free transfers.

News of Carroll's permanent signing was broken on Twitter by Jack Sullivan, the thirteen-year-old son of David Sullivan. SuGo seemed completely oblivious to how this looked to the outside world. Sullivan Jr's Twitter account was being used to spread rumours and gossip and confirm transfer activity. It's still happening now. Forget lies, the amount of money being spent, and the sale of our heritage, the fact that the board were happy to sit by and watch a teenager break news to the footballing world via his Twitter account was shocking. It was like some spoiled brat getting an expensive toy to play with. No, it wasn't *like* that: That's exactly what it *was*. It got worse when the thirteen-year-old tweeted asking fans what they thought about signing Ilombe Myobo from Ghent, a player convicted ten years previously of taking part in the gang rape of a fourteen-year-old girl. Jack Sullivan's tweet read:

> How would you feel if we signed Mboyo of Gent? Terrible crime when he was 16, can he ever be forgiven? What do you think?

We think your dad should confiscate your phone, Jack.

The only major permanent departure was Gary O'Neil, who left on a free transfer for QPR. I liked O'Neil. He had joined in the middle of the Avram Grant crisis season and never let us down. Euphemistically called a 'squad player', he took a decent corner, crossed the ball well and had a good engine. I liked him a lot. He made 40 starts for West Ham, 16 sub appearances and scored 3 goals.

Pre-season had gone well, which was a bad sign as far as I was concerned. Good pre-seasons often breed contempt. The best signing of the close season for me was Adidas as kit manufacturer. Macron had been okay, but they were a little bit shit, weren't they? I always preferred Adidas, they just looked better. The new kit was smart, not fussy, with blue sleeves and claret body, a white collar and the three white stripes extending down the shoulder and sleeve. New sponsors Alpari meant we could also get rid of those fucking annoying electronic odds generator boards run by SBOBET that always drew my eye away from what was going on at pitch level.

As the first game of the season approached, social media had been full of confident posts given the over-achievements of last season, the signings we had made and the fact the fixture computer had been kind to us, not having to face one of the 'big six' until 6 October.

The first game of the new season was against newly promoted Cardiff City at Upton Park. A Jarvis cross actually found its intended target in the penalty area, Joe Cole turned and released a shot into the bottom corner for the lead. Kevin Nolan struck a sweet second half shot to double the advantage and wrap up the points.

A well-earned point in a 0–0 draw at St James's Park followed, giving us 4 points from the opening two fixtures and 3rd place in the formative table.

Ricardo Vaz Tê reminded Big Sam of his ability with a magnificent free kick to give us the lead in the League Cup 2nd round tie against Cheltenham Town at Upton Park. The mohican had gone, he was looking trim and sharp but struggled to get game time.

Ravel Morrison had also struggled to get game time under Allardyce and had been sent off on loan to Birmingham, but he played against Cheltenham and scored a great second goal, juggling the ball on the edge of the area and firing a low shot beyond the grasp of the keeper. Adrián made his debut in goal and gave away a penalty, rushing off his line and mistiming his challenge. But 2–1 was enough to see us through to the next round and another home tie against Cardiff City.

Stoke City came to Upton Park and stole the points with a 1–0 win courtesy of a Jermaine Pennant free kick. Sky saw fit to televise our game at St Mary's against Southampton, which was an entertaining if worrying 0–0 draw in which Jääskeläinen made a number of fine saves, and Collins appeared to handle in the area before later blasting a good chance over the bar. The holy grail of the clean sheet had been achieved, but it was

Keystone Cops-style defending and our goal remained intact more through luck than judgement.

Everton exposed our defensive frailties for all the world to see at Upton Park. Everton, now managed by former Wigan boss Roberto Martínez following David Moyes's departure for Manchester United, played a slightly more expansive game than his predecessor, but this did not make it any easier for us to get behind them. They remained one of our toughest opponents in the Premier League era.

Ravel Morrison struck from the edge of the box early on to give us the lead, though it took a massive deflection. Leighton Baines equalised with a thunderous free kick. Nolan won a penalty in the second half which was dispatched with his normal efficiency, but then disaster struck as he received a second booking and was sent off for a challenge on that horrible little shit Ross Barkley. Noble had quite clearly got the ball first, but Barclay went down like he'd been shot, and we were left with ten men. From the resulting free kick Baines repeated his party trick, but to the opposite corner before the customary goal from Romelu Lukaku sealed our fate.

The match against Cardiff City in the League Cup was Allardyce's hundredth in charge of West Ham. His overall league record remained impressive, despite the stuttering start to this campaign, with 37 wins from 89 matches – giving him a win percentage of 41 per cent. But those figures were skewed by a season in the Championship – a season littered with costly draws. Big Sam had shown that he wasn't that fussed about the cups, and indeed since taking over in June 2011 the only cup tie we had won had been the game against Cheltenham a few weeks before.

We went into a 2–0 lead inside seven minutes against Cardiff, before they pulled it back to 2–2 (no side of mine would ever surrender a two-goal lead). But Vaz Tê scored a late equaliser to take us through to the fourth round against Burnley at Turf Moor.

44

SOMEWHERE ONLY WE KNOW

TOTTENHAM HOTSPUR 1, WEST HAM UNITED 2
LEAGUE CUP FIFTH ROUND, 18 DECEMBER 2013
Oysters. Jesus, they feel like a big runny lump of snot
in Worcester sauce going down your throat.

League form continued to be worrying. We lost 1–0 away at
Hull to a debatable penalty, and the next two fixtures did not
offer up much hope, Tottenham away and Manchester City at
home. Tottenham away was goalless after sixty-five minutes. I
would have taken a 0–0, but when Winston Reid poked home
from a corner after a bit of pinball in the six-yard box the odds
looked better. White Hart Lane was not an easy place to win
though, and we had not won a game there since 1999. We had
more bite and desire in midfield as Noble's pass found Vaz Tê
and he was fortunate to find the net with a bit of a powder-puff
shot, but we celebrated like it was a 25-yard piledriver. Nothing
lucky about the third from Morrison as he picked up the ball
from a pass by Diamé in our own half and accelerated like a
greyhound past two Tottenham defenders, leaving them both
on their backsides, then chipped over the keeper for 3–0. Ec-
stasy! To win at White Hart Lane is always a nice feeling, but
to round it off with a goal like that, which really rubbed their
noses in it, was extra special. It also went a long way towards
spelling the end of the road for André Villas-Boas as Tottenham manager, resulting in the laughable appointment of
Tim Sherwood.

Allardyce, in typically modest fashion, claimed to be a tactical genius and said that had he been Italian they would be

calling him 'Allardicio', or something like that. Actually, Sam, if you were Italian they would be calling you 'Il Fatso'.

As is the West Ham Way, after a fine result like that, and all fired up, we lost at home 3–1 to Manchester City, but it was closer than the scoreline suggested. Even so, just 8 points from 8 games had to be improved on.

Morrison's goal against Tottenham earned him a call-up to the England u-21 squad and he played against Lithuania, scoring twice in a 5–0 win. Maybe Big Sam had been a good influence on him and persuaded him to leave his bad boy days behind him. Maybe.

A 0–0 draw was a point well earned at the Liberty Stadium against Swansea City, a game notable mainly for Sam laughing uncontrollably at Chico Flores as he failed to win a free kick after going down clutching his face. Tosser. That's Flores, not Big Sam. Well, you know what I mean.

We won, rather unexpectedly, at Burnley in the League Cup with two penalties converted by two different players: Jack Collison and Matty Taylor. I say it was unexpected because Sam again seemed not to be taking it too seriously and, given our league position, that was probably justified. Dan Potts made a rare start alongside the delightfully named Pelly Ruddock, who I assumed was the love child of Pelé and Razor. Pelly Ruddock Mpanzu had, in fact, signed from Boreham Wood in 2011 and made his debut against Burnley. He and another youth prospect Leo Chambers also played but, despite impressing, it seemed the kids were not alright, as it was the last appearance either would make for the West Ham first team. Danny Potts would only play twice more.

As soon as I had worked three months at FSCS I was on the phone to Barclays asking for a job. A week later I was back at my old desk, with my old team leader, picking up much of the same work I had left behind in June. It was like taking off a tight pair of shoes and popping on a comfy pair of slippers. My team leader Gerard Donachie was the most sarcastic man I had ever met. A good man, a Liverpool fan, he had championed my request to come back. It was good to have friends in high places.

The 0–0 draw at home to Aston Villa marked possibly the lowest ebb to date of the Allardyce era. West Ham dominated possession but did not pose any kind of threat. It was one of the dullest 0–0 draws I had ever seen. But worse was to come. We lost a lead to go down 3–1 at Carrow Road then lost a fourth home game of the season, a tame 3–0 to Chelsea.

Out of the relegation zone on goal difference only, we faced a Fulham side level on points with us but 5 goals worse off. We beat them 3–0 with goals from Mo Diamé just after half time and a late extra two from both Carlton and Joey Cole. Once again, the indignity of losing to West Ham was too much for the opposition and they sacked manager Martin Jol.

The conversion work on the Olympic Stadium got under way with the moving of the floodlights to accommodate the new roof. Vice-chairman Brady looked on what she had done, and she was well satisfied. It all seemed a long way off and still nothing to worry about. There was still time for an earthquake to strike with its epicentre at Westfield.

Pulis against Allardyce was never going to be a feast of flowing, entertaining football, and that was how it proved at Selhurst Park. Watching the game was akin to having pins stuck in your eyes. Marouane Chamakh, who had failed to impress in his loan spell with us, naturally scored the winner for Palace in a 1–0 win. A 4–1 defeat at Anfield meant the wait went on, ticking over to fifty long years. The game did, however, feature two own goals: Demel scored for Liverpool and Škrtel scored for West Ham. Nolan got a straight red. Best forgotten.

When I said the Villa game marked a low ebb for Allardyce, I was forgetting the Sunderland game. People actually paid money to go and watch it. People had taken time out of their hectic schedules to go and observe this shower of shite that was served up to us. I saw a lot of disappointing defeats in my time, but as 0–0 draws go, this felt like a defeat. It was truly shocking. Yes, Downing and Carroll were out injured. Yes, Nolan was suspended. But really? Sullivan stuck his nose in again during an interview in *Football Focus* that day, stating the rest of the season was damage limitation. Inspiring, cheers Dave. Could there be any lower watermarks?

It certainly was not the type of form you wanted to be taking into a cup quarter-final at White Hart Lane. But that was what we had so we had to make the best of it. The team that took on Spurs was put together out of necessity rather than any cunning Allardicio style tactical genius. He started with Collison, Taylor, Diarra, Jarvis and Joey Cole in midfield with Carlton on his own up front. I watched through my fingers. Tim Sherwood looked like a supply teacher who had taken a wrong turning and ended up running the school sports day. He blagged it pretty well for the first hour or so, as Adebayor put Spurs 1–0 up on 67 minutes and it looked like another cup run coming to an end.

But the night was far from over. In one of those rare moments when previously ineffective players suddenly found their sweet spot, Taylor fed Jarvis to fire in an equaliser past Lloris, then Diamé crossed for Maïga to get in a weak but accurate header that saw the French keeper clawing at thin air. Tottenham had already packed their bags and gone home by the time Maïga hit the bar and Collison had another good effort saved. Jubilation for a second time in the space of a few weeks at White Hart Lane; it almost made the dross in between easier to bear.

45

RATHER BE

WEST HAM UNITED 3, SOUTHAMPTON 1
PREMIER LEAGUE, 22 FEBRUARY 2014
Go Compare! Go fuck off.

Remember that low ebb I was talking about? I was forgetting January 2014.

The euphoria of beating Tottenham at White Hart Lane for the second time in the same season was short lived as the semi-final draw paired us with Manchester City, completely ignoring my prayers for a two-legged semi-final against Sunderland. Whoever says these things are not fixed needs only to look at this draw and subsequent League Cup draws. City against struggling West Ham and Manchester United against Sunderland.

We lost away at Old Trafford and at home to Arsenal, both 3–1 in a routine fashion, then drew 3–3 at home with West Bromwich Albion in a see-saw game in which we led 1–0, trailed 2–1, led 3–2 then threw it all away. Il Fatso was running out of excuses. Having claimed to be a tactical genius in October, his touch seemed to have deserted him as his reliance on clean sheets seemed to be at the expense of showing any form of attacking intent whatsoever. Yes, Carroll was still injured, but even when he did play, especially away from home, he stood on his own, hands on hips in the opponents' half, watching in the vain hope that the ball might come his way.

The West Bromwich Albion game was the first match of the season in which we had won a point and conceded a goal. We drew 0–0 in the other four draws, and the games we had won had been with clean sheets. So you could see Allardyce's argument. But the games in between were rank. It seemed that if we conceded a goal there was no plan B. Reliance on clean sheets it all very well, but only if you have a team capable of keeping a clean sheet more often than not.

We should have been able to manage this against Fulham at Craven Cottage on New Year's Day, but we could not, and lost 2–1.

There had been increasing pressure on Il Fatso to play some youth. It had worked at Burnley in the League Cup and, with decent signings at a premium, it seemed a good way to see some new players come through.

But Big Sam was an arrogant man and did things his way. When we clamoured for 4–4–2 at home in the Championship season he refused to listen, and we kept drawing. When he eventually did try it, we lost a game that probably merited a more cautious approach. He almost did things to prove a point, deliberately and methodically so that it would go horribly wrong and would be enough to shut people up.

We had been begging him to give youth a chance, but successive promising youth team players had been sold or packed off on loan.

The cup tie against Nottingham Forest at the City Ground was the ideal opportunity. He took it with both hands. As if to prove that you can't win anything with kids, he played the following side against Forest in the FA Cup third round:

Adrián, Diarra, Potts, Driver, Downing, Jarvis, Whitehead, Moncur, Lletget, Maïga and Morrison, with subs Turgott, Fanimo and Burke.

Five kids in the starting XI and three on the bench. Il Fatso was making his point, and he made it well. The 5–0 defeat against Forest was humiliating, on a professional level for the club, but also for those poor kids who were effectively hung out to dry. 'See?!' you could almost hear Allardyce crying with glee, 'That's what happens when you play kids!' Yes Sam, that's what happens when you name eight in your squad of fourteen. No one was fooled by it.

The argument was also made that with a League Cup semi-final coming up midweek at the Etihad, he had to preserve his experienced players. It was true that we were in deep shit with injuries, and the team that took to the field against Manchester City looked like it was beaten before it had even crossed the line. It certainly was beaten when it left the field: 6–0 in a League Cup semi-final for the second time in our history. No plastic pitch or absent manager to blame this time.

A 2–0 win at Cardiff at the weekend said more about Cardiff than us. Andy Carroll finally made an appearance, but as one came in, one went out, with James Tomkins seeing red. He wasn't the only one seeing red. Cardiff fans had been seeing red all season as their owner Vincent Tan had decided red was their lucky colour. In a move that made SuGo look positively sane, he disregarded Cardiff's entire identity and made them wear red shirts at home. (Their nickname is the Bluebirds, Vince.) Well, it wasn't very lucky as they turned out to be shit. They must have been because we beat them for a third time that season and we were hopeless.

Newcastle beat us 3–1 at Upton Park, then the formality of the League Cup semi-final second leg saw us unable to even raise enough enthusiasm to avoid a record aggregate defeat. At least in 1990 Bonzo roused us against Oldham to win the second leg 3–0 and give them something to think about. This time it seemed it wasn't even damage limitation. We lost the game 3–0, the tie and our self-respect 9–0 on aggregate. In a desperate attempt to drum up some interest the game was offering 'kids for a quid' tickets, but if it had been free I doubt if many more than the 14,390 who did turn up would have bothered.

When something like that happens you expect a reaction. If there is no reaction then you really are in trouble. Fortunately, something stirred as we gained a point in a 0–0 draw at Stamford Bridge. The most entertaining aspect of this was José Mourinho's post-match comments:

This is not the best league in the world, this is football from the nineteenth century.

> The only [other] thing I could bring was a Black and Decker
> to destroy the wall.

This was a bit rich coming from one of the most negative managers in the history of the game. The reality was that we had come for a point, as we did at most away games. But most home teams had enough about them to find a way through, something Allardyce stubbornly refused to address by setting up differently. Results like this made it even less likely that he would change, but we enjoyed the moment.

The January transfer window closed with limited activity having taken place. Roger Johnson came in on loan from Wolves, bringing with him the unfortunate epithet 'Roger the Relegator', as he had gone down with both Wolves and Birmingham in previous seasons. It seemed a strange choice. I've always been slightly baffled by the selection of players who have 'experience' because that often means they have experience of the wrong things. Like taking 'experienced' England players to the World Cup. Why? All they have experience of is losing and missing penalties. If the right experience is what you want, take Bobby Charlton, Geoff Hurst and Martin Peters.

In another bizarre move that was clearly agent-driven, two players of the same nationality but from different clubs arrived on loan. Antonio Nocerino from A.C. Milan and Marco Borriello from Roma both signed until the end of the season. I was a little concerned that we might have another Tevez and Mascherano situation on our hands, but these names, while well respected, were hardly in their category. Pablo Armero, a Colombian defender playing for Napoli, also joined on loan to the end of the season.

Răzvan Raț was released after just a few months at the club, and Maïga, struggling with form, and Ravel Morrison, struggling with discipline (having developed one of those niggly intermittent faults) went off on loan to QPR to the end of the season. Jack Collison, struggling with injury, went to Wigan on loan.

Having grabbed a foothold in the relegation zone, it was important that we built on it to lever ourselves out. We had a decent record at home to Swansea, and with Carroll, Reid, Downing and Jarvis all fit we looked a different proposition. Carroll twice set up Nolan to score and the game was effectively over, but not before Flores had gained a little revenge for Allardyce laughing at him in December, as he again went down clutching his face. This time the referee was Howard Webb, so Carroll was sent off. Vice-chairman Brady criticised Flores in her column in *The Sun*. She just didn't know when to shut up; it wasn't really any of her business.

Carlton came in for Carroll at Villa Park, but it was Nolan again who grabbed a brace. He seemed to be the only West Ham player who knew where the net was, and it was just as well. The 7 points from the last 3 games had lifted us up to 15th place, 2 points clear of the relegation zone. But better was to follow as we beat Norwich City 2–0 at Upton Park, then Southampton 3–1 to lift us up to 10th on 31 points, 6 clear of relegation, earning Il Fatso the manager of the month award for February 2014. We would never hear the last of it. Surely the lowest low had now passed.

46

WAVES

WEST HAM UNITED 2, TOTTENHAM HOTSPUR 0
PREMIER LEAGUE, 3 MAY 2014
Miranda Hart. Complete oxygen thief. About as funny
as a smack in the mouth in my opinion.

I have already skirted around the issue of social media and its effect on the way you support your football team, but now may be an opportune moment to explore that in a little more detail. If everyone liked yellow, what would happen to blue? This is a phrase (or something similar) used in Brazil to demonstrate that everyone has a different perspective, and an opinion.

Opinions are great. Like my view of Miranda Hart. They keep debate fresh, they help to explore all avenues when it comes to trying to fix a problem. The fact that she is so popular shows that it takes all sorts to make a world.

But when you mix opinions with the anonymous right of reply afforded by the internet, you have a potentially explosive combination.

I never thought I would refer to Dr Henry Kissinger in one of my books, but in his 2014 work *World Order* he warns that an individual with enough computing power could 'access the cyber domain to disable and potentially destroy critical infrastructure from a position of near-complete anonymity.'

This is the issue we are facing at a personal level too. People can say what they want without fear of the consequences. They can threaten, they can spread lies and be as offensive as they like because unless the police and internet providers get involved, no one can be certain who they are.

Kissinger highlights that the 24/7 news cycle we now have means that politicians have less time for reflection before speaking or commenting. If politicians struggle to provide a coherent response when put on the spot, how are members of the public supposed to cope? I doubt if you would hear Boris Johnson respond to an awkward question by inviting you to ask him to his face at the Podium. Although, now I think about it...

Opinion on Kissinger is divided. Some see him as a Nobel Prize-winning diplomat, others see him as nothing short of a war criminal. Whatever your view, you have to admit he makes a good point:

> One needs to differentiate between information, knowledge and wisdom. In the internet era they tend to get mixed up. The more time one spends simply absorbing information, the less time one has to apply wisdom. And then there's common sense.

Kissinger reckons if there is a third world war it will probably start in cyberspace and escalate in ways that no world leaders could predict. I swear Kissinger must have done some of his research by trawling through West Ham fan pages on Facebook.

As I found out initially with reviews of *The Legacy of Barry Green* and my badly thought-out blog, internet critics can make printed-word critics look like pussycats by comparison.

It often starts off with a reply beginning with the word 'Actually', which is another of my irrational hatreds. When someone says the word 'Actually', what they are saying is that what you have just said is completely wrong: this is the truth, this is how things are.

Things then move on to 'Do you seriously think that...?' and then 'What complete nonsense.' Although some people skip that entirely and go straight to the personal insult.

It's easy to be critical. After all, I have made enough criticisms in this book to last me a lifetime. But it's an interesting mentality – how not being able to see that person somehow gives you the right to be rude in a way you would (hopefully) not dream of if you were face to face. If you would be that rude to someone's face, then fair play to you.

Reflection, as Kissinger alludes to, is vital. We make comments on social media without thinking them through. You can delete but you cannot unsee. It's particularly dangerous because it's purely verbal. You cannot see body language. You don't know the circumstances of the other person. At any given time we could be pressing a button or triggering a response in someone. If we understood the other person full, the chances are we wouldn't say it.

All of this was starting to come to a head within the STOP! Hammer Time Facebook page, and in particular, over the various merits and defects of Allardyce. Generally, the out brigade were more vociferous and aggressive than those who preferred to keep the status quo. It was the same with the Scottish independence and Brexit campaigns. Those seeking change seemed more willing to be aggressive than those who wanted things to stay as they were. And they didn't care who they upset in the process.

Before the days of social media, people still had opinions, it's just that you rarely heard them. Unless someone went to the trouble of writing an article for a newspaper or fanzine, or got themselves on the radio or TV, you would not hear it. Given the limited medium for opinions to be expressed, it meant that the level of influence on people was more or less black and white. You were generally yes or no. In or out. Organising a protest must have been a nightmare. Quite how the suffragette movement managed to organise itself without a WhatsApp group boggles the mind. How Rosa Parks managed to get her point across without posting a selfie sat on a bus is quite amazing. But as we would see in 2018, social media does not a successful protest make.

Social media has changed the playing field. Sometimes it is a positive thing. People who may have been labouring under a misconception may suddenly find the truth. But more often than not it's nothing more than the recycling of lies dreamed up by an attention-seeking cunt put forward as fact by people who have merely googled something to try to prove their point.

There are definite groups of people, particularly on football forums. There is the type that deliberately say something outrageous to attract attention. There is the type who will watch a thread where everyone broadly agrees, then take the opposite view for the hell of it. There are people who just snipe at everything – even the most positive of things. I remember one example – I posted a video of our 2–1 win over Manchester United in 1986, a glorious game that makes me go misty-eyed just thinking about it. The post received 114 positive comments, but the final one was this: 'Alan Dickens, the man who wasn't the next Trevor Brooking.' That successfully killed the mood of goodwill and positivity. Well done you.

At least it didn't descend into mudslinging. This normally is the domain of the troll. The troll is the person who not only says inflammatory things, he or she says outrageous things, often aimed personally at individuals to get a reaction, then sits back to watch the shitstorm that inevitably follows.

There is a need for instant gratification now. The days when I would print off my copy and send it by first-class mail (or fax at a push) to Gary for publication in OLAS, which he would then type in by hand, are long gone. But they were only twenty years ago. That was surpassed by the days of the floppy disc, then e-mail, and now with Facebook and blogging you can upload your opinions instantly. Regrettably, that also means you can upload them before having the chance to think them through.

The instant-gratification brigade is pandered to by the broadcast media, who now show live Premier League press conferences. The FA Cup draw now displays the number of the ball with the allocated team, so your heart skips a fraction of a second earlier when you hear the number of the ball rather than the name of your team. Madness. In Brazil, they interview players on the pitch at half time while they are on their way to the dressing room. Personally, I've never seen the point of interviewing players full stop. 'The fans were great.' 'The three points was the main thing.' 'It was a great team performance.' Insert any combination of the above statements, and that's what you normally get.

Sometimes an opinion is down to taste or point of view, yet you can still be judged. Music is a prime example. There is pressure to like stuff that's cool. But what is wrong with liking stuff that isn't? Just because you don't like it, doesn't make it shit. It just makes it different. People are really, I mean really, nasty about Phil Collins, Coldplay, and other perceived-to-be 'bland' artists. But to some people they mean a lot. It doesn't make them bad. Miranda Hart is, mystifyingly, very popular, and has a much more successful career in her chosen field than I do. So who am I to judge? Sorry Miranda, I'll move on now.

I'm often swayed by someone's opinion because it is stated with such conviction. Take a little time to check things out and an opinion stated with conviction can start to crumble like an Avram Grant back four. Even if it's clearly bollocks, people need to read broadly and make up their own minds. Alas, these days it is easier to pick up an opinion without the need to research or verify facts first. My main takeaway has always been: don't believe anything you see on social media because someone somewhere is trying to manipulate you and they have an agenda for doing so.

Back on the pitch, 4 wins on the spin and 5 undefeated after the horror show at the start of 2014 should have signalled a turn in fortunes, but a 1–0 defeat at Everton and a 3–1 reverse at Stoke were compounded by a 2–0 home defeat by Manchester United and their beleaguered boss David Moyes. Wayne Rooney scored that goal from inside his own half, which the popular press always lose their shit over, conveniently forgetting that he fouled James Tomkins before setting himself up unmolested to strike the shot. The BBC said he 'outmuscled' Tomkins. Outflabbed, more like.

It meant that when Hull City came to Upton Park on 26 March in front of Uncle Rupert's cameras, a win was desperately needed to maintain or extend the 6-point advantage we held over the teams currently occupying the bottom three.

Now, remember those nadirs I was referring to? Well, I forgot Hull at home, March 2014. This was, without a doubt, the single most irritating show of arrogance and petulance I had ever seen from a football manager.

Hull goalkeeper McGregor was sent off after a foul in the box on Diamé. Noble, reliable as ever, scored from the spot. From that point we should have gone on to win easily. But suffice it to say, we made such heavy weather of it, it was embarrassing.

Hull started the second half brightly and Huddlestone's free kick deflected off Jelavić and flew past Adrián in goal, who was rooted to the spot.

It was turgid stuff, like watching someone push a rock up a hill, only to slip and see it go rolling back to the bottom again.

Then we finally had some luck. Guy Demel put in a speculative cross, James Chester stuck out a knee and the ball looped up over replacement keeper Harper to restore the lead.

If it was poor before we took the lead, afterwards it was worse. We could not have complained any more if we had been losing. The din inside Upton Park was awful, the likes of which I had never heard before, at least not in such a negative way. After the final whistle, tactical genius Il Fatso cupped his ear to the fans. The moment he did that, he lost any respect I had for him, and I hadn't had a huge amount to start with.

Not only that, but every West Ham fan seemed to lose patience with Allardyce at that point, though some continued to defend. He became one of the first divisive figures on social media causing people to fall out. I couldn't wait for the season to end, and hopefully for Il Fatso to fuck off.

We won 2–1 at Sunderland in another excruciating display then lost at home to Liverpool, although admittedly more as a result of poor refereeing than anything else. We were going through the motions. 3–1 at the Emirates, 1–0 at home to Palace, 1–0 at the Hawthorns. Fortunately, everyone else around us was shit so by the time Tottenham came on 3 May a win would have seen us safe.

Australian midfielder Mile Jedinak scored Palace's winner

from the penalty spot but did not celebrate. He showed remarkable restraint out of respect for his compatriot, young Dylan Tombides.

Dylan had been making good progress, and made his debut against Wigan in the League Cup in September 2012. Having done so, we expected to see a lot more of him. But by December 2012 he was back receiving chemotherapy. He recovered sufficiently to feature in the Asian under-22 tournament in January 2014, but on his return to England he was told that his condition was terminal. His cancer had spread to his liver and he died on the morning of 18 April. Another example of how football needs to be put into perspective. Cancer is a bastard indeed.

His legacy is the Dylan Tombides DT38 foundation, a charity which raises awareness of testicular cancer and of the education of young people on the subject. A statue was erected in his honour at the Perth Oval in 2015. Keep checking, lads. Then check again.

Other than the fact that we had already beaten them twice that season there was little to indicate from current form that we might beat Tottenham again. They must have been sick of the sight of us, as Younès Kaboul got himself sent off, and a few minutes later Harry Kane diverted Andy Carroll's header into his own net. One of his own from one of their own. Kane definitely got the last touch and claimed it.

Downing then scored his first goal for West Ham but credit for the assist has to go to the Tottenham wall, which parted obligingly for Downing's effort to sneak through to make it 2–0. The supply teacher in the dugout did not look impressed and it seemed he would shortly be off looking for a fresh challenge.

The season ended with a listless 2–0 defeat at the Etihad, City taking their overall aggregate against us that season to 14–1. Liverpool needed to beat Newcastle and for us to beat City to win the title. I do hope no one put money on it. City won the title under the leadership of a charming 60-year-old Chilean by the name of Manuel Pellegrini.

47

AM I WRONG

CRYSTAL PALACE 1, WEST HAM UNITED 3
PREMIER LEAGUE, 23 AUGUST 2014
Trying to find the end of the Sellotape. Surely there
should be a law against it?

The podcast stable that produced *STOP! Hammer Time* did, from time to time, arrange live podcasts for the listeners to attend, with a famous guest to draw in the numbers. In May 2014 it was Julian Dicks. Such was the popularity of the podcast that around sixty people crammed into the function room at the Horse and Stables pub near Lambeth North tube station for the event, which I helped to kick off by arranging a quiz. I set a question relating to the number of times Julian had been Hammer of the Year. The question was:

'Julian was Hammer of the Year three times, but who was he runner-up to in 1989?'

A broad Bristolian accent bellowed out from the back of the room. 'Four times! Not three!'

They say footballers don't care. But Julian clearly did. We had a great time with him that night. He regaled us with stories of when he first joined the club and how John Lyall looked after him, even picking him up from his temporary accommodation and taking him to training during the first few weeks, and how he would get into Lyall's Jaguar having to put up with his chain-smoking, too scared to ask to open a window.

As a collective group, West Ham fans were exhausted at the end of the 2013/14 season, and they had, on the whole, had enough of Il Fatso aka Allardicio, Hippo Head, Big Sam, or whatever you wanted to call him.

Before the season had even finished there were rumours that SuGo had approached A.C. Milan boss Allegri, rumours that were quickly denied by Sullivan. At the end-of-season awards ceremony, he took the unprecedented step of apologising to fans:

> I want to apologise to the supporters for this season… it's not been good enough. We all take responsibility and we will work hard to improve things in the future. We will sit down next week and look at what we need to take things forward.

Allardyce seemed to take this as a personal slight, which it was, if you think about it. This was yet another example of Sullivan saying what he thinks the fans want to hear, without fully thinking it through.

The rumour mill quickly began to grind. It seemed SuGo had not learned the lessons of the Martin O'Neill debacle and discreet enquiries were allegedly being made about the recently sacked David Moyes and the then Napoli boss Rafa Benítez. Why they felt unable to sort things out with Allardyce first, then start making enquiries, is something I will never understand. Clearly they were unhappy with Allardyce. He had done what was asked of him, now he could go. But 'crisis meetings' were held, and he was allowed to keep his job, albeit without any apparent talk of a contract extension, which was due to expire in the summer of 2015.

It came across like this: we tried to find someone better but couldn't. Premier League survival is what really matters. Sam has kept us up two years in a row. Let him have another go.

Allegedly there had been talks about the style of football played and there had been demands made for a more fluid, expansive style of play, to which Il Fatso had allegedly agreed. I was sceptical. Asking Allardyce to play attractive football was like asking a gay man to be straight. He might be able to pull it off for a while, but you cannot be something you are not.

Joe Cole was allowed to leave and headed off to Aston Villa. Jack Collison, still struggling with injury, went off to Wigan on a permanent deal. George McCartney was released; Callum Driver and Jordan Spence also went their own ways. Matty Taylor went to Burnley. Morrison, still unable to show any form of enthusiasm for playing for West Ham and pictured twice on Twitter wearing other teams' shirts, was sent to Cardiff on a three-month loan. Diarra went without leaving any sort of impression; Maïga went on loan again, for the whole season, to Metz.

Coming in was Argentinian international Mauro Zárate. This was exciting. I could not see this being an Allardyce signing. He had far too much flair for an Allardyce player. We had seen already how flair players were dealt with – generally sent off on loan to Cardiff, while Kevin Nolan continued to huff and puff in midfield.

But there were more new faces coming in. Cheikhou Kouyaté was signed from Anderlecht, probably as a replacement for Mo Diamé who was making noises about wanting to move. Aaron Cresswell, a young English full-back signed from Ipswich, and Diego Poyet, son of Gus, and Charlton's player of the season the previous year, came in. Striker Enner Valencia (who had been impressive in the World Cup for Ecuador) and Carl Jenkinson, an unused right-back at Arsenal, came on loan, as well as Diafra Sakho, an exciting young Senegalese talent playing in Ligue 2 in France. This was all good, positive stuff, but more was to come. Alex Song was still in his prime at twenty-seven when he came to us on loan. This was the sort of player who normally only came to us when they were looking to draw their pension. The summer signings were completed with Morgan Amalfitano, who was contracted to Marseille but had been on loan at West Bromwich Albion the season before.

This, to me, was a good transfer window. Players left who had no future at the club, while coming in were exciting young players of proven pedigree like Cresswell and Jenkinson, to fill positions that had been crying out for attention in the team.

The new Adidas home kit harked back to the halcyon days of 1985/86. The away kit, however, was a bizarre concoction in sky blue with a navy sash, which reminded me of the uniforms in *Thunderbirds*. There was also a third kit, for no apparent reason, which was a sickening shade of purple.

A good start was needed and what better way to achieve that than with a home game against Tottenham Hotspur, a team we had beaten three times during the previous campaign. But the supply teacher had gone and in his place was Mauricio Pochettino. Recently purloined from Southampton, they had someone in place who not only looked like he knew what he was doing, but probably did.

Mark Noble missed a penalty, a real collector's item. It had been given for handball against Kyle Naughton who was harshly sent off. James Collins was also sent off for two bookable offences and, with the game looking like it was heading for 0–0, debutant Eric Dier stole in at the death to grab victory for Tottenham.

At Crystal Palace I bumped into my old school mate Del Shave and had a quick pint with him before going to meet up with the STOP! Hammer Time team to watch Palace v. *Thunderbirds*. As it turned out, Thunderbirds were go, as we won 3–1 with a couple of cracking goals, I missed the first by Zárate because I was having a piss, and the second from Stewart Downing was a real peach from outside the box.

Carlton added a third after Palace had pulled one back and it was a perfect day overall: beautiful sunshine, a West Ham victory with spectacular goals, great company and a short bus ride home.

Sheffield United came to Upton Park in the League Cup for their first visit since the Tevez affair had been concluded. There were appeals for calm all round, and the fans in the Sir Trevor Brooking Lower were cleared out to make way for the travelling hordes of Blunts, but in the event none of that was necessary as they brought down only a handful of fans and the game was a non-event. Sakho scored his first goal for West Ham in a 1–1 draw but then missed the vital spot-kick as we went out 5–4 on penalties.

On the Saturday of the Southampton game I was out in Stockholm with Elaine on a short break. What a beautiful city Stockholm is. It seems Elaine conveniently knows a Brazilian living in just about every European country, which is great for claiming free accommodation and specialist local know-ledge. As it happened, we were in Stockholm at just the right time for the crayfish festival, just as the crayfish were ready to eat. The tradition is to eat them until they are coming out of your ears while drinking various flavours of frozen vodka, which is a very dangerous game. I could not get a signal and found out the result of the Southampton game after the event: a 3–1 defeat.

So with three league games played we had one win and two home defeats. Despite all the new signings it seemed that noth-ing had changed, at least in terms of results.

Mo Diamé got his dream move to a big club looking to win trophies: Hull City. As luck would have it we played them next. Naturally he scored to put Hull 2–1 up. Enner Valencia had scored his first West Ham goal and Diafra Sakho secured a point for us. Diamé moaned that Allardyce had played him out of position, so every time a scout from Liverpool or Manchester United came to see him, he looked shit. That was why he ended up at Hull. No, that's not the reason, Mo.

Jack Collison showed that not all professional footballers are completely selfish toss rags, penning a 2,800-word letter to the fans to thank them for their support during his time at the club. What a guy.

Something clicked against Hull, then something really clicked as the next game against Liverpool was one of the best performances since we had returned to the Premier League. The Reds had been runners-up the previous season and had played some great stuff under Brendan Rodgers, but in the Saturday evening kick-off, West Ham were at their throats from the start and were 2–0 up inside the first ten minutes. Despite all the new signings on show it was the old guard who combined for the opener, and Downing crossed for Tomkins to head back across goal, leaving Reid to find it harder to miss than score. Reid was in imperious form and it was his interception in midfield a few minutes later that broke to Noble, who fed Sakho to float a ball over Mignolet into the net with Valencia following up for good measure. Sterling pulled one back, but maybe in hindsight, West Ham never looked like losing their grip on the game. In the dying minutes Downing passed a neat ball in to Morgan Amalfitano who stroked the ball in at the far post for 3–1.

It was a moment to savour. Since returning to the Premier League we had not really competed with the big boys, but this performance showed we could go toe-to-toe with them and come out on top. That said, the next game was also against one of the big boys. We went toe-to-toe but lost. Importantly though, we gave them a game. At Old Trafford Manchester United raced into a 2–0 lead, but Sakho scored for a third game in a row to pull one back and we were unlucky not to get a point. Indeed, Wayne Rooney's cynical foul on Stewart Downing in the second half was a measure of how twitchy Manchester United were after we scored. Rooney was quite rightly sent off, but we had them on the run. Had Kevin Nolan had a shave, his stubble might not have been offside, and we would have claimed a point. To me though, this was a sign of real improvement.

We beat a very poor QPR side (who were at this time managed by Saggy Chops) at Upton Park 2–0, with Sakho scoring again after a first-half own goal by Onuoha. At Turf Moor, the Thunderbirds were go again. The value of quality crosses was evident, as first Sakho headed in for his fifth in a row from a pin-point cross by Cresswell, then Valencia cracked in a bullet header from a cross of equal quality from the opposite flank from Jenkinson. The full-backs seemed to be the key. They were marauding forward and getting good crosses in. We had a good box-to-box man in Kouyaté, and pace and strength in Downing, Sakho and Valencia. In addition, Adrián was playing well in goal. Burnley couldn't live with us. Although they pulled one back, Carlton added a third to wrap up the points and remarkably lifted us up to 4th place in the table.

48

ALL ABOUT THAT BASS

WEST HAM UNITED 2, MANCHESTER CITY 1
PREMIER LEAGUE, 25 OCTOBER 2014
People who put their bags on the seat next to them on the train.
Then look at you like filth when you ask to sit down.

I wasn't able to get to the City game, but I had a good excuse. It was Mum's eightieth birthday party. We held the party at our flat – afternoon tea – with the occasion added to by the game being on the TV in the background, and Dad, me, my uncle Peter and nephews all being somewhat distracted by the goings on at Upton Park.

Morgan Amalfitano tapped in from a few yards out after Valencia had powered down the right and cut the ball back. Valencia ended up in row five of the Sir Trevor Brooking Lower, in among the City fans. Although we played well, City had us on the rack at times. We didn't control the game as we had against Liverpool, but we always looked like we could score. Sakho, seeking his sixth goal in as many starts, found it as Cresswell put in another great cross for Sakho to head goalwards. Joe Hart appeared to have kept the ball out but the GDS system adjudged it to have crossed the line. City pulled one back, but we held out for another famous victory.

The West Ham Way had been up for debate again. Allardyce had questioned it when he joined in June 2011. Now Alex Ferguson criticised us in his autobiography. He asked what the West Ham Way was if we had not won a trophy for 34 years, and why, every time we had played them, we had either been crap or lucky (to paraphrase). Sounded like a huge bunch of sour grapes to me.

The cost of the conversion of the Olympic Stadium was also back in the public eye, with another £35 million agreed to be paid by the LLDC to the contractors Balfour Beatty, taking the overall estimated cost to the public purse around the £600 million mark. Frankly, I found the whole thing embarrassing. I did not want to be associated with this; it was like we were stealing. But at the same time, most of the cost had been the initial construction, and what was the point of having a stadium of that size sitting there doing nothing? The other discomfort was that it felt like we were not only leaving our spiritual home but moving to somewhere that would be unpopular not just with our fans but with everyone else's too.

The win over City cemented 4th place with 16 points from 9 games. It seemed I had been a little harsh on Il Fatso. Perhaps he had been merely doing what he could with the resources available to that point. Now he had a squad to be reckoned with, he was getting results. The key seemed to be the attacking full-backs and quality crosses which had been sorely missed despite us spending a fortune on Matt Jarvis to come in and do that precise job, and Andy Carroll, who was permanently fucking injured, and only just coming back to fitness after missing the start of the season.

A point won from 2–0 down at Stoke was again down to quality crosses. This time Stewart Downing from the right teed one up, admittedly at an awkward height, for Valencia to dive waist-high to pull one back. Valencia himself then sent a ball back across the area that caused so much confusion Downing was able to score. Mark Hughes opened a new bag of lemons.

Carroll was available for home game against Aston Villa and perhaps wisely was named on the bench, with the team playing well without him, and Sakho, having missed the Stoke match, was on course to beat a Premier League record by scoring in all of his first seven starts. Villa were struggling in 16th and looked to be there for the taking, so inevitably the game ended 0–0, so Sakho did not get the record. Carroll came on and had a couple of decent chances. He was Allardyce's man, so he started the next game away at Everton.

I was trying to keep in touch with the game from a supermarket in Calais, but even from the red wine aisle I could see that Lukaku was offside for Everton's opener.

Zárate levelled just after half time and tempers flared when McCarthy went over the top on Amalfitano, which sparked a scrap involving almost every player on the pitch. McCarthy, not for the first time, was the aggressor, but both he and Reid got a booking for their trouble. McCarthy should have been sent off, but was still on the pitch when Leon Osman, playing his 400th game for Everton, scored the winner.

The next three games yielded maximum points in a quite bizarre conclusion to the opening half of the campaign. Alan Pardew's Newcastle were beaten 1–0 at Upton Park with a goal from Aaron Cresswell, West Bromwich Albion were beaten 2–1 at the Hawthorns with Carroll and Nolan on the scoresheet, then Swansea were dispatched 3–1 at Upton Park. It was remarkable: 27 points from the opening 15 games of the season, 8 wins and 3 draws. Liverpool and Manchester City were even put to the sword, and Manchester United were given a good game at Old Trafford. Sitting at 3rd place in the Premier League table, a draw at Sunderland and a home win over Leicester City only served to heighten the optimism felt by the average West Ham fan going into Christmas 2014. Then it was Chelsea away on Boxing Day. Pretty much safe already. Nothing to fear. We'd go for it, right?

49

UPTOWN FUNK

WEST HAM UNITED 2, EVERTON 2
(WEST HAM WIN 9–8 ON PENALTIES)
FA CUP THIRD ROUND REPLAY, 13 JANUARY 2015
Keyboard warriors. Trolls. Malcontents.

The win over Leicester proved to be the high-water mark of the season. Ongoing negotiations between Allardyce and the board had failed to result in the offer of a new contract and it appeared that this was having an adverse effect on Il Fatso's motivation.

The S!HT team organised another live podcast, this time with George Parris. George was a pivotal member of the 1985/86 team that finished 3rd in the old first division. Also on the bill was Olympic silver medallist and well-known West Ham fan Kriss Akabusi. A good friend of the podcast, Kriss often made an appearance, taking over the show much to the amusement of everyone involved. The next day at work, I took a break from being fair and reasonable to show my colleagues the photos from the event. A colleague Bob Wetherall told me a story about Akabusi visiting his sister-in-law's school shortly after winning his silver medal. He gave a speech then the headmaster asked if the kids had any questions. Apparently one child put her hand up and asked, 'I'd like to ask Kriss how often he masturbates.' Cue stunned silence. Cue typical hysterical laughter from Akabusi. He didn't answer the question though.

Diafra Sakho was rewarded for his fine start to his West Ham career with an improved contract, then promptly injured his back. It seemed that Allardyce, however, was not going to be rewarded for engineering such a fine start to the season.

While I had some sympathy for him, the Boxing Day game against Chelsea at Stamford Bridge illustrated to everyone what a frustrating manager Allardyce can be at times. We had a chance to really attack Chelsea. We'd had such a good start to the season, who would have flinched if we had lost 4–0 but had given it a good go?

But no, the holy grail of the clean sheet was the first priority again, and it was therefore just a matter of time before we conceded; the team was simply not set up to counter conceding a goal away from home. As soon as we conceded it became solely a matter of damage limitation. We lost 2–0 and I was furious with Allardyce.

Form took a little dip with a home defeat to Arsenal and three draws in a row over the new year. West Bromwich Albion should have been a fairly straightforward 3 points, but they had the newly appointed Tony Pulis in the stands, and with West Ham winning 1–0 at half time he was seen to jog down to the dressing room to have a word. Whatever was said appeared to work and again an Allardyce side had no answers after conceding a goal.

In the FA Cup we were winning 1–0 at Goodison through a James Collins header until the last minute when Lukaku managed to squeeze in his now mandatory goal, so we faced a replay at Upton Park that was much less than welcome given the fixture congestion around Christmas and the new year. At least that was the story put out by Premier League managers – the reality of the situation is that top flight teams have big squads full of players whose *raison d'être* is to play football. And chairmen want income through the turnstiles. They can complain as much as they want about fixture congestion, I will never believe them while they arrange friendlies as soon as they get knocked out of the cups.

It didn't help that transfer activity in the January window was limited. Possibly this was because SuGo had no intention of renewing Allardyce's contract in the summer and we had built up enough fat in the first half of the year to live off through the second half which, if we did not invest, or show confidence in the manager, would inevitably deteriorate into a bore fest.

Only two players came in: Doneil Henry, a Canadian international defender who was signed from Apollon Limassol for an undisclosed fee, then immediately went out on loan to Blackburn Rovers; and Brazilian left-winger Anderson Luiz de Carvalho, better known as Nenê, who joined as a free agent. He had scored 36 goals in 76 games for Paris Saint-Germain. None in 8 for West Ham.

Ravel Morrison was finally released from his torture, as were we. What a wasted talent that young lad was. He was linked to a move to Lazio, but as far as Allardyce was concerned it could have been Pluto. The guy was a nightmare. Zárate clearly was too creative for an Allardyce team so he was sent to QPR on loan and the saddest and most notable departure was Ricardo Vaz Tê who went to Turkey after being released. He had been an important fixture at the club and a key member of the squad that got us promoted in 2012. Possibly not a Premier League quality player, he will always be remembered for his winner at Wembley. In all he made 47 starts (14 as substitute) and scored 19 goals, although only 5 of those came in Premier League matches.

Next came another draw at Swansea. This time a belter from Andy Carroll earned a point, before the replay against Everton at Upton Park. The game is remembered as a classic, but if the truth be told the first hour or so was pretty dull. West Ham played at home in their horrible purple third kit. Maybe horrible is too strong a word – there was nothing wrong with it as such, I merely hated what it represented: commercialism of the highest order. We played at home in a purple kit. What was that about if it wasn't to sell shirts? West Ham play at home in claret and blue. End of. Stop messing with things to squeeze a few more quid out of the fan base.

Valencia scored early in the second half, but Everton came

back through a Mirallas free kick to force extra time. Everton were down to ten men, after Aiden McGeady was sent off, but Lukaku had not yet grabbed his statutory goal against West Ham, which he eventually did in extra time. It looked like the purple shirt was a bad omen. Enter, stage left, Carlton Cole. On as a substitute, he scored his last ever West Ham goal to tie the game up at 2–2 and sent it to penalties.

Everton went first. I won't go into the detail; but Naismith missed for Everton and with the scores tied at 4–4, Downing had the opportunity to win the tie, but Everton keeper Robles saved. To sudden death. Gareth Barry scored, Carlton Cole scored (make *that* his last goal for West Ham!), John Stones, Valencia and Jagielka made it 6–7. It was gut-wrenching stuff and impossible to watch, even though the prize was essentially a fourth-round trip away at Bristol City. It's not like it was the final. But Everton have special scumbag status in my eyes and we had not won in our last fifteen meetings. This was important.

Amalfitano equalised. Séamus Coleman and Carl Jenkinson made it 8–8. Each time an Everton player stepped up, it looked so easy for them. Every time a West Ham player walked up they looked terrified. It was a reflection of my own state.

Only James Tomkins of the outfield West Ham players had not taken a kick, but as Everton only had ten players the only remaining available player was goalkeeper Joel Robles. He struck his penalty goalwards, but it smashed against the bar, crashed down and came out.

Now who would take our next penalty? We only had Tomkins and Adrián left before we had to start again. Adrián stepped forward purposefully before performing one of the most iconic acts of West Ham's recent history. As he started his run up, he tore off his gloves and threw them to the ground. This was confidence of the highest order. It said: 'I won't be needing these again.'

And he didn't. Adrián Scored. West Ham won the tie 9–8 on penalties. The roof came off Upton Park and we had beaten Everton at last.

For the second time in eight years, West Ham's shirt sponsors went into administration. Alpari was a Forex trader, whatever that is, something to do with gambling on foreign exchange rates. Clearly something that looked odds-on wasn't, and all their contracts were void.

West Ham's shirts were still carrying the Alpari logo when they played Hull City at Upton Park the following Sunday. A dour goalless first half was characterised by the lumping of long balls up to Carroll, which was largely ineffective. In the second half we got the ball down and scored three times, something that must have irked Il Fatso immensely.

Diafra Sakho had missed the African Cup of Nations due to his back injury but became available again to play for West Ham before the tournament had actually finished, coming on to score the winner in the fourth round of the FA Cup at Ashton Gate. This did not go unnoticed by the Senegalese FA. However, Allardyce explained that his back was still fragile, and he was unable to fly any distance.

The fifth round paired us with West Bromwich Albion at the Hawthorns on Valentine's day, but before that we had a customary defeat at Anfield to participate in. Well, when I say participate, we were there. Well, when I say we were there; there were eleven players wearing shirts on the pitch. It was like they knew that we could not win at Anfield and therefore did not even make the effort.

Manchester United at home is always a different story, however, and as Ferguson had pointed out we were always desperate or lucky when we played them. So lucky, in fact, that they had to come from behind twice in both games played at Upton Park in 2012/13, and won by cheating in 2013/14. So, we were both desperate and lucky as Kouyaté juggled the ball on the penalty spot and swivelled to sweep the ball home just after half time and relied on a late (and I mean late) equaliser from Daley Blind to nick a draw. In the press conference, Allardyce tongue-in-cheekily criticised United for playing the long ball. Louis van Gaal failed to see the funny side and in his next conference produced a number of documents with circles and arrows on them, explaining that they were not a long ball side. Me thinks he doth protest too much.

The form in no way reflected the first half of the season. I put this down to lack of investment in the transfer window, and the fact Sam secretly knew he was leaving. I wasn't sure who to detest more over this: Allardyce for not being professional about it – after all he might have had his contract renewed if we had done well – or SuGo for dragging their heels over holding talks to renew or extend his existing deal. Or they could have bloody well got rid of the guy if they didn't like him. But it was hard to fire him after the start we'd had. In any event, give us some football we can watch. Not a turgid 0-0 at St Mary's and a 4-0 battering by West Bromwich Albion at the Hawthorns in the FA Cup. All that effort in the shootout against Everton had been for nothing. At St Mary's, Carroll hobbled out on crutches and did not play again that season, Quelle surprise. More surprising perhaps, was that Adrián's red card for denying an obvious goalscoring opportunity was rescinded on appeal.

50

LOVE ME LIKE YOU DO

TOTTENHAM HOTSPUR 2, WEST HAM UNITED 2
PREMIER LEAGUE, 22 FEBRUARY 2015
Phone calls that tell you about the accident you had.
I think I would know.

It was hard to know who cared less: the board, the manager or the players. One would have thought that even if the manager's position was in doubt, the players would have taken it upon themselves to show a modicum of effort. But this was 2015. Things did not work like that. Il Fatso knew that with his reputation and history he would land another job by August 2015 with no problem whatsoever. Players knew that whatever happened, they were likely to get another Premier League club on similar or better wages. Fans could not make such calculating choices. We were stuck with being West Ham fans. Players these days behave like naughty schoolchildren. They do what they want, when they want and engineer situations to get the coach sacked if they don't like his methods. It seemed clear that most of the players quite liked Allardyce, but he couldn't be arsed, so many of them weren't bothered either; it was a vicious circle.

I suppose it would be fair to say that I was not making a huge amount of effort myself. But then I wasn't being paid huge sums of money to represent the club. I still had not taken a season ticket, picking and choosing my games as I felt like it. It was partly my choice because of the style of football (September to December 2014 excepted) that we had been witnessing. Something was nagging away in the back of my mind though, that the final season at the Boleyn, regardless of who was in charge, I would not want to miss out.

As was often the case, we made a bit of effort at White Hart Lane, much to Tottenham's chagrin. We went 2–0 up through Kouyaté and Sakho, the latter scoring from an impossible angle. We were still leading 2–1 with ninety minutes on the clock when Tottenham were awarded a penalty after Song inexplicably placed his hands on Harry Kane who went down like he had slipped on his own drool.

Time was well up by the time the ball was placed on the penalty spot, and Adrián saved the kick. As the time had only been extended to allow the penalty to be taken, that should have been the end of the game, but referee Moss allowed Kane the opportunity to bundle in the rebound.

From that point the season descended into farce. The first nineteen games had yielded 31 points and saw us sitting in 6th position just before Christmas, and as high as 3rd in early December. The second half of the season yielded a mere 16 points and saw us crash down to 12th.

Crystal Palace beat us 3–1 at Upton Park and Chelsea also beat us 1–0 at home (though it has to be said Hazard was fortunate not to be given offside). But again, no plan B after going behind. Arsenal rolled us over 0–3 at the Emirates before we sneaked past Sunderland 1–0 with a goal from Sakho. Leicester City started their incredible run that saw them escape relegation. When they played us they were in bottom position with 19 points. They somehow managed to win 7 of their last 9 games, taking 22 points in total from a possible 27 to finish the season safe in 14th place. West Ham, of course, gifted them that start.

Aaron Cresswell scored a great free kick at home to Stoke, but it was only enough for a point. Manchester City beat us 2–0 at the Etihad. I met up with Stuart the QPR fan for the trip to Loftus Road, witnessing another drab affair, and though we did our best to gift the opposition a lifeline, Charlie Austin fluffed his lines, failing to convert from the penalty spot. QPR were destined for relegation.

The season wound down with a win over another team doomed for relegation: Burnley. That match was harder work than it should have been, with a Noble penalty being the only difference, then Aston Villa beat us 1–0 at Villa Park. Everton were not so much a bogey team as a bucket of snot team – coming from behind to win at Upton Park with Lukaku scoring again – and finally Newcastle United, who needed a win to be sure of staying up, could not have wished to play a more obliging team on the final day.

Normally a manager would be looking to plan for the next season, knowing that he had time on his contract. Clearly you cannot legislate for getting the sack, but while the first half of the season made it impossible for SuGo to sack Allardyce, in the back of their minds they clearly felt there was a better man for the job, as did the majority of fans. But the way the whole thing was handled meant that from being in a position to break our record points haul for a Premier League season, we plummeted to 12th position and finished the season with a whimper.

At least the podcast finished the season on a high, with a live recording featuring legendary goalkeeper Phil Parkes. I had become friends with Phil's daughter Marie and asked her if Phil would be willing to take part. Between us we arranged it and had a great evening, firstly taking about modern issues, then, much more enjoyably, wallowing in the good old days. It's where I wanted to be. As the question-and-answer session drew to a close I raised my hand and asked host Phil Whelans if I could approach the desk to say something on the microphone. I explained how I had seen Billy Bonds in Bromley a few weeks before and explained to Elaine that the man over there was one of West Ham's greatest ever players. Her reaction was to tell me to go and get a selfie with him. But I knew how private a man Billy is, and didn't want to disturb him. I explained to Phil Parkes that I regretted it afterwards, and all I had really wanted to do was to go and tell him 'thank you.'

Thank you for being a club legend. Thank you for all those hours of pleasure watching you from the North Bank in my youth. Thank you for being the manager who brought us into to the Premier League. Thank you for being our record appearance holder. Thank you for lifting the FA Cup twice. No selfie. No autograph, just thank you.

Now I may never get the opportunity again, so I wanted to be sure that I thanked Phil Parkes for being the greatest goalkeeper ever to represent us. After the season we had endured, with players and manager taking a largely laissez-faire attitude, it was refreshing to spend time in the company of people like Phil Parkes. I really hope I meet Bonzo sometime soon, so I can thank him as I had intended.

No sooner had the whistle gone on the final game of the season at Newcastle than an official announcement was made that Il Fatso's contract was not being renewed. Another embarrassing situation, badly handled. It was mixed emotions for me as I never wanted him to come in the first place. He systematically disrespected the traditions of the club and made himself wholly unpopular. He played a negative style of football designed to keep a clean sheet but had no plan B when the opposition scored. He boasted and bragged about his achievements. He was never a West Ham man. That said, I appreciated, by whatever fine margin, that he did get us promoted at the first attempt. He did keep us in the Premier League for three seasons. He did all that was asked of him, and it was not part of his brief to be liked.

The search for a new manager started. Sullivan told the club website:

> I am dedicating every waking minute to recruiting the best available manager to drive our club forwards … What is clear from our discussions so far is that this job is attracting names it wouldn't have done five years ago.
>
> When you combine our move to one of the best stadiums in Europe in 16 months' time with the Board's ambitious vision and significant transfer budget you have an extremely exciting prospect for the right man.
>
> I want to appoint a manager you all feel excited by and one

that will honour the Club's traditions and history. With your support, an ambitious manager and the Board's drive and commitment I can see the next few years being game-changing for our Club.

Coincidentally, Slaven Bilić had just been sacked as manager of Beşiktaş in Turkey. Contrary to Sullivan's statement, the same names continued to be linked to the role: David Moyes, Rafa Benítez, etc. It was as if SuGo were obsessed with playing bland, banal football, and far from looking to honour traditions, they were stripping our identity piece by piece until there was nothing left, to finally, after giving the club a full lobotomy, transplant us into the Olympic Stadium after we had been bullied and beaten so much that we would not object.

At the end of May, Carlton finally left West Ham, by my estimation, for the third time. Good old Carlton, I loved him. I don't think anyone would deny he had limited ability, but he was wholehearted, and to us, sometimes that means more. I don't think some people will ever understand that. He would not have played as many games and scored as many goals if he was rubbish. Carlton made 182 starts for West Ham and 111 sub appearances (a total of 293 appearances), and scored 68 goals. That put him second in the list of Premier League appearances behind Mark Noble. I would miss his steaming head when being interviewed on a cold winter's night.

51

WANT TO WANT ME

WEST HAM UNITED 3, FC LUSITANS 0
EUROPA LEAGUE QUALIFYING FIRST ROUND, 2 JULY 2015
Snapback baseball caps. They look really shit.

So Slaven Bilić was the man chosen to replace Allardyce. He was appointed on 9 June 2015. This went some way to pacifying me, and was proof that SuGo did actually have the traditions of the club at heart in appointing a former player, and a popular former player at that, as manager.

On the whole I was happy with the selection, but there were two things that bothered me. Firstly, I recall interviewing Bilić for the fanzine outside Roker Park in 1996 when there were rumours of a possible move to Tottenham. He stuttered his way through the interview saying he was happy at West Ham, but he had a family and had to think of the future, neither confirming nor denying anything. The second thing was the 1998 World Cup incident that got Laurent Blanc sent off and suspended for the final. It did not sit easy with me. I have a long memory for stuff like that.

In the end, you could not reasonably call Bilić a West Ham legend. He had always been up front about the fact that he would probably move on, and in the end it was Everton who came calling, but Bilić allegedly insisted on staying to the end on the 1996/97 campaign to ensure our safety. The extent to which that was a noble gesture is questionable, given that he played in the team that got us into a mess in the first place. Whether he was a West Ham legend or not, he had a history with the club, which none of the previous three managers had. That was going to be an important factor during the final season at the Boleyn.

Darren Randolph, the Republic of Ireland international goal-keeper, joined from Birmingham City, and Spanish midfielder Pedro Obiang signed from Sampdoria.

Young Norwegian midfielder Martin Samuelsen came from Manchester City, but the key signing arrived on 26 June, when France international Dimitri Payet signed from Marseille on a five-year deal valued at around €10 million. Just as Carroll had been Allardyce's man, it seemed Payet was Bilić's man; he had said right from the start this was who he wanted and to their credit, the board went out and got him. I had to admit I had never heard of him, but then I hadn't heard of half our signings. It was a far cry from the days of there being just one or maybe two signings at the close of the season, probably from Scotland or the lower leagues, and generally, names you would have heard of.

Four time hammer of the year Julian Dicks was also a major summer signing, coming in as part of the coaching staff.

So Bilić had set out his stall, and he had to do it quickly. Il Fatso's legacy had been qualification for the Europa League via the fair play system, which meant we had to play in the first qualifying round on the ridiculously early date of 2 July.

Shortly after my birthday on 22 June, Elaine's father was taken ill so she went out to Brazil to help her sister and her mother look after him. It did not look good. I expected her to be out there for a while, but the difference this time was that she had a visa and the legal right to return – as long as she did not stay out of the country for more than ninety days.

I missed her, of course, but I knew she was away because her dad was very poorly and in hospital. I called twice daily to get updates, but had one eye on the calendar to make sure her visa did not expire. I had read a story of a British man married to a Japanese woman for twenty years, and she had permanent leave to remain in the UK, but not a British passport. She went home to tend to her sick mother but it took months. When her mother eventually died she was denied entry back to the UK as her 'permanent' leave had expired. You think we give foreigners too many rights? Not all of them. In fact, those who deserve these basic rights are often denied because of the shitstorm stirred up by racists who complain about foreigners coming here and taking our jobs. Ill-informed nonsense. The exact same folk who are happy to cheer on Croatian Slaven Bilić, Frenchman Payet and Senegalese Sakho and Kouyaté.

The problems surrounding the internet, mainly involving brainless wankers taking things to ridiculous extremes, had doomed the STOP! Hammer Time Facebook page since it hit 4,000 members. It seemed the site was now just a permanent bitch-fest and was not a pleasant place to be. As a result, three of the original members of the S!HT page, Jacqui Hughes, Matt Liston and James McFadyen, got their heads together and created a page called Upton Parklife, which was membership by nomination only. That way, there was a chance of keeping tossers at arm's length, and it seemed to work. It was the place to be. Plenty of good-humoured banter without a hint of trolling. Anything that even resembled that was quickly stamped on.

We had a Friday music night where people posted their favourite songs on a nominated subject. It was a place where the internet-weary could seek comfort and solace. I am proud of my contribution to the new page. I started something called 'Almost West Ham'. I travelled home on the bus through Lewisham, where there was a shop called 'Sakhi Fabrics', a café called 'Kem's', and a restaurant called 'Tompkins'. All nearly West Ham players' names (Kem's being almost the late Ken's café of Green Street), but not quite. I posted pictures and soon everyone started positing pictures of things they had seen with crossed hammers, players' names, or painted claret and blue. It is still going on now.

I had swallowed my pride and got down on my knees in the ticket office, asking for a season ticket for the 2015/16 season, calling in the offer that had been made to me in May 2013 after much wringing of hands. Dad was now well beyond the stage where he wanted to come, but I was able to take a seat in the Bobby Moore Upper, row P, seat 17.

On July 2 I met with Jacqui Hughes, Jim Grant and actor Phil Nice (who was also a good friend of the podcast) at the Black Lion in Plaistow for a few pre-match beers on a warm July evening before taking my new seat and introducing myself to my new neighbour Gavin, who would share the ups and downs of 2015/16 with me. Fortunately, Gavin was a great guy, and we immediately hit it off – I was on my own with a solitary ticket for the first time since 1990. It was good to make a friend right away.

A quite bizarre scenario saw Upton Park crammed to the rafters on 2 July for a European qualifier against a tiny team from Andorra. There were two reasons for this. The arrival of Slaven Bilić, and the fact that it could be the last European tie at the Boleyn.

The new Umbro kit looked smart. It was a balmy evening, we won 3–0. It was going to be a good season. The return leg in Andorra finished 1–0 to West Ham thanks to a goal from Elliot Lee.

That set us up for a second-round qualifying tie against Birkirkara FC of Malta. This was not quite so straightforward, although by rights it should have been. The first leg at Upton Park ended 1–0 thanks to a last-gasp James Tomkins goal, and we lost the away leg by the same score, which meant the tie went to penalties. I had subscribed to Premier Sports, who had a special deal of showing the Birkirkara tie live on a three-month trial. We won the shootout, but it was closer than it should have been. The third qualifying round saw us up against FC Astra Giurgiu of Romania. This looked like a proper European tie against decent opposition. At 2–0 up in the first leg we looked home and dry. But James Collins was sent off and we collapsed, conceding two away goals to draw the tie 2–2. If felt like a defeat.

In the midst of all the Europa League activity the small matter of the transfer window remained. As well as Carlton, who went to Celtic, Guy Demel, Jussi Jääskeläinen, Nenê and Dan Potts were all released. Matt Jarvis went on loan to Norwich to see if he could not put in any crosses there instead. After a falling out with Bilić, Morgan Amalfitano was packed off to Lille.

We signed centre-back Angelo Ogbonna from Juventus for €11 million, and Carl Jenkinson and Alex Song extended their loans for another season. Stewart Downing returned to his hometown club of Middlesbrough for £5 million. Raw talent Michail Antonio signed from Nottingham Forest for around £7 million, Nikica Jelavić from Hull for £3 million and Victor Moses on a season-long loan from Chelsea.

Young Argentinian midfielder Manuel Lanzini joined from UAE side Al Jazira on a year-long loan. Known as 'the Jewel', Lanzini was formerly of River Plate and came with a glowing reputation, but if he was so great why was he playing in the UAE?

We did not complain when he opened the scoring in the second leg to give West Ham the lead on aggregate and an away goal of our own. But there the good news ended. Astra Giurgiu scored twice to win the tie 2–1, thanks to Bilić having played a largely weakened side with one eye on the Premier League campaign which started that weekend.

Elaine's dad made a remarkable recovery. It had not looked good and she and her sister had taken turns to camp by his hospital bed, waiting for what appeared to be inevitable. Indeed, at one stage a nurse had unplugged his machine and was wheeling him off down to the mortuary in anticipation. But Senhor Iran was made of sterner stuff, and within a few days he was up and about, jumping around like a toddler. Elaine was able to come home.

52

DON'T BE SO HARD ON YOURSELF

LIVERPOOL 0, WEST HAM UNITED 3
PREMIER LEAGUE, 29 AUGUST 2015

*Carling, Heineken, Carlsberg. What is the point? Might as well have a
glass of water. On the other hand, I can't stand poncey perfumed beer
they will only let you have in two-thirds of a pint because it tastes so
horrible. Just give me a pint of IPA.*

The Premier League season started away at Arsenal on a gloriously sunny day. The performances under Bilić in the Europe
League qualifiers had not filled me with sufficient confidence
to make me think we might have a chance of a good result,
but I was not worried; we had winnable home games against
Leicester and newly promoted Bournemouth to follow. Then it
was Liverpool away after that, so I set my expectation level at 6
points from the opening 4 games.

The Europa League matches had been a struggle. But pre-
season was encouraging, with Payet looking like real class. But
I had seen enough pre-seasons – this was my fortieth – to know
that it was no indication of how the season was going to go.

Petr Čech made his debut in goal for Arsenal and was caught
in no-man's land as Payet floated in a perfectly flighted free kick.
Čech didn't know whether to stick or twist and before he could
decide, Kouyaté had headed the ball in for 1–0. He was similarly embarrassed in the second half when a Zárate shot from
outside the box found its way past him, but to be honest, we
could have played another ninety minutes and Arsenal would
not have scored. It was our day.

To say I went to work with my chest puffed out with pride

was an understatement. If this was what we had to look forward to then bring it on. We made Arsenal look second rate – and on their own turf. Payet ran the show, Kouyaté looked strong in midfield, Noble mopped up everything and his distribution seemed to have improved. The young Reece Oxford even had Mesut Özil in his pocket.

I met up with the S!HT crowd at the Black Lion the following Saturday full of confidence. Despite their strong finish to last season, surely Leicester were there for the taking? How many years did I say I had been supporting West Ham? Forty, was it? Should I have known better than to go into a game full of confidence? Almost certainly.

Leicester tore us a new one in the first half and went in at the break 2–0 up. They had won their opening game against Sunderland and looked really good. This Algerian fella Leicester had, what was his name? Mahrez? Where the hell had he come from? Well, Algeria, I suppose. Leicester taught us a lesson in the first half, but in the second we looked much better. Payet pulled one back and we should have had a penalty, but Leicester held on. In the final minute, Adrián came up for a corner. We lost possession and in an attempt to retrieve the ball he put six fresh stud marks in Jamie Vardy's chest. It was clearly an accident, but referee Taylor had little option but to send him off. It wasn't a disaster, but it wasn't far off.

I made a note to be less smug for the visit of Bournemouth, but it seemed to make no difference. Bournemouth raced into a 2–0 lead just as Leicester had a week before. Injuries to Carroll, Valencia, and Zárate meant that Kevin Nolan was pushed forward into a more advanced role supporting Diafra Sakho. That clearly wasn't working as he was replaced by Matt Jarvis at half time. Ogbonna was having a complete nightmare and was replaced by Tomkins after thirty-five minutes. It seemed to be one step forward and two steps back. Cresswell made a heinous error, allowing Callum Wilson to score Bournemouth's second.

We got it back to 2–2, with Noble winning a penalty that he converted himself, then Kouyaté firing in from close range, but

Bournemouth were like an elastic band stretched to the limit, and it was only a matter of time before they would ping up the other end and score again, which they did. After that, Jenkinson got sent off, giving away a penalty for the fourth. That made it 5 red cards in 9 competitive games under Bilić, and I had to wonder if it had been such a great idea to bring Julian Dicks in as a coach.

Maïga, back from his loan spell in France, slotted in a third, but we looked unlikely to take anything from the game. Poor old Darren Randolph in goal had conceded 8 for Birmingham in the Championship the last time he had played against Bournemouth. I bet this has left him with an irrational hatred of Bournemouth. Thank god we had taken 3 points from Arsenal because the two home-bankers had yielded nothing. We had shown good signs upfront, but defensively we were a shambles. How many would it be at Anfield?

The answer to that question was 3. But for West Ham! I had sulked at home that day, studiously avoiding the score, worried that it might run to double figures. Eventually I cracked, as I always do, and did a double take when I saw were 2–0 up. This was a big deal indeed. It was like a British man winning Wimbledon. It was like England winning the World Cup. It was something that had last happened so long ago the majority of the fans that witnessed it this time around would not have been born the last time it happened. To put things in perspective, the last time West Ham won at Anfield, the Beatles were at number one with 'She Loves You', the average house price was £3,160, a brand-new Ford Cortina would set you back £675 and you could fill it with four-star petrol for five bob a gallon (that's just over five new pence per litre for all you teenagers). In other words, it was a fucking long time ago.

The thing was, we didn't just win at Anfield, we tore them apart. The 52-year wait seemed to make the final outcome all the more conclusive. Lanzini converted a Cresswell cross, then picked Lovren's pocket on the right wing to put in a cross for Noble to score. Liverpool had been reduced to ten men after

Coutinho's foul on Payet earned him a second yellow, but any Liverpool side with seven men would normally be able to see us off at Anfield. Parity was restored when Noble was also dismissed for a second yellow. He clearly got the ball, but as it was a second yellow the decision could not be appealed.

Sakho added a late third to put an extra layer of shine on a result that was already polished like a brand-new Ferrari.

This was not just a win. This was something we had been waiting for since Charlie had the measles, as my dad would have said. For those of us of a certain age it was potentially the start of a new future, one where we played away from home at the big clubs without fear. Or it could be a blip. It was probably a blip.

See, I told you we would get 6 points from the opening 4 games.

53

WHAT DO YOU MEAN?

WEST HAM UNITED 2, CHELSEA 1
PREMIER LEAGUE, 24 OCTOBER 2015

People who park in the street outside my house. They may be perfectly entitled to do so but I really hate it. Especially that tosser from number 35.

Payet was proving to be a real find. Except he wasn't really a find, Bilić had been on his case for some time and he was an exceptional talent. As with most exceptional talents he tended to be a bit moody and unreliable, but so far so good. Against Newcastle he scored both goals to give us our first home win of the campaign, putting us on 9 points from five matches. It was such a shame we had messed up so royally in games we could have won. But that was the West Ham Way. It looked like Bilić would fit the bill perfectly.

Another blip at the Etihad. Victor Moses fired in a long shot that England keeper Joe Hart failed to get down to, low to his left. Who knew? Sakho added a scrappy second, but we were not complaining. De Bruyne pulled one back before half time and it looked like it would be backs to the wall in the second half, but we held on, not so much through discipline and keeping our shape, but by causing City more headaches than they caused us.

After winning at Arsenal, Liverpool and Manchester City it was disappointing to go out of the League Cup at the first hurdle away at Leicester. Leicester, for god's sake. What were they ever going to achieve?

The need to get back on the property ladder had been nagging away for some time. Since leaving Bradford I had been renting for five years, effectively pumping £12,000 a year down the drain with no appreciating asset. As soon as the house in Bradford had crept back up to the value I needed to clear my debts, I sold it. Mum and Dad were struggling to sell their first-floor maisonette in Shirley, near Croydon. They were desperate to move to a ground-floor flat and had found the perfect place. They stood to lose it if they did not sell quickly. My brother-in-law Alan had a light-bulb moment, and I bought their flat. As West Ham drew 2–2 with Norwich at Upton Park, twice coming from behind, I was ferrying our possessions as best as possible in a rented van, but it was no good, we had accumulated so much stuff we had to hire a professional removal firm. It had taken me six trips just to move all our pot plants. Rock and roll.

Another 2–2 draw at Sunderland, again coming from behind. Struggling Sunderland were shortly to part company with boss Dick Advocaat (the football manager with the funniest name ever?). Sunderland's form had been snowballing, but they could easily have been 4–0 up instead of by just the 2 when Jenkinson stole into the box unattended to convert a Moses cross for 2–1 immediately before the break. Jermaine Lens, having scored a magnificent goal to put Sunderland 2 up, then got himself sent off and suddenly West Ham took the initiative. Lanzini was in acres of space to get a shot away that the keeper could only parry to the feet of Payet who made no mistake. We could have won, but that would have been greedy.

I went off to Brazil for a holiday with Elaine, who was still anxious about her dad. We arrived just in time to watch online as we won 3–1 at Crystal Palace. Jenkinson again showed his worth going forward, putting us in front before Dwight Gayle won a penalty for Palace before getting sent off. Red cards were a prominent feature of our games that season. Two late goals sealed it. Zárate chipped in a perfect cross for Carroll to head down and Lanzini couldn't miss. Payet rounded it off with a lovely chip right at the death.

This was great to watch. The likes of Zárate being given a run in the team, and Lanzini and Payet all brought new dimensions.

Payet's passing was something else. Most players can find a colleague with a pass. But often it's a pass straight to their feet. It does nothing for the move other than to retain possession. Payet passed the ball into space for players to run on to. He passed the ball at a slightly different angle so that defenders didn't read it. And he scored goals. He wasn't especially quick, but he had a lightning-fast brain. I loved him.

The home game against Chelsea was being shown live on Fox Sports in Brazil so I was able to watch the full ninety minutes, beer in hand. Senhor Iran insisted that I use his recliner, and who was I to contradict my father-in-law? Zárate scored with a low shot in the first half and Chelsea had Matić sent off for two bookable offences. Fabregas thought he had scored, but there was still 0.5mm of the ball that had not crossed the line. Hard cheese, Cesc, better luck next time mate.

José Mourinho's protests earned him a space in the stands surrounded by West Ham fans, who made him feel very welcome, especially when Andy Carroll came on as a substitute and scored the winner on 79 minutes. The place went mental. By which I mean Elaine's parents' front room. I believe it was quite brisk at Upton Park too, as we held on for 3 points to take the total for the season to 20, good enough for 3rd place in the table.

A mix-up with flights meant I ended up coming home twenty-four hours before Elaine, but I was at the airport long enough to see that we lost 2–0 at Watford. This was inexplicable after the last few performances. Bad day at the office, move on.

In the time it took between me landing at Heathrow and Elaine finally arriving she had agreed with our friends Orlando and Fabiano that we should go to Austria for the weekend of 22 November – and Fabiano had booked the tickets. But it was Tottenham away! Meh.

I was back working at the Ombudsman Service and was able to make up some of the time I had lost by going on holiday by working on Saturdays, so I did that on the day of the Everton match before driving to Plaistow and parking up by the Black Lion to meet the usual suspects for a pint before the game.

Manuel Lanzini curled a superb shot into the top corner, that postage-stamp-sized space that the goalkeeper cannot reach, but playing against Everton we always needed at least 2 goals to allow for Lukaku. He equalised, and James McCarthy cynically clattered into Dimitri Payet. Roberto Martínez had a reputation for playing attacking football, but at times it was attacking in the literal sense. Payet was targeted from the start and had already been kicked up in the air several times by the time McCarthy put in the crunching scissors challenge that eventually forced him to withdraw early in the second half. My love for Payet had grown game by game, but on this occasion in particular, before he got chopped in half by McCarthy, he did a little drag back in the centre circle and nutmegged Ross Barkley with such cheek I nearly peed my pants.

We had to settle for a point and would be without Payet until the New Year. It would be a real test to see how we would cope without him. We had already seen how the team struggled after his departure in the Everton game. I hoped that we would not prove to be a one-man team.

54

LOVE YOURSELF

WEST HAM UNITED 2, SOUTHAMPTON 1
PREMIER LEAGUE, 28 DECEMBER 2015
Mrs Brown's Boys. *People actually enjoy that mindless pap?*

I found myself in Salzburg, Austria in a beautiful winter wonderland as we kicked off against Tottenham at White Hart Lane. It seemed that without Payet we were not all that. We were beaten 4–1 in a game that was a throwback to the darkest days of Il Fatso. Carroll was isolated on his own up front, hardly getting a kick. Still, at least he was playing.

Without Payet it would have been easy for form to fall through the floor, but we managed to avoid defeat in the next five games. Unfortunately we also managed to avoid victory, drawing all five. West Bromwich Albion at home was a struggle, and although Zárate scored with a spectacular free kick, that was to be the only highlight. Three goalless draws followed. Not sure if that had ever happened before. Away at Old Trafford we were unfortunate. Louis van Gaal was not proving universally popular with the home crowd, who booed loudly and headed for the exits well before the end, seemingly resigned to the fact that their heroes would not score.

Against Stoke at home, Antonio made his first start, huffing and puffing without reward. Away at Swansea we looked similarly bereft of ideas without Payet pulling the strings. I checked on his progress daily.

On Boxing Day we drew the fifth game in a row against an already seemingly doomed Aston Villa side with only 7 points to their name from a possible 51. It looked like it might be 7 from

325

54 when Aaron Cresswell planted a firm shot in the bottom corner, but Villa earned a penalty to equalise and we again seemed unable to find the angles to make life uncomfortable for them.

So, from being third after beating Chelsea on 24 October (despite only losing two games since then), we went into the game at home to Southampton having slipped to 10th on 26 points and only 9 points above the drop zone. Mind you, we still had a very pleasant view looking down on Chelsea in 15th.

I was concerned now – a win was vital against Southampton to avoid getting sucked into a relegation scrap. The table was so compressed it could easily happen.

The signs were not great as Southampton took a first-half lead, but Antonio equalised with an unorthodox goal, and Carroll came on to perform his party piece, scoring the winner from the bench.

Although we hadn't lost since the Tottenham game five weeks earlier, we hadn't won either, and the relief was palpable. More of a relief was that Payet's recovery was ahead of schedule, and it looked like he would play some part in the game against Liverpool at Upton Park on 2 January.

It was now getting very real. Every home game was a final something. Final game at Upton Park against Southampton. Final league game at home against Liverpool. Final New Year bank holiday fixture. Having been fairly ambivalent about the move, my emotions were starting to rise with each passing game.

Payet started on the bench for the Liverpool game. Such was our energy and commitment that the first goal came from a move finished by Antonio, which he had started himself on his own goal line. Within seconds the ball was up the field and in the net. Payet came on and suddenly the engine was purring again. A delightful flick in the centre circle got everyone up off their seats if they weren't already standing. This was what we had been missing.

Carroll scored a second and West Ham completed a league double over Liverpool for the first time in fifty-two years, having beaten them 1–0 at Upton Park in January 1964, the same season in which we last won at Anfield.

In the FA Cup we drew Wolverhampton Wanderers at home and I had tickets in the East Upper. Although I had my season ticket in the Bobby Moore, I had wanted to sit in as many different parts of the ground as possible for the final season at the Boleyn. So this was another last. My last game in the East Stand. Elaine came with me, and we were also sat with my nephews and their girlfriends. We had to sit and lean forward as the old TV gantry blocked our view if you sat upright. Also, from that seat, you could not see any of the Bobby Moore Upper of the West Stand Upper. But it had to be done.

We gained some revenge for the 4–3 defeat at home to Bournemouth by winning 3–1 at the Vitality Stadium, or Dean Court, to you and me. Enner Valencia bagged his first goals of the season and Payet the third in a comprehensive win, which was as good as our defeat at Newcastle in the next match was bad. The occasional rubbish performance away from home in a season that had produced so many great performances already was inexplicable. But it was the West Ham Way. Bilić understood that better than any manager since Bonzo. Even Curbishley didn't really understand it, and tried to strangle the life out of the team. Bilić got it by the bucket load, and for that reason, was quickly becoming a god and he was therefore excused the off-day at St James's Park.

The home game against Manchester City was switched to the Saturday evening for TV. Under the lights, Valencia sparkled again and grabbed another brace: first scoring after just 53 seconds, then reacting to a quickly taken throw-in to put us back into the lead. Drawing 2–2 at home to the champions was no disgrace, but with us having won at their place earlier in the season, expectations were at another level. By the time we played Liverpool at Anfield in the fourth round of the cup we were justified in believing we could win – and we nearly did, going a third game without conceding to Liverpool, but this time earning a replay. Maybe the last FA Cup replay at Upton Park?

Aston Villa's miserable run towards relegation continued at Upton Park with a 2–0 defeat to a less-than-inspired West Ham. We didn't have to be all that inspired to beat that Villa team to be fair; they were shocking.

Another inexplicable away day at Southampton ended in a 1–0 defeat before Liverpool came back for the fourth-round replay at Upton Park. I had been vending my personal services, so to speak, between Barclays and the Ombudsman Service since 2009, with only that brief break in 2013. The all-too-frequent call into a meeting with the project manager meant that contractors were being let go. I wasn't one of them, but it set alarm bells ringing and I was back on the phone to Barclays. By 8 February I had returned on a free transfer.

In the other transfer window, the only significant acquisitions were Sam Byram, a young full-back drafted in from Leeds United as Carl Jenkinson had to return to Arsenal with a long-term injury, and Emmanuel Emenike, a Nigerian international striker on loan from Fenerbahçe until the end of the season. Zárate had finally had enough, and went off to Fiorentina for £1.6 million.

I savoured the moments before the Liverpool replay, taking the time to walk around the Green Street junction with Barking Road and take pictures, knowing that the number of remaining nights like this was limited. Certainly nights containing such drama would be in short supply. West Ham took the lead through an acrobatic volley from Antonio, but Coutinho equalised with a free kick that bizarrely went under the defensive wall, and beating Darren Randolph, who was the chosen goalkeeper for FA Cup matches.

The game ebbed and flowed into extra time and looked like it was heading for a penalty shootout until in the final minute of extra time, Angelo Ogbonna's head was found by a cross from Payet and Upton Park went wild as the ball hit the back of the net. When I got home and watched the highlights, the commentator pronounced Ogbonna's name 'Ogboner'. I still chuckle at that.

Given the long gap between the original tie and the replay, we only had to wait twelve days for the fifth-round tie at Blackburn. In between, we again showed our powers of recovery away at Norwich, coming from 2–0 down to draw 2–2 again. This was alright up to a point, but there were days when the powers of recovery were not so strong. It would be nice not to be 2–0 down in the first place.

This is the conundrum faced by any manager of West Ham United. As fans, we demand entertaining football. But we can't afford to lose too many games either. A cavalier attitude is fine, but these days there has to also be an element of pragmatism – and it is slowly killing the game.

Blackburn away was one of the performances of the season. Nearly 7,000 Hammers fans had made the trip and created a fantastic cup-tie atmosphere. It wasn't looking good when Rovers went 1–0 up, but by half time Victor Moses and a Payet free kick gave us a 2–1 lead. Rovers had Taylor sent off and the game opened up even more. Kouyaté was also sent off, harshly, for clipping the heels of Adam Henley in between a brace for Emenike. The decision was harsh, and was later rescinded on appeal. Payet rounded things off in added time with a quite superb goal. Picking the ball up on half way, beating his man with a turn, he didn't so much beat the rest of the defenders in his path, as simply run away from them before slotting the ball home.

The joy of winning 5–1 was tempered somewhat by the news that our quarter-final opponents would be Manchester United at Old Trafford, but on current form, and with Payet in the team, anything could happen.

Il Fatso was now managing Sunderland, dragging them from the brink of relegation to the brink of survival. Apart from the fact that they were playing in green and yellow, they looked like any of the West Ham teams he had set up away from home – with little idea what to do after going behind. Antonio was proving to be a real find, and it was his goal that the proved the difference in a 1–0 win in bleak, blustery Saturday morning conditions.

I was desperate to get a ticket for the quarter final at Old Trafford, and spent the morning of the Sunderland game on the internet waiting for tickets to become available. Eventually I had success. I had a feeling in my gut we were going to win. But it could have just been last night's curry.

In midweek we put a significant spoke in Tottenham's title-charge wheel, beating them 1–0 at Upton Park, with Antonio scoring the winner. Leicester City had unexpectedly hit the front. Everyone assumed they would fold at some point, but they hadn't. They just kept on winning. It was a story that gave us all hope. Leicester's cause was helped by the fact that only Tottenham were applying any serious pressure to them. Both Manchester clubs tripped up on a regular basis and Chelsea, having got rid of Mourinho, still languished in the bottom half of the table, while Arsenal's ambitions were yet again set no higher than fourth.

All of which meant that if we could string some results together we stood a chance of qualifying for the Champions League. Ridiculous as it sounded, the ten-point pledge was starting to make sense. After the Tottenham game on 2 March we sat in 6th place on 46 points, just 1 point behind Manchester City in 4th, but having played one game more. Manchester United in 5th also had one more point than us. To be rubbing shoulders with these giants had been unthinkable a couple of years ago. Was it that the ten-point pledge was going well? Would the move to the Olympic Stadium attract bigger names and push us to the higher level? Or was it just that Dimitri Payet was playing out of his skin and carrying the team through some shoddy defensive performances?

55

7 YEARS

WEST HAM UNITED 1, MANCHESTER UNITED 2
FA CUP SIXTH ROUND REPLAY, 13 APRIL 2016
Cyclists bombing through the Greenwich foot tunnel at full
pelt despite the 'Cyclists Please Dismount' signs.
What makes you above the law, you helmets?

Before the game at Goodison Park I had been directed to some Everton fan forum pages on the internet and was shocked by what I saw. There were Everton fans openly advocating targeting Payet and suggesting that not only should he be taken out of the game again, but he should have his leg broken.

There are some horrible people in the world. There are some particularly horrible people who follow football and some pretty nasty types who have mastered the art of using a keyboard. All three seemed to have combined in this message board, and left me feeling physically sick.

Sometimes you want to take a screen shot and send it to the manager or the players and say, 'Look! This is what they are saying, this should motivate you!', but unless you had Slaven's mobile number, how would you even start? Twitter has made things a lot easier of course – there is now a way of contacting players directly with your thoughts, even if it is highly unlikely that they administer or even read their pages themselves.

Clearly no one had sent them the screenshot as Lukaku got his contractual obligation out of the way early, on 13 minutes. Kevin Mirallas was sent off before half time, but that didn't stop Aaron Lennon making it 2–0 on 56 minutes. Lukaku had a golden opportunity to kill the match off with a penalty, but he struck it tamely. We were wretched. By the time Antonio pulled one back on 78 minutes it looked like too little, too late. What could we do in the remaining 12 minutes? It is often said that 2–0 is a difficult lead in football. It seems like a stupid thing to say, but there is some sense to it. Often, 2–0 leads are over-turned. And this is because it is in that zone where one goal gives the other team momentum, and makes you look over your shoulder and doubt yourself. That is exactly what happened to Everton, and it couldn't have happened to a nicer bunch. Sakho equalised three minutes after Antonio's first and we would have taken it. It was the fourth time we had levelled from 0–2 down that season. But we had never, as yet, gone on to win. That was all about to change as Payet found himself in the six-yard area in the last minute to bag a win that as little as fifteen minutes before had seemed impossible.

I had to pinch myself. These things did not happen to West Ham. They happened to other teams playing against us – not to us. I loved it. It was particularly sweet that Payet should score the winner given the abuse being levelled at him on the Everton forums pre-match. One might almost say it was karma. Instant karma.

With that result still fresh in our minds we headed to Old Trafford in a buoyant mood. For the first time in a long time we headed into a sixth-round tie ahead of Manchester United in the table by 2 clear points, but having played a game more, and only 1 point behind City in 4th.

But this was the cup, so league form was merely an indica-tion of what might happen. It was a season of things happening for the first time in a long time. We beat Liverpool at Anfield, we went into March ahead of Manchester United in the league and I travelled to an away game on one of the club coaches.

After years of making my own way to games and enjoying the flexibility it afforded us, it was nice to be able to sit back and relax, and let someone else do it all. We arrived in good time, and as Colin Milne was on a different coach, we met up in the Old Trafford car park to find the rest of the S!HT crew in good voice at the Matchstick Man pub just a short walk away. I could not believe how confident everyone was. One of the things I love about being a West Ham fan is our ability to indulge in gallows humour, and our natural pessimism. It felt quite strange to be going into a game, especially at Old Trafford, feeling confident of a good result. Watford beat Arsenal in the early game. Crystal Palace and Everton were the other semi-finalists awaiting the outcome of our match. Whoever won this would win the cup – surely this was effectively the final?

I sat high up in the away end with Michael Mowatt and another former OLAS writer, Philip Pitt, who I had reacquainted myself with through S!HT. It was a beautiful sunny day. We were playing well, but it always seemed that United might have the edge. But then on 68 minutes a free kick was given for West Ham a few yards outside the penalty area. Payet put it in the only place de Gea could not reach. Surely that was it.

We hadn't reckoned on Bastian Schweinhundt, though, clattering into Randolph in an obvious foul, which allowed Anthony Martial to score an equaliser. Everyone looked at the officials. The officials looked at everyone, shrugged, and said, 'What?'

No matter. A replay it would be, and we would claim our place in a Wembley semi-final then. We were confident we had done the hard bit.

But form dipped, and officials ganged up on us in the intervening period. At Stamford Bridge we were twice in the lead, but referee Bobby Madley wasn't in the mood to co-operate. Fabregas was guilty of an outrageous bit of gamesmanship, dragging the ball well back behind the spot where Madley told him the kick should be taken from to equalise with free kick after Lanzini had scored a peach of a goal to give West Ham the lead. Carroll stepped off the bench to repeat his party trick, and it seemed enough to give us the double over Chelsea, but Antonio's foul on Loftus-Cheek was deemed to be inside the area, not a yard outside, as it actually was. Bobby Madley gave the penalty in the last minute. The game might as well have been reffed by Stevie Wonder. Had we had VAR in 2016 we would could have won the FA Cup and qualified for the Champions League. Maybe. Three points would have put us in 4th place, probably temporarily, but it would have been a psychological boost heading into the home game with Alan Pardew's Crystal Palace.

But before that, Mr West Ham, Mark Noble, had a richly deserved testimonial match at Upton Park: a West Ham United XI against a West Ham All-Stars XI. It was a magnificent day, a warm sunny March afternoon with a carnival atmosphere brought about by the fact that no one cared who won, just that they should be entertained, and heroes past and present should be allowed to score at every opportunity.

And they did. Craig Bellamy opened the scoring for the All-Stars, then after having a shot saved by David James, who seemed to have lost, or more likely dropped, his copy of the script, Mark Noble was allowed to score. Adrián added to his cult-hero status by dribbling from one end of the pitch to the other and scoring, then Alex Song scored his only ever goal in a West Ham shirt and Sakho walked the ball in for 4–1. Teddy Sheringham scored for the All-Stars before Sakho made it 5–2. Then came a real sight for sore eyes as two West Ham legends combined: Ian Bishop crossed from the right corner of the penalty area and Dean Ashton scored with an acrobatic volley that made me cry tears of happiness tinged with sadness that he was taken from us so early. Had he stayed fit, I am convinced we would have gone on to great things. We would certainly not have been relegated in 2011. That means we would never have had Allardyce... I really try not to resent Shaun Wright-Phillips, but it's difficult.

Ashton scored a second, by which time I'd lost track of the score, but all that was needed was for Paolo Di Canio to get one in, which he duly did. I felt a little guilty for feeling sad that Dean Ashton could no longer play football when we were reminded of what real tragedy is, as Taylor Tombides chipped in a lovely goal at the end, and looked skywards towards his brother Dylan. I think the game ended 6–5 but, as if we hadn't had enough fun, they had a penalty shoot-out which ended 7–7 after eleven penalties each.

In the next match Payet again scored an outrageous free kick against Palace, but it was only enough to get another 2–2 draw. Kouyaté was again sent off, again seemingly harshly, and again overturned. This time it was Mark Clattenburg. But the successful appeal did not give us the additional 2 points. The officials had cost us dearly. Football managers get banned for saying as much, so I will say it for them: the referees were crap. As Ron Atkinson said, 'I never comment on referees and I'm not going to change for that twat.'

It did knock the stuffing out of us a little bit, and when Arsenal went 2–0 ahead at Upton Park in a Saturday lunchtime kick-off, it seemed the wheels had finally come off. But Andy Carroll at least had other ideas. He pulled one back from a great Cresswell cross from the left, then before half time he juggled with the ball on the penalty spot before falling into a semi-bicycle kick to level it up. With the momentum still favouring the Hammers after the break, Antonio crossed from the right to allow Carroll to complete his hat-trick. We understandably went potty, and at 2–0 down of course we would have ripped your hand off for a draw, but when Arsenal made it 3–3 there was an inevitable feeling of disappointment.

No matter what happened in the sixth-round replay against Manchester United it would be the last cup tie to be played at the Boleyn. I have spoken earlier about how officials cost us in the league campaign, but think of it this way: had Manchester United's goal at Old Trafford been correctly ruled out and we had won, maybe our league game against Manchester United would not have been postponed, and the last game at the Boleyn would have been a 1–4 hammering at home to Swansea. Perhaps it was meant to be.

It was another emotional day at the Boleyn; by this point they all were. I had seen some amazing cup ties down the years: a 2–1 win over Norwich in the fourth round in 1984, a 4–0 win over Sheffield United in 1987 and, of course, Stuart Slater's rite of passage against Everton in the 1991 quarter-final. It is to my deep regret that I was not old enough to be going on my own when we won the cup in 1980. It's why I don't like managers prioritising the league over the cups. I still want to see it happen before I die.

In the end, the final cup tie at the Boleyn ended in disappointment. After a lacklustre first half, United took a two-goal lead with us only managing a James Tomkins header in reply. In a frantic finish, Kouyaté thought he had equalised but was ruled offside. Replays later showed he may have been level. Scratch what I just said about officials. They are all twats.

56

ONE DANCE

WEST HAM UNITED 3, MANCHESTER UNITED 2
PREMIER LEAGUE, 10 MAY 2016

16-year-old X-Factor *contestants who say, 'I'm singing "Without You"
by Mariah Carey.' It's not by Mariah Carey. It was written by Pete Ham
of Badfinger and the definitive version is by Harry Nilsson. Similarly,
'I Will Always Love You' is not by Whitney Houston and 'Run'
is not by Leona Lewis.*

Out of the cup it seemed we could finally concentrate on the league. But we kept on throwing away leads. Leicester City had been the surprise package of the season under Claudio Ranieri. They played some amazing football and were about to go on to win the Premier League title. But we did our best to trip them up; Jamie Vardy scored, then got sent off for two bookable offences, the second being a laughable dive to try and win a penalty. We were leading 2–1 through goals from a Carroll penalty and a terrific drive from Cresswell. But then referee Moss gave Leicester a penalty for an innocuous-looking challenge by Carroll on Schlupp. It looked a lot like a bit of evening up to me.

I wasn't there: I was at the christening of Lisa and Stuart the QPR fan's unexpected arrival Eiddwen. She was born in November 2015 and suffered several complications, which I am happy to report are all sorted now and, at the age of two-and-a-half, she has been discharged from the hospital's care. A cuter kid you will not meet, she really is a miracle child.

Things like that always help to put football into perspective. I think of this every time I see someone blowing their top on social media over a delayed substitution or a refereeing decision. It's really not important.

At home to Watford we won 3–1, Carroll starting the scoring, then two penalties for Mark Noble. It was almost a relief to have a run-of the mill game that ended in victory and kept us in 6th place on 56 points, 3 behind Manchester United and 4 behind Arsenal in 4th, but having played a game more than both. Qualification for the Champions League was now looking like a forlorn hope, but we still had an excellent shout of qualifying for the Europa League.

Those chances were boosted by a 3–0 win at the Hawthorns, thanks to Noble scoring a second successive brace, with both from open play.

It set us up nicely for the final Saturday afternoon match at the Boleyn, against highly beatable Swansea City. It was something to do with the West Ham Way though. Something that said just when you start to get ahead of yourselves, you should have a swift kick in the nuts to remind you of your place. Swansea delivered four kicks in the nuts in swift succession and the vast majority of the 34,907 in attendance walked away with their tails firmly between their legs.

It had been a poor performance. But we had to get it out of our systems with the final game against Manchester United coming up in only three days.

It was a strange atmosphere in the Black Lion pre-match. There was a celebratory feel to it because of the season we had enjoyed, and an optimism about the future in the new stadium. But this was also tinged with sadness; we knew that this was the last time we would meet in the Black Lion (before a game at the Boleyn anyway) and it was impossible not to feel emotional about the fact that for me, a forty-year association with this particular corner of east London, though not a native, was coming to an end. I could understand why for those born and bred in the area it was a much bigger deal. But then David Gold was born at 442 Green Street – has he ever mentioned that? And he couldn't wait to get us moved out, drop the keys off at Barratts, and tell them to get on with razing the place to the ground. It stank a little bit in my view: that these guys purported to be our saviours, yet were looking to change everything about the club systematically and without so much as a nod to tradition.

One thing they had got right was the matchday programmes for that season, each one sporting a style from years gone by. I did like that. But I could not imagine that SuGo or Brady had come up with it.

I left the pub early to go and soak up some atmosphere. Matt Liston came with me and it soon became clear as we entered Green Street that there was a problem with congestion. Four or five police vans were parked across the street, which made it very difficult for people to pass from the tube station to the Barking Road end. Thousands of fans had turned up without tickets to be part of the final day. Anyone who had not antic- ipated that this would happen must need their head checked. The Manchester United bus had tried to pick its way through the crowd and inevitably some fucking idiot threw something. That was always going to make the back- and possibly front- page headline, no matter what happened in the game.

It was a little scary squeezing through the gaps between the police vans. But we made it, and popped out the other side like champagne corks. Kick-off was delayed by forty-five minutes as the crowd found its way inside to their seats. Matt took his seat in the West Upper, while I went around to my seat to join Gavin for the last time. Fortunately, he had got there early and saved my T-shirt which was on my seat. T-shirts had been left on each seat as a memento of the final game. We were supposed to wear them to create a sea of claret and blue, but mine is still carefully preserved in it plastic wrapper.

It was a spine-tingling evening to which the football was almost secondary. As everybody knows, the game ended 3–2 to West Ham after we had been leading 1–0 and then trailed 1–2. It was the history of West Ham encapsulated in a single game. It was the West Ham Way.

Several things stuck in my mind that night. The first was the togetherness of the fans. It was probably the last time I actually saw everyone in the same mood, there for the same reasons, and not bitching with each other about something. The second was the brass band that played 'Bubbles' at half time. I had everything under control until that point, but will admit to shedding a little tear at that moment as 'Bubbles' was played to the correct tune, not the way it is sometimes strangled by West Ham fans, who always set off with too much enthusiasm and far too high, then have to switch register halfway through.

Finally, I will remember the anti-climax of the show after the game. The underwhelming interviews conducted by Bianca Westwood and Ben Shephard. They were doing their best, bless them, but I had lost interest by that stage. It was dragging things out beyond the point to which it became a celebration. The game was over. There would be no more here. I was feeling tired and emotional and wanted to leave. But I felt it disloyal to leave while there was still stuff to see, no matter how naff.

So I stayed until the end, but the memory of that night is sullied a little by the crapness of the finale. Like you could top coming back from 1–2 down against Manchester United to win 3–2?

So that was that. The Boleyn was gone. Off up into broad sunlit uplands in Stratford. Not before the small matter of a 2–1 defeat on the final day at Stoke which meant that after enjoying such an entertaining season we finished rather disappointingly in 7th on 62 points. Southampton snuck up on us at the end and robbed us of 6th. Seventh was still good; we finished above Liverpool and Chelsea, but the top six is that area we are constantly told we needed to be in. As it happened, 7th was still good enough for a Europa League place, with Manchester United qualifying via the league and by winning the FA Cup.

We would start the new era at the new stadium with European football. What could possibly go wrong? All we needed to do was stick together. Don't bitch and fight. Keep winning. It would be fine.

57

CLOSER

WEST HAM UNITED 2, WATFORD 4
PREMIER LEAGUE, 10 SEPTEMBER 2016

*People who drop litter, especially from a car window. I can feel my
blood starting to boil right now just thinking about it.*

That summer of 2016. The optimism, basking in the glory of
finishing in 7th place, and having one of the top players in
Europe in our squad. It was a feeling I will remember for a long
time. It is particularly sweet in hindsight when juxtaposed to
the bitterness that followed so soon afterwards.

But through June and July 2016 we were a top Premier League
side with a manager whose stock was rising by the day, particularly through his punditry on ITV's coverage of Euro 2016, and
when he climbed on to the table when Payet scored for France it
seemed impossible that I could love the guy any more.

England, of course were a disaster. Having beaten Wales and
drawn with Russia and Slovakia to make the knockout stages,
they lost to Iceland. Joe Hart had a nightmare, but no more so
than anyone else who played for England that night. At least
Joe Hart didn't play for West Ham, eh? Also, I was grateful for
the fact we would not have to face France in the quarter-finals
and risk being destroyed by a West Ham player. That could have
made life very awkward.

Despite the general optimism about the new stadium, it was
clear that in order to maintain the momentum we had gathered
in 2015/16 we would need further significant investment in the
squad, not only to push on, but to keep those top-quality players already with us happy, and show that we meant business.

A little odd, then, that transfer activity seemed so muted. The biggest signing was already there, we had Manuel Lanzini on a permanent deal. If SuGo thought that would appease us they were wrong. The other names coming in were not inspiring. Algerian winger Sofiane Feghouli, Gökhan Töre (on loan), Håvard Nordtveit, and youngsters Domingos Quina and Toni Martínez all signed in July. Sorry, but unless you play FIFA 17 all day every day, you were never going to have heard of any of them, except perhaps Töre, a Turkish international born in Germany who had been a youth team player at Chelsea. His stats at Beşiktaş were not especially impressive and did not fill me with confidence, but then, neither did any of the other signings.

Of those discarded, Elliot Lee went off to Barnsley, Joey O'Brien was simply released into the wild (he was recently captured by poachers and made to play for Shamrock Rovers). He had been a good player for West Ham; he knew his limitations and was happy to make the odd substitute appearance towards the end, but I don't recall him ever seriously letting us down. He ended up with 89 starts, 16 sub appearances and 3 goals. Much more of a loss, however, was James Tomkins, who was sold to Crystal Palace for £10 million. Quite how this came about was a bit of a mystery. If Tomkins wanted first-team football, surely he knew the score with our injury record and it would only be a matter of time before he got a run in the side. If it was Bilić or the board that wanted to sell him – who was the replacement? We had an ageing Collins, Ogboner, and an injury-prone Reid. Nordtveit could play centre-back, but then so could I at a push. A crazy sale in my opinion.

Tomkins had come through the ranks and been a loyal servant to us up to that point; he had made an impressive 225 starts for West Ham, 16 substitute appearances and scored 11 goals.

I was worried about the way the new season was shaping up. We had Chelsea away on the opening day, pushed back to the Monday evening of 15 August for TV, and had to start our Europa League campaign in Slovenia against NK Domžale on 28 July.

Everything seemed to be unravelling before the season had even started. A prestigious friendly against Juventus had been arranged for 7 August, but the early start to the Europa League campaign meant that there would be a game played there three days earlier, which rather pissed on that particular firework.

The away leg in Slovenia was a torrid affair: a Mark Noble penalty gave us a vital away goal, but the game was lost 1–2. Not a disaster, but we did not play well. Nordtveit looked hopeless, Feghouli similarly so. The omens were not great, but with the away goal it meant a 1–0 win at home would be enough. If we could call it home, that it is. Philip Pitt had been to choose seats for us in my absence on another trip to Brazil. He rang me from the virtual reality stadium store set up in the Westfield Shopping Centre at Stratford to say he had looked at the more expensive band one tickets and they were all a long way from the pitch. He had been offered seats in the corner of the East and Bobby Moore stands, block 141, row 12, which gave a much better view. I trusted his judgement and told him to go ahead. My eldest nephew, Mark, had bought four tickets in block 230 and younger nephew Sam had bought two in 242. The scatter-gun approach to selling season tickets had been one of the first ways in which people had been rubbed up the wrong way. Band one holders were called in first for their appointments, but with the capacity at the London Stadium being 20,000 higher, people were invited to nominate friends, not necessarily existing season ticket holders, to buy tickets with them.

SuGo quite rightly wanted to ensure that we sold as many season tickets as possible, but in the first season at the new ground that was never likely to be a problem. This was merely fanning the flames of resentment among the lower band holders. As a band three holder at Upton Park, by the time my appointment came around many of the 'better' seats had gone, but Philip managed to secure great seats in 141 which, as far as I could see, provided a superior view to those in some of the band one spots.

The first competitive game at the London Stadium came on

4 August. I met Colin Milne at the Hamilton Hall pub in Liverpool Street and we took the train to Stratford in plenty of time to get to the Stadium and soak up a little atmosphere. It was clear to me that the walk to the stadium from Stratford station was going to be a pain in the arse on a weekly basis and I would have to find an alternative route quickly.

I walked in full of anticipation. I had been inside the stadium three times before, twice on 10k charity runs and once for the Paralympics. This was the first time I had been there to watch a game. As I took my seat in row 12 of block 141, it really didn't seem all that bad. As I had been in the upper tier of the Bobby Moore Upper at Upton Park, I was closer to the pitch than I had been before, but as I looked to my left it was obvious that as the running track pushed the stands away from the field, those even in the lower tiers on the halfway line were a long way from the action.

This was not what we had been promised. All the hype surrounding the move, the artists' impressions, the rhetoric coming from the board, everything had pointed towards seating covering the running track and fans being as close to the action as possible. I was lucky. In the corner I was very close, comparatively speaking, but I could see why others might have had cause to complain.

The other thing that struck me was that the stadium did not appear to be finished. The lower tier seats seemed to be constructed on scaffolding. Is that what they meant by retractable seats? I'd had a vision of a button being pressed and everything folding away like some sort of James Bond gadget.

I had been a cautious advocate of the move, having seen what I had seen at the Paralympics and on my runs, but this was not what I had signed up for. Demolition work had already started on Upton Park so it was time to swallow hard, move forward and make the best of it.

The whole experience of the London Stadium move has already been well documented in Brian Williams' excellent book *Home from Home*, so I won't be going into too much detail about the games since the move, but concentrating more on what happened among us fans and our relationships with the stadium, the board and each other.

The first competitive game ended in a 3–0 win with Kouyaté scoring the first 2 goals and Feghouli banging in an impressive third. We were drawn to face FC Astra Giurgiu again in the final play-off for a place in the group stages of the Europa League. With them having knocked us out twelve months before, this was a chance for a bit of revenge, but first the Premier League season had to get underway.

In the meantime though the 'prestige' opening game for the London Stadium saw West Ham take on Italian champions Juventus. West Ham were decked out in another money-making memorial kit in navy blue with the Union Jack on the breast, used only for this game, and never used again in a competitive fixture. It was a shame because it was a nice kit – but yet another way to hold the average fan by the ankles and shake him until every last penny has been drained.

The game itself was unremarkable, as most pre-season friendlies are. West Ham came back from 0–2 down to 2–2 with two Andy Carroll headers but a third for Juventus from Simone Zaza wrapped up the win for the old lady.

The transfer window up to that point had been completely underwhelming. Rumours of big name signings such as Carlos Bacca, Michy Batshuayi and Alexandre Lacazette had not come to fruition mainly, it seemed, from the fans' perspective, because Sullivan was always trying to get knock-down deals, insulting the selling clubs with derisory offers.

In a final attempt to land a marquee signing, André Ayew was signed from Swansea City for £20.5 million. Not only did this stink of desperation to those connected with the club, the reek was so strong that fans of other clubs could smell it too. The smell must have been particularly pungent in Dimitri Payet's house, where he must have wondered what the hell was going on. Here he was after winning all the plaudits possible the previous season, helping France to get within a whisker of winning the Euros, and now he was being asked to play in a team with Håvard Nordtveit. Swiss youngster Edimilson Fernandes was signed for €5.5 million, and with the full-back situation desperate, veteran Spanish right-back Álvaro Arbeloa was signed on a free transfer from Real Madrid. Seriously? Was that the best we could do? He was about seventy-five, for god's sake.

Payet, rightly or wrongly, seemed to be getting special treatment. He didn't train like the others, he was allowed additional time off in the summer because of the European Championships. His salary was reportedly significantly higher than anyone else's at the club. This was not likely to breed a good team spirit in an already fragile atmosphere.

Aaron Cresswell suffered an injury in a pre-season game and there was no cover at left-back, so another random lunge into the transfer market resulted in Arthur Masuaku, a French left-back of Congolese descent, coming in from Olympiacos for £6.25 million.

Come the opening game of the Premier League season it would be easy to say we were unlucky to lose 1–2 at Stamford Bridge, and given that James Collins had equalised Eden Hazard's penalty 13 minutes from the end, a draw looked the likely outcome. However, referee Anthony Taylor's refusal to brandish a second yellow at Diego Costa after a ludicrous challenge on Adrián meant he was still on the pitch to take advantage of hesitant defending in the final minute to give Chelsea the victory. But in reality, Chelsea were the better organised and stronger team. It was a pale shadow of the performance we had put in at Stamford Bridge a few short months earlier and, to add insult to injury, or rather, to add injury to insult, André Ayew picked up a knock that would keep our record signing out until late October.

Away at Astra Giurgiu, a Mark Noble penalty again seemed to have done most of the hard work in the tie, earning a 1–1 draw, a better result than we had there twelve months earlier. All we had to do was get a better result at home and we were in the group stages. At the new fortress that should be no problem.

We had a 100 per cent record in competitive games so far and were yet to concede a goal.

Bournemouth was the first home game on a gloriously sunny Sunday afternoon, and the S!HT crowd gathered at the Podium bar by the Orbit. This really didn't seem so bad. At that stage they sold Peroni on draft, a better alternative to the piss-coloured water that had been the usual fare in that bar, being Heineken. It was a bit lively though, and the staff didn't have much of an idea how to pour it, which meant long queues to get served. But no matter; teething troubles. There was a barbecue going on, a nice sunny day, pint of Peroni and good friends. The only trouble was there was one of those pesky football matches about to spoil everything.

A dire affair ended in a 1–0 victory for West Ham with Antonio scoring the winner. But over and above the standard of the performance there was something else bothering me. There were a lot of familiar faces around but a lot of new ones too. I have always been in favour of bringing new blood into the club and as it seemed the additional 20,000 season tickets had all been snapped up there was a mix of regulars, families and, dare I say it, tourists.

The tourist fan gets a rotten press. Whether you like it or not, it's really no one's business what people do on their holidays. If I want to go to watch Paris Saint-Germain, buy a scarf that is half PSG and half Marseille, and sit quietly watching the game, would you expect me to be criticised by the average PSG fan? I don't think so. So why was such vitriol aimed at tourist fans within the London Stadium? Why were there fights breaking out in the stands between people wearing the same colours? Why was I seeing people at each other's throats? This was our first Premier League game in the new stadium and instead of being a day of celebration, for me, it was a day to forget.

The blame lies not with tourist fans, not with new season ticket holders, not with season ticket holders who have been going for over forty years, but fairly and squarely with whoever decided that tickets should be randomly distributed.

The seating arrangements at Upton Park evolved over a number of years. When I started going, the North and South Banks were completely terraced for standing, as was the lower tier of the East Stand. Shortly before that the lower tier of the West Stand was also terraced. So, as fans, we had been brought up watching football standing up. I shudder to think now what some modern fans would think of going to football and the only way to tell the score was by the number of times you got moved to a completely different part of the terrace by a writhing sea of bodies. There were times when I saw virtually nothing (being of diminutive stature) and times when I came out of games with pockets full of lager, or worse. It was not for the faint-hearted.

After Hillsborough and the Taylor Report, Upton Park went all-seater, but even so there were still areas of the ground that were known as being more boisterous than others. The Bobby Moore Lower was a prime example, where the majority of fans stood for the whole of the game, regardless of what was happening on the pitch. Stewards largely turned a blind eye to this. It was an arrangement that worked well for many years between the Bobby Moore stand opening in January 1993 and West Ham leaving the Boleyn twenty-two years later.

So, what happens when you take all those people from their seats in the Bobby Moore Lower and mix them in with new people who only have experience of watching games from a seated position? What happens when you mix them in with people who have their wives and children, maybe even elderly relatives with them, who want to sit down to watch a game? Then add to the mix a bunch of twelve-year-old stewards, who are not actually employed by the club, and who would not say boo to a goose. What happens? It kicks off. Big time, as Slaven would say. I held my head in my hands as I walked back to the station. I knew that this was going to be hard work.

Speaking of which, the Romanians came back the following Thursday and knocked us out of the Europa League. No European football, a stadium that was going down like a sack of shit with the old regulars, a string of desperate transfer window signings and a proper 3–1 hiding at Manchester City for good measure. If things are measured in months, then I could not wait for August 2016 to end because it had, quite frankly, been crap.

There were to be yet more questionable signings, though. Argentinian striker Jonathan Calleri signed on loan from Deportivo Maldonado in Uruguay. He had previously been on loan at São Paulo in Brazil so I asked some of my contacts about him, and they reported back positive things: he had scored 3 times in 5 games there. Argentina's early exit from the Olympic football tournament in Brazil facilitated his loan to us to the end of the season. More baffling was the arrival of Simone Zaza on loan from Juventus for a crushing €5 million loan fee and an option to buy at €20 million at the end of the season. Although that was eye-watering money for a man who had shown he did not even know how to take a penalty, at least SuGo had not committed themselves to a permanent deal. If he was rubbish we could send him back. If he was decent we had a fixed price for him. I think I could tell which of the two it would be though.

The board continued to anger and irritate. Club legend Tony Carr, who had been granted a testimonial in 2010, and was the man who nurtured so many young talents at the club, was asked to reduce his working week from five days to one. Who can afford to do that? It was effectively a dismissal, which was confirmed, allegedly by post.

But it wasn't just the board, though. The sponsors were getting in on the act. Betway criticised Bilić's decision to persist playing Antonio at right-back on their Twitter account. Their criticism may have been warranted, but they are the sponsors! They needed to wind their necks in.

Against Watford, West Ham looked to have put all the troubles behind them; Lanzini and Payet were pulling the strings for Antonio to score twice, and the second goal was set up by a cheeky rabona from Payet. It looked like we would run riot. The pre-match rendition of 'Bubbles' had been stirring and there seemed to be real togetherness among the fans. Then it all fell apart. I made my excuses five minutes before half time to go and get the beers in. By the time I had collected Sam's season tickets from Matt Liston and returned to my seat ten minutes into the second half we were 2–3 down and everyone was at each other's throats again.'

Whoever was to blame for West Ham playing like a bunch of twats, it wasn't the people asking others to sit down. It wasn't the people leaving early. It wasn't the people who didn't sing. But they seemed to be getting the blame.

I have been known to leave a game a few minutes early. I'm a busy man and I like to beat the traffic. But some of the abuse being hurled at people in block 141 for leaving early was, quite frankly, embarrassing. Interestingly, there is no such abuse thrown at people who arrive late. Surely that is just as bad an offence? Or turning up so pissed that you sleep through most of the game with a mixture of dribble and vomit running down your chin. Thanks for your support guys.

It seemed that there was a running battle among supporters to prove they were somehow bigger or better fans than the next man, and it made me sick. It was fucking pathetic. We were all West Ham fans, or we wouldn't be there. How we individually choose to support the team is a matter of choice that only the individual can make. But if you live in a glass house, don't throw stones.

The atmosphere towards the end of the Watford game was so toxic I thought the club were going to have to issue gas masks for the next home match. We lost 4–2 at the Hawthorns after being 4–0 down and, while we did at least show some signs of fight, they were fleeting.

The cup game against Accrington Stanley was memorable for one thing only. I spent the entire second half watching the game with Marie Parkes and her partner, Paul, keeping one eye on the big screen but having much more fun talking to Marie about what it was like being the daughter of a legend and whether it had been difficult to carve out her own identity, and whether she was sick of being introduced as Phil Parkes's daughter. It was all fascinating stuff. We watched as Payet lined up a free kick in the final minute of added time and duly scored. It was a relief. It would have been nice to spend another half an hour chatting with Marie, but I had work the next morning.

I was there, supporting the team. But I wasn't being given much to support. The flair of the previous season had gone and the suffix 'United' after West Ham was a sad misnomer. The unity the fans had shown in expressing their love of the Boleyn on leaving in May was now mirrored by vitriol and hatred for anyone and anything to do with the new stadium by some sections of the support, presumable a guilty reaction to not doing more to try to prevent the move in the first place.

But promises had been made that placated us. Many of us believed them, even supported the plans. Now I felt particularly foolish. But it was done. So I had to try to make the best of it. It was a shame that others did not seem so willing. Constant moaning never changed anything.

I had worked out early on that going to Stratford station was a non-starter on match day, so got into the habit of getting off the DLR at Pudding Mill Lane and making the ten-minute walk to the Podium Bar. On Sundays I could park free at Elverson Road DLR station, so the journey was actually a lot easier for me. But I was aware that for the majority of fans it wasn't, particularly with weekend engineering works.

The S!HT crew met in the Podium before the game against Southampton convinced that things could not get any worse. How wrong we were. A terrible performance, more unrest in the stands and a 0–3 defeat proved to be the nadir of the first half of the season. We ended September with just the 3 points gained against Bournemouth, which put us in the bottom three.

The home match against Middlesbrough coincided with my dad's eighty-third birthday, so I had to miss it to take part in the festivities. I therefore didn't get to see Payet's amazing goal in the 1–1 draw. I watched it later on *Match of the Day*, and it was indeed an impressive goal, but it seemed like the defenders allowed him the freedom of the London Stadium. The last time I saw such a mazy dribble ending in a goal was when Adrián scored in Mark Noble's testimonial.

58

SHOUT OUT TO MY EX

LIVERPOOL 2, WEST HAM UNITED 2
PREMIER LEAGUE, 11 DECEMBER 2016
Playing music after goals. Does my head in.

Despite the draw against Middlesbrough we were still in deep shit, and still playing like a bunch of strangers. And even with some of the changes being made by the stadium management, the stewarding continued to rile the home fans, who continued to get under each other's skin. What we needed was a big performance at home to bring everyone together. It seemed obvious to me after the Watford game, that when things were going okay, people had no time to bitch about the stadium or each other. It was clear from looking at social media forums that there were enough idiots out there being influenced into thinking one thing one week and another the next. The only way to solve the issue would be to start winning.

We got our second win of the season at Selhurst Park against Crystal Palace, and thankfully, Manuel Lanzini scored to ease the pressure on Bilić somewhat before I went off to Brazil on holiday. I watched on a dodgy link as Winston Reid gave us another 1–0 win at home to David Moyes's Sunderland. The last-minute strike suggested the performance had been less than convincing.

Chelsea came to visit in the League Cup on the back of an excellent start to the season and were hot favourites to progress. I had taken an internal flight to the north of Brazil and was on the beach in Porto de Galinhas, trying to connect to the hotel wi-fi to keep up with the game. By the time I managed to find a connection we were already 2–0 to the good, thanks to goals from Kouyaté and Fernandes. Through the magic of the internet I was able to keep in touch with friends at the game. They told me it was the best atmosphere yet and that maybe there was hope. As I suspected, all we had to do was keep on winning to stop the hate. Gary Cahill pulled one back, but West Ham were through to the last eight. Somehow.

The next day we went snorkelling off the reef near the hotel and met a really nice couple from Porto Alegre in the south of Brazil. Alessandra and Marcello were from the same town but supported different teams. Alessandra supported Grêmio and Marcello supported Inter. It was the equivalent of a couple from Manchester supporting City and United. As usual with these holiday meetings, we exchanged numbers and I told Marcello if he was ever in London to let me know and I would arrange tickets and we would go to a game. How many times have we done that?

The airline cancelled our flight home and lost our bags, so we spent a night in Recife with only our hand luggage and a hastily purchased toothbrush each. It meant I was back in Rio Claro twenty-four hours later than anticipated and was in danger of missing the commentary on the game at Goodison Park against Everton. On the bus going back to Rio Claro I had no wi-fi and therefore allowed international roaming on my phone, using it for a total of eight minutes to find that we had lost 2–0. Lukaku again. Those eight minutes cost me £37. I wouldn't have minded so much if we had won.

I stepped back off the plane at Heathrow on 5 November, dropped my bags at home and headed straight for the London Stadium for the home game against Stoke. After two weeks in temperatures over 30 degrees it was a bit of a shock to the system, and my neighbour Philip did not come so I was on my own watching the game, something I had got used to years ago, but having become accustomed to company, I missed it. Most of the people around me were too angry for me to want to make friends, or muttered things under their breath that made me feel they would not welcome any conversational ice-breakers. The usual crew turned up late behind me, with the usual suspect so pissed I don't know how he managed it. Either he got up especially early to start drinking or he had a very weak liver.

We took the lead through a dubious goal, but then a rush of blood to the head from Adrián gifted Stoke an equaliser. It was pretty rank, and a reasonable summary of the football we had seen at the London Stadium thus far.

We played better at Tottenham, leading 1–0 and 2–1 before Bilić made the baffling decision to withdraw Payet. He wasn't having the best of games, it was true, but he kept the Tottenham defence occupied, and gave them that little element of doubt in their minds when they came forward, knowing that losing the ball could spell disaster. As it was we had taken off our only outlet going forward. Nordtveit looked completely out of his depth and gave away a last-minute penalty, going in rashly on Son, allowing Kane to get an injury-time winner after he had already equalised, tapping in a Son cross which Randolph, in for out-of-favour Adrián, could only palm into his path. Ogboner had it covered, but the communication appeared to be non-existent.

It wasn't going to get any easier. In the next 4 matches we had to play Manchester United twice, then Arsenal and Liverpool. From those games we managed 2 points, which was 2 more than I was expecting: a 1–1 draw at Old Trafford and 2–2 at Anfield – but the main point of concern was the way we had crumbled in the League Cup quarter-final, also at Old Trafford, eventually losing 4–1. Payet looked completely disinterested and played a suicidal ball across our own area which was intercepted for one of United's goals. He was looking more and more disillusioned by the moment.

We also got unceremoniously dry-humped at home to Arsenal 1–5, with Alexi Sanchez scoring a hat-trick. It was reaching the stage where I started dreading home games. I hated it.

It was too early to be talking about 'must-win' games, but the midweek fixture against Burnley was shaping up that way.

As I walked towards the Podium Bar that night I took a photograph of the stadium and had to admit from a distance it looked impressive illuminated at night. Burnley had only managed 1 point and 1 goal away from home by the time they came to play us, so on paper we looked like the perfect opponents for them.

Andy Carroll at least seemed to be fit, making his first start since August. The game was far from a classic. Mark Noble bundled in the rebound after his initial penalty had been saved by Tom Heaton. Three points was three points, though, and it was enough to lift us four clear of the relegation zone, and with a home game to come against Hull City, perhaps a chance to get a run of results together. A run of dodgy 1-0 wins maybe. Against Hull, our goalpost was man of the match.

The tribulations of football were once again put in perspective for me when I found out that my former team leader at Barclays, Gerard, was seriously ill in hospital, having suffered a severe bleed in the main blood supply to his brain. The news was blunt and shocking. He would not recover. He was just 39 years old. He was 'locked in', which I understand means he was aware of what was going on around him, but could only communicate by blinking. He died a few days later, leaving a wife, Sarah, and two young boys, Callum and Finley. Just a few days previously he had been sending me sarcastic text messages during the Liverpool v. West Ham game. I struggled to understand it.

Most of us working at Barclays knew Gerard, so it was a muted unofficial Christmas party that was held in Shoreditch the night before the Hull game. My dad's health had also been deteriorating, and we got results from an X-ray which showed that his prostate cancer had spread to his lungs and bones. I had been trying to break it gently to Elaine that Dad didn't have long – I meant weeks, not months – but she refused to accept it until one day we popped in to visit and Dad looked like a ghost and could hardly speak. His eyes still lit up when he saw Elaine and he managed to stand up for a hug, but as we left Elaine started crying as the penny finally dropped.

Christmas was difficult. We always entertained, and we struggled to get Dad up the stairs to our maisonette, but once there we played him all his favourite Peter Sellers records and he seemed quite happy. We could not know exactly how much pain he was in as he rarely complained.

On Boxing Day we went to see him again, and his face lit up again when he saw that we had won 4–1 at Swansea. It was the last time he would be in a position to understand a West Ham result, so I'm pleased it was such an emphatic one in our favour.

Without any warning whatsoever, Elaine's father, Senhor Iran was taken into hospital in Rio Claro. His heart was weak, but he had been managing quite happily since his scare in June 2015. On 30 December 2016 we arrived home from work, busying ourselves in our normal routine when Elaine's phone rang. It was her sister. Her father had passed away that afternoon.

We sat on the edge of the bed and both cried our eyes out. Elaine for her dad, and her mum, and me for Elaine's mum and dad, and for Elaine herself, but also for me, my mum and my sisters, knowing we would have to face this in the near future.

I checked out flights but Elaine had already missed the only one that would get her to Rio Claro in time for Senhor Iran's funeral the next day. They don't mess about in Brazil. She decided to wait a few weeks and go and visit once the dust had settled, partly because there was nothing she could do, but I also knew her, and I knew that she wanted to be here to support me through what was coming.

By the time we played Manchester United, losing on 2 January, for my dad it was just a matter of when. New Year's Eve had passed without being celebrated as such, just a cursory nod to the passing of a horrible year.

Miraculously, the friends we had made in Brazil back in October got in touch and my nephew duly obliged and handed over his tickets for them to use. It was all very strange. I met them for a drink beforehand, but I was distracted, glancing at my phone every few minutes to see if I was needed.

Marcello and Alessandra were very understanding and

generously each brought me a scarf from their favoured teams of Grêmio and Inter as a thank-you for procuring the tickets. Elaine and I met them in London the next day for lunch but again I was on edge, and knew that it would not be long before I got the call.

That call came at 8.30 a.m. on 5 January 2017 – and I refer you back to the first chapter of this book. Exactly seven days after Elaine lost her dad, I lost mine. The sense of loss within the household could not be measured.

The following Saturday we had a home game against Crystal Palace. This turned out to be a good thing, as I met with nephews Mark and Sam, Mark's partner Kerry-Ann, and Jamie and Jessica to have a drink in Dad's honour. I watched the first half in block 141 but the usual numpties were doing my head in, and I wasn't in the mood. So I went up to block 230 and watched the second half with Sam. Feghouli opened the scoring, then Carroll added his goal-of-the-month-winning bicycle kick before Lanzini finished off a 3–0 win. It seemed Il Fatso's Palace, like his West Ham and Sunderland sides before them, also had no plan B after going behind.

59

SHAPE OF YOU

WATFORD 1, WEST HAM UNITED 1
PREMIER LEAGUE, 25 FEBRUARY 2017
Rucksacks on the tube or in lifts. Take them off. You twats.

I took part in a quiz in London with Phil and Jim from S!HT, Craig Climpson and his father, Danny, Michelle Gabriel and Trevor Drane. All of us had met through S!HT and we had formed a team to take part in a fund raiser for Pride of Irons. We won. The prize was a tour of the London Stadium.

That would be a London Stadium without Dimitri Payet, who had begun behaving like a spoiled brat and refused to play after his request to leave had been turned down. It was a difficult one. We would have been within our rights to let him rot in the reserves, but that would also have run down his transfer value. Better to let him go and get a decent fee for him. Our hand was slightly forced, knowing that there was really only one club he wanted to go to. In the end a £25 million fee from Marseille was a £15 million profit and represented as good a deal as we were likely to get.

The important thing was not to waste the money on players like Robert Snodgrass. To be fair, Snodgrass had impressed for Hull and ran the show during the game in December. Although, having said that, the man of the match was still a lump of wood. We bought him, so whether you thought that was a waste of money or not, the important thing was that the chairman did not undermine him by saying that his own son had begged him not to sign him. Anyway, we had Robert Snodgrass. And José Fonte. Marvellous.

What we hoped was a mini revival continued against Middlesbrough at the Riverside. A 3–1 win that was notable for Andy Carroll's brace meant that maybe he was finally back to his best. And Jonathan Calleri's last-minute third was also significant for one unlucky punter who had stood to win £250,000 on Sky Sports' Soccer Six, as with ninety-four minutes gone he had all six scores spot on. Calleri's goal was meaningless in the end, but cost Ian Alger of Basildon £245,000, as he only collected £5,000.

Still, the disappointment of an unfulfilled promise is not the same as actual loss. Manchester City at home in the league was beyond disappointing – it felt like a real loss, even though the expectation bar was set remarkably low. At the Pride of Irons quiz I had met Danny Francis, who had been on the editorial team of Hammers News in the '90s when I had been writing for them. He now had an official role with the club and he gave me his e-mail address to allow me to send him some text and a picture to slot into the programme in memory of Dad. His funeral had been the previous Wednesday and the wounds were still open, but the little postage stamp-sized tribute in the programme meant a lot. It also helped to ease the pain of the 4–0 defeat. Just 12–1 over a three-game aggregate in games against City that season: we must have been improving. It was 14–1 in 2013/14, after all.

Manchester City were a different class, and Bilić didn't seem to have a clue how to set up against them, as, to be fair, many managers didn't. We tried to play football and took a pasting. We could just as easily have gone defensive and taken a pasting.

If we take City out of the equation, the mini revival continued away at Southampton with another 3–1 win that took us up to 9th place on 31 points. Looking at the remaining fixtures there was no reason why we could not finish comfortably in the top half.

In fact there were several reasons. Not least the fact that Carroll had picked up yet another knock against Southampton and would miss the next two games. Also, the fact that we failed to win any of the next 8 games. I have to take partial responsibility for us failing to beat West Bromwich Albion at the London Stadium. We had fought back well from 1–0 down to be leading 2–1 with goals from Feghouli and Lanzini. At that point, with five minutes to go, I made my excuses and left. As I walked back across the green towards Pudding Mill Lane DLR station, who should I see but cushion-faced TV presenter and celebrity West Bromwich Albion fan Adrian Chiles.

I am not usually one to gloat. After all, I rarely get the opportunity, and I hate it when other people do it. But I couldn't resist a quick 'Tough luck Adrian!'. No sooner had the final syllable left my lips but a roar went up from the away end as Jonny Evans equalised in added time. So I'm sorry. That was my fault.

Not long after this, Elaine went off to Brazil for ten days to see her mum after the unexpected loss of her dad. I busied myself by going to Watford with Jim Grant, Colin Milne and Michelle Gabriel. I had forgotten what a tight little ground Vicarage Road is. Maybe I had become accustomed to the wide, open spaces on the concourses of the London Stadium, but this seemed very poky as I went for a half-time piss and could hardly turn around.

I gave up smoking in 2002, but it has always puzzled me why people feel the need to smoke in the bogs in football grounds. And not always just tobacco either. Why is that? Do you have a crafty fag on the tube? I doubt it. Would you smoke on a petrol station forecourt? Unlikely. It's a very odd thing. An irrational hatred, you might say.

Oh the game. It ended up 1–1, thanks to André Ayew equalising an early Troy Deeney penalty.

Unfortunately, there would be no repeat of the League Cup win over Chelsea as they came and quite clinically took 3 points on their way to the title in their first season under Antonio Conte. Bournemouth, Leicester and Hull were all games that we should have taken points from, but we failed miserably. We just could not put a run together.

Arsenal away was not a game we expected to win but it was a game we at least expected to compete in. Disappointment again on both counts, as we lost 3–0. From being 9th on 4 February we had slipped back to 15th by 8 April when Swansea City came to the London Stadium enjoying something of a revival under Paul Clement.

I sat up in block 230 with Sam and watched in horror as Antonio pulled up with what looked like a torn hamstring. Kouyaté scored just before half time and it proved to be enough. While not mathematically safe, it looked like we had probably done enough to stay up. After the euphoria and optimism of the summer, it was a bitter experience to be feeling grateful just to survive in the top league. This was not the next level. This was not part of the ten-point pledge.

The triumphant S!HT quiz team took the tour of the London Stadium, not accompanied by a club legend but by a recorded message. It was interesting to see the dressing rooms and sit in the manager's chair. But it was a little bit like being shown around a sausage factory. With no sausages.

60

SYMPHONY

WEST HAM UNITED 1, TOTTENHAM HOTSPUR 0
PREMIER LEAGUE, 5 MAY 2017
People who ask to look at your records
and touch the vinyl. Stop right there.

We edged towards safety with a 2–2 draw at the Stadium of Light, with David Moyes's Sunderland equalising late on in front of three Sunderland fans and a dog that had wandered in looking for its ball. This dispelled the myth that fans in the north-east will turn up to watch the grass grow. Mind you, this had been a particularly shit season for Sunderland even by their standards, but they still managed a point against us. Something they had only managed in 1 other of their previous 7 games.

Goalless draws against Everton at home and Stoke City away followed. I was grateful for the 0–0 against Everton for no other reason than it stopped that prick Lukaku scoring against us for a tenth successive game, which was something that I was getting a bit sick of.

Although unbeaten in 4 games we were still not mathematically safe when Tottenham came to the London Stadium for our first ever Friday night Premier League game. Tottenham, for their part, were still in with a mathematical chance of winning the title. Their run going into the game was impressive: they had won 9 consecutive games and, given our patchy form, it seemed that we would have to wait until the final game of the season to ensure our safety.

But this was Tottenham Hotspur, and part of the West Ham Way over the years has been to put a spoke in the wheel of teams chasing the title. I'd seen us do it to Manchester United more than once. The atmosphere inside the stadium was one of unity. After all, whether you are a tourist, whether you are sitting down or standing up, pissed or sober, asleep or awake, smoking in the bogs or intently watching the game, we can all agree that we hate Tottenham.

Lanzini's second half goal meant it was virtually impossible for Tottenham to win the title. They had gone all Spursy. Rachel Riley, the lovely numbers girl on *Countdown*, was part of the presentation team on the *Friday Night Football* show. And, just when you though it impossible to find her any more attractive, she said on national TV that Spurs had lost their bottle. More importantly – some might say less importantly – the 42 points made us mathematically safe with just 2 games left.

Before the Liverpool game I made a pilgrimage back to the Boleyn and met Jim Grant for pie and mash at Nathan's. I had promised myself I wouldn't do it. I didn't think it would affect me. But despite the fact the West Stand was only eighteen years old, seeing it ripped open and exposed really hurt. The Bobby Moore Stand had gone. The place I used to sit, the piece of space that I occupied in the final season was just that. Fresh air. After the joy of beating Spurs at our new home, I should not have gone back to the Boleyn. It merely put me in a bad mood, particularly as we lost 4–0 at home to Liverpool in a display that lacked anything positive. It meant that despite ending the season with a 2–1 win at Turf Moor, I was in a foul mood at the end of our first season at the London Stadium.

We had been tricked. The board must have known it was going to be like this, but it seemed they didn't care. The most important part of their ten-point pledge was that they would listen to fans. This wasn't happening – things needed to change.

It would have been useful to have had some peace and quiet, with the club staying out of the headlines. But there was to be no such luck. After being close to agreeing a £20 million naming rights deal, Vodafone inexplicably pulled the plug.

West Ham were unlikely to have seen any of the money, as

the LLDC were entitled to income from naming rights as part of the agreement. But the termination of the deal without proper explanation did not look good.

It could have just been that West Ham's name, like most of the home performances, was dirty. HMRC conducted a dawn raid in connection with alleged fraud. It appeared the investigation related to the transfers of players between the UK and France and the payment of income tax and NI contributions since 2010. Newcastle United were raided at the same time and their managing director Lee Charnley was arrested. He was later released without charge. It then emerged that there was no fault at West Ham's end as the allegations surrounded the transfers of several players, including the free transfer of Demba Ba to Newcastle in 2011.

But stuff like that stank the place out. It didn't stop 90 per cent of season ticket holders renewing, with only 5,000 fans deciding it was not for them anymore. Why should the board care? They allegedly had a waiting list of 50,000. The 90 per cent who renewed, if they were like me, did so on the basis that it was not ridiculously expensive, and things could not possibly get any worse.

The Supporters Club, which had been left high and dry by the move to the London Stadium, was saved from closure by the formation of a new committee. The premises in Castle Street were clearly no longer viable for match days, but the new committee set about liaising with the board to find suitable premises near the London Stadium.

The new fixture list came out in June and it soon became apparent that the first three fixtures would have to be played away due to the athletics World Championships taking place at the stadium. We had Manchester United away, Southampton at home and Newcastle away as the first three matches, but the Southampton game was switched to St Mary's, as was the second-round League Cup tie with Cheltenham Town, which had originally been drawn at home.

Brady was a guest on Sky Sports' *The Debate* and explained the potential impact. She played down the consequences and confirmed that this situation would never happen again, it being part of the contractual arrangements when negotiating the original lease. Odd though, that we had only just found out about it.

She claimed Bilić had said that we have to play all the teams anyway, so it didn't matter in which order. But he would say that, wouldn't he? What Brady didn't address was the fact that three away games in a row would almost certainly mean zero points going into September; almost certainly it would mean we would be bottom of the table and playing catch-up. A home fixture is vital, and especially a winnable one against the likes of Southampton, to get early momentum.

She showed her complete lack of understanding of the way football works by going on to say it was balanced out by having three home games in a row in March. It might be too late by then. It was unfortunate, but it appeared that the agreement was indeed made some time ago and there was nothing that could be done. The twattish face of social media reared its ugly head again though, when some West Ham fans questioned why the barriers erected to prevent football fans entering Westfield shopping centre were not in place for the athletics. Really? Do you need me to draw you a diagram?

The board continued to suffer from foot-in-mouth disease. I just wanted them to shut up. Joe Hart joined the club on loan and I really couldn't understand why. We had two good goal-keepers and Hart had been off-colour for some time, having had a disastrous Euro 2016 and during a difficult loan spell at Torino. It was a big name. He would sell shirts in China.

Sullivan just could not keep his trap shut. Of the trio in charge only David Gold appeared to have any sensitivity to what the fans might be feeling, after all, he was born at 442 Green Street, did he ever tell you that?

Sullivan said on the club website:

He is the best goalkeeper I've worked with and I fully expect him to be equally as good [as he had been at Birmingham for Sullivan] for us this coming season.

Lovely. Just what Adrián, clearly – at the very most – the second-best goalkeeper he had ever worked with, wanted to hear.

The pot was bubbling away on social media. It seemed that we were lurching from one crisis to another every day of the week leading up to the new season. In reality these 'crises' were quite often nothing more than a storm in a teacup, magnified infinitely by the power of social media and its destructive ability to spread lies and over-react. And the 2017/18 season would see that happen by the bucket load.

61

DESPACITO

MANCHESTER UNITED 4, WEST HAM UNITED 0
PREMIER LEAGUE, 13 AUGUST 2017
Panic and hysteria created by social media. Can't stand it.
Take a breath before you write anything.

The transfer window had to be a success. After two failures in succession, it was clear there was no strategy and no individual at the club who had the nous to source players who would fit into a particular system and pursue them systematically with realistic offers that did not insult the selling club.

It had not always been that way under SuGo. When Il Fatso identified Matt Jarvis as the man he wanted to supply killer crosses for Andy Carroll, the board went out and got him – albeit the news we were desperate to sign him probably pushed his price up by a couple of million. The fact that Jarvis couldn't cross the road without falling over was not SuGo's fault. Similarly, the fact that Andy Carroll had glass ankles was not their fault. Transfer windows that had seen the likes of Sakho, Kouyaté, Valencia, Payet and Ogboner join could only be deemed a success – so what had gone wrong?

There can be little doubt in my mind that part of the problem lay in a lack of communication between Bilić and the board, and Sullivan, in particular, making ridiculously low bids for players they had no intention of buying to placate the fan base chomping on the social media bit for every scrap of news twenty-four hours a day, seven days a week. At least the fruit of his loins seemed to have wound his neck in a bit and wasn't embarrassing us quite so much on Twitter, but Sullivan himself seemed to have adopted a director of football (DoF) role, and wasn't particularly good at it.

His attempts to sign William Carvalho from Sporting Lisbon descended into farce. Sporting said they never received an offer. Sullivan said the offer was accepted but confirmation was not received before deadline day. Accusations flew left, right and centre, with Sullivan eventually publishing the e-mails he had sent to Sporting, which frankly looked like they had been drawn in crayon by a five-year-old. It was an unseemly mess. When were they going to distance themselves from first-team affairs? There was one positive outcome however: Sporting President Bruno de Carvalho nicknamed SuGo the 'Dildo Brothers'. That was funny.

Bilić has to take part of the blame for not being clear what system he wanted to employ and what players he needed to fill those roles. But we are not privy to conversations he may have had in private with the board.

Aside from the Carvalho farce, this transfer window didn't appear to be going too badly. Hart came in on loan, albeit in my view, he wasn't really required. I just hoped there was not some clause in his contract about 'game time' ahead of the World Cup.

Javier Hernández had been on our radar for some time, but he finally joined for £16 million from Bayer Leverkusen.

Marko Arnautović was another player I had long admired at Stoke, though he seemed a little surly and, alongside Andy Carroll, would mean we had far too many top knots at the club. He signed for a massive £20 million that made me nervous, but by this time it was really not a huge sum of money for a top-flight player.

Pablo Zabaleta came in from Manchester City on a free transfer and Sead Hakšabanović (I shall call him Sead), a young Montenegrin, was signed from Swedish club Halmstads BK for £2.7 million. He was classed as one for the future, which in modern parlance meant he would go off on loan to a Championship club and never be seen again.

On the way out, Arbeloa had hardly been noticed and retired

from the game. Some would argue he retired when he arrived. Nordtveit went to 1899 Hoffenheim where he promptly had a rude awakening against Liverpool. I think £18.99 was the transfer fee we received for him. Enner Valencia had struggled to find the form that had served us well in 2014/15 and did no better on loan at Everton, so was sold to Mexican side Tigres.

Now we had Joe Hart, Darren Randolph was deemed surplus to requirements. He and Ashley Fletcher were sold to Middlesbrough for a combined fee of £11.5 million which, on the face of it, looked like good business. Sofiane Feghouli had also struggled to make an impact and was sold to Galatasaray for £4 million.

Pre-season was neither here nor there. We lost to Werder Bremen over two games in the space of two days at the end of July, then got battered 3–0 by Manchester City *again* in a friendly that was inexplicably arranged in Iceland. The run-up to the season was becoming a bit of a joke, and again, all part of the money-spinning process, with games shown live on TV and lucrative incentives offered to take part in tournaments abroad. The days of playing Southend, Colchester and Leyton Orient seemed a distant memory.

The three away games to open the season ended, predictably, in three defeats. Also predicable was that Lukaku would score for his new club Manchester United on his debut on the opening day. It took him just over half an hour, adding a second in the 52nd minute. Although the last 2 goals from Martial and Pogba came on 87 and 90 minutes, they did not skew the scoreline away from an accurate reflection of what happened. To use a technical footballing term, we were pants.

We did at least show some fight at St Mary's against Southampton, but we were not to know they were crap too, and Zabaleta completely forgot he wasn't playing for Manchester City and would not get away with a last-minute challenge in the area. So, after hauling us back to 2–2 from 2–0 down, Hernández's efforts were in vain as Southampton converted the last-minute penalty.

We did win at Whaddon Road against Cheltenham in the

League Cup, but made heavy weather of it, still looking defensively shaky.

If we had been unfortunate at St Mary's, we were simply awful at St James's Park, where newly promoted Newcastle tore bits off us, winning 3–0 with only timid resistance.

As I had suspected, Bilić was under pressure right away: the opening three fixtures had been away from home. No one outside the top six can cope with that sort of a start to the season.

Martin Keown is not necessarily my favourite pundit, but he called it on *Match of the Day* 2 the next day:

> You wonder if it's going to be time to change the manager … It seems so early in the season but he's going to have to have a good look at himself. Is he up for the job? It didn't look like he was up for it yesterday.

Bilić looked like a broken man, standing hands on hips in the technical area, like the captain of the *Titanic*.

He had the international break, at least, to consider his approach for the next game at home to Huddersfield, who had enjoyed a start as good as ours had been bad, taking 7 points from their opening 3 games – 2 of which had been at home, proving that it's important to have a home game or two early on.

The game had been moved to a Monday night for the benefit of TV. It meant that everyone had the chance to move further away from us before we got to kick a ball. It meant a win would not be enough to lift us out of the bottom three. It looked like we might have to settle for a point, though, as it was not until the 72nd minute that Pedro Obiang fired in a shot that took a looping deflection and nestled in the Huddersfield net. Ayew added a second from typical range a few minutes later. A clean sheet. A 100 per cent record at home. Off the bottom. But it was far from convincing.

Obiang was fast becoming a key member of the squad, and at the Hawthorns he was the only player who seemed to want to break the deadlock, with a shot from the halfway line that hit the bar. But 0–0 seemed to have stopped the rot away from home. It still wasn't convincing, though. There was a lot of work to do. But the tools Bilić had at his disposal were limited. Arnautović had been sent off at Southampton and was suspended, Hernández was blowing hot and cold. Ayew wasn't the answer, although that depended what the question was. The defence, despite two clean sheets, and indeed a third in the cup against Bolton at the London Stadium, did nothing to paper over the cracks that were obvious for all to see.

My poor mum, having lost her husband in January, now had to deal with the loss of her only brother as my Uncle Peter passed away. As with Dad, it was not completely unexpected but equally, as with Dad, that made it no easier to deal with. Peter was a very kind and funny man who always claimed not to be a West Ham fan, but one day produced about 100 West Ham home programmes from the 1960s. 'Thought you might like these,' he said. They were from games he had attended at Upton Park. He had never mentioned it before then! We all miss him terribly.

Before the home game against Tottenham I met up at the Podium with Gavin, my former neighbour in the Bobby Moore Upper, and we reminisced about the good old days of 2015/16. It had been pretty poor fare since coming back to the Premier League in 2012. That first season was okay, the first half of 2014/15 wasn't too bad either, but 2015/16 was the only decent full season we had enjoyed in the last six. It didn't seem fair, and it certainly didn't seem to be in line with the ten-point pledge. We had been promised world-class football in a world-class stadium. What we had was third-rate football in a seething concrete mass of hatred.

The 100 per cent home record soon went as we went 3–0 down to Tottenham, who seemed hell bent on revenge for us screwing up their title plans a few months before. We had been drawn to play Tottenham in the League Cup at their temporary home of Wembley in October. I would be in Brazil. In forty years of watching West Ham I had not yet seen us play at Wembley. Now I was going to miss another opportunity. I started making enquiries then about tickets for the league match scheduled for 31 December. I was not intending to miss that.

Hernández and Kouyaté scored to give the score line a bit of re-spectability, but it was another defensive shambles and we seemed to be back to square one. We had to beat Swansea on 14 October. Again, a tepid, frustrating performance punctuated by unrest among the fans saw us go into the final minute at 0–0. Substitute Diafra Sakho made a rare appearance and popped up with the winner that produced a massive sigh of relief more than a cheer.

The arguments were well under way on social media between those who had every faith in Bilić and wanted him to stay, and those who thought he was a busted flush and should go.

Personally I loved him. He understood the West Ham Way – even if at times he went too far in trying to apply it. In many ways he was the perfect manager for West Ham. I was torn, but I accepted maybe a change was needed. But the usual question posed to those who suggested such a thing, and not usually as politely, was: who would replace him? Many were advocates of Rafa Benítez, but why would he come to West Ham? Once again, the shambolic way in which the club was run would pre-vent us bringing in a top-class candidate. It seemed that no one at board level understood the fans.

The Supporter's Advisory Board provided some interface, but it was limited. I hated the way the board rode roughshod over the wishes of the fans and managed to cause offence to someone, it seemed, on a daily basis. So when I saw an advert for a fan liaison officer role to organise communication chan-nels between the board and the fans, I applied. I did not expect to get the job. Indeed, if I had been offered it, I doubt if I could have afforded to take it. But I didn't even get to the first round. I was disgusted. I felt my experience at least warranted an inter-view. But applications were being handled by the job-search website Indeed, and if the CV didn't tick all the boxes, there was no wriggle room, and no appeal. Computer says no.

I was back in Brazil as we gave away another lead late on at Turf Moor to draw 1–1, and despite efforts to find a broadcast of the home game against Brighton I was unsuccessful – in the end I was glad as we were trounced 3–0 at home by a team that had only scored one goal away from home to that point, and who would go on to score only 10 goals away from home all season. Three of them came that night.

It was another low. Another night of speculation over Bilić's future. For now, he remained at his post.

I tried again, this time half-heartedly, to find the Tottenham cup tie in Brazil. I knew it was on ESPN but only online. I phoned one of the local sports bars who assured me they had it so I dragged Elaine out at 5 p.m. along with her sister, brother-in-law and niece to the bar in question only to find that the game being shown was Chelsea against Everton. 'É a mesma coisa, né?' ('Isn't it the same thing?')

I now had free data usage in Brazil, so it didn't cost me £37 to find out we were 2–0 down at Wembley. The mosquitoes were doing my head in so we went home. ESPN were a bit slow with the updates. The ticker tape banner across the bottom still said Tottenham 2 West Ham 0 so I went to the fridge to get a beer. When I came back it said Tottenham 2 West Ham 2. Surely this was a mistake? But then André Ayew's name came up as the scorer of both. Surely that couldn't be a mistake? Before I had finished the beer it said Tottenham 2 West Ham 3 (Ogboner). I sent a message to my Tottenham-supporting colleague Derek Thomson, saying that if we held on I would bring him back some Brazilian beers. He said in that case, he was quite happy to lose. Tottenham fans are so easily bought.

It was quite a night. One of those nights that defines us, and the reason why Bilić was such a good fit as a coach. In among the rough of 3–0 home defeats to Brighton and 4–0 shellackings at Old Trafford, came a result so beautifully unpredictable that you had to keep going just to see what would happen next.

What happened next was that we went 2–0 up at Selhurst Park against a Crystal Palace team that had lost their opening 7 games without scoring a goal, but who were showing signs of recovery under new boss Roy Hodgson. Ayew set us up with a rare strike from outside the area and Hernández scored the goals.

Palace pulled one back, but going into the last minute we had possession in the Palace half. Antonio should have kept the ball down by the corner flag, but instead, he put a tame cross into the hands of Palace keeper Wayne Hennessey. Palace worked the ball up field to find Wilfried Zaha on the left side of the box who fired a shot – down to Hart's left – that stole them a point.

The draw for the quarter-finals of the League Cup was almost as farcical as our season to date, as the live link went down conveniently to allow the draw to be made without anyone seeing it, as the four remaining 'big' teams were kept apart. We got Arsenal away. Manchester United were away at Bristol City, Chelsea would play Bournemouth and Manchester City would play Leicester. Conspiracy theories were rife, and for once I thought there might be some substance.

As with last year I had hardly had time to acclimatise to the British winter after three weeks in Brazil before I found myself standing on the roof of the Podium drinking horrible Heineken and dreading the ninety minutes that lay ahead. The new security measures that had been brought in by the stadium management meant I had to leave a good half an hour before kick-off to make sure I was in my seat in time, but many others hadn't bothered, and I wished I hadn't either as Liverpool's team of highlighter pens strolled to a 4–1 win.

I stayed to the end – but many others did not. Andy Carroll picked up on this in the press, criticising those who left early: 'They really should be staying.' Why? He went on to explain:

> You never know what's going to happen. They walked out at half-time against Tottenham when we were getting beaten 2–0 and we turned it round … They should be supporting us no matter what. We should be playing better – it's us to blame. But they should be helping us out a bit.

He didn't say anything about people turning up fifteen minutes late and sleeping through the entire match.

62

HAVANA

WATFORD 2, WEST HAM UNITED 0
PREMIER LEAGUE, 19 NOVEMBER 2017

People who walk away from cash points failing to tell you it has no money in it. How hard would that be? Or, when you tell the person behind you it has no money in it, but they go and try all the same. What is it? You think I'm just overdrawn?

Perhaps given SuGo's record for allowing contracts to run down, it was surprising that Bilić was sacked. Sullivan suggested Bilić had effectively lost the will to carry on with the job and was completely exhausted, despite the fact the season was only three months in. In a way, I felt relief for Slaven. The level of suffering was so obvious that, had he been a dog, he would have been put down weeks ago. In an open letter to the fans published on the official website he thanked the fans for their support:

> It has been far more than just a job for me. Having worn the claret and blue shirt as a player, I felt that connection when I returned as manager and I have always known how truly special this club is.

God bless you Slaven, all the best.

Since David Moyes's name had been linked with the manager's role for years, it seemed that SuGo had finally made their dream appointment, so it was somewhat baffling that they only gave him a contract to the end of the season.

The appointment did not go down well with West Ham fans generally. Those in favour cited his overall record with Everton, taking them to a Champions League spot on limited resources and the fact that, despite being nominated by Sir Alex Ferguson to succeed him, he was left with an ageing squad that was on the wane and was essentially stitched up.

Those against pointed to his inability to maintain momentum at Manchester United, as well as his successive failures at Real Sociedad and Sunderland.

If I'm honest, I was underwhelmed by the selection, but it had been obvious this was who we were going to get. At least he brought in Stuart Pearce as part of the coaching team.

My biggest concern was the length of his contract. If SuGo thought he was so amazing, why was it so short? Tony Cottee also called it on Sky Sports:

> As soon as there is uncertainty at a football club, players switch off, players lose concentration, and that's what happens. So I don't want to read that David Moyes has got it until the end of the season …
> Why not give him a [long term] contract? If he's your choice, he's your choice. Give him a three-and-a-half-year contract or whatever it is, because you can't say, 'Well, we'll see how it goes'.

The appointment of Moyes on such a short-term deal brought comment from the popular press also. I would rather stick pins in my eyes than read the *Daily Mail*, but I am told they were particularly critical, and people seem to believe what is written in the *Daily Mail* like it's some sort of gospel.

It said that the team which was many people's second favourite was now wandering around like a lost soul:

> Part of Brady's legacy is that most neutrals no longer care whether West Ham stay up or go down.

Sadly, many devoted West Ham fans felt the same way and almost wished for relegation in the hope that it would force the current ownership to consider their positions.

Moyes started his tenure with a tricky fixture away at Watford.

Anti-board feeling was both vocal and visible in the form of chanting and banners. Sadly, attempts were made by stewards to remove some of these, which were not offensive, but were simply expressions of free speech.

Some people on Facebook and Twitter were not so reserved. Brady was often referred to as 'The Tranny' on some pages. There is no need for that. The open hatred towards the board would not help. They had thick skins.

The 2–0 defeat at Watford was a run-of-the-mill as they come. It seemed the days of the managerial 'bounce' were well and truly gone, as we were looking no different than we had done in the previous 14 games of the season. Often new managers who come in are able to breathe life into a team and extract a performance that defies logic. Clearly the players were as underwhelmed by Moyes as we had been.

A story emerged on BBC local news the next day about West Ham fans calling 999 because they were so worried about West Ham's poor performances. The Essex Police control room tweeted:

> Ringing 999 because @WestHamUtd have lost again and you aren't sure what to do is not acceptable! It is a complete waste of our time.

I was incensed. It was clearly an attempt by Essex police to raise awareness of the abuse of the 999 system. I have read of people calling 999 when their boiler broke down, or even when a kebab shop ran out of chilli sauce. It is an irresponsible waste of police time. But quite often people making these calls have issues themselves. I was interested to know more, so submitted a freedom of information request to find out exactly how many calls were received by Essex police in relation to West Ham's form.

I didn't think it was fair that with our reputation already in tatters, the police should pull us up as an example. I was confident there would have been between zero and one calls made. So why drag us into it?

I updated the Upton Parklife Facebook group and received

unexpected criticism. I was told that I was wasting police time just as much, and what's more, I was behaving like a Spurs fan. I was also told I needed to go with the flow and get a sense of humour.

Okay, three things. Firstly, this was a serious issue in my view and submitting an FOI request would not mean a uniform would have to plough through loads of call data looking for the relevant information. Secondly, Spurs fans would not have seen the funny side at all. I did – but also, I recognised that it was a serious matter. The police should be trusted to uphold the law, not to make flippant and/or untrue statements on Twitter. Finally, if there had been more than one call from West Ham fans, these people needed to be found and helped.

When the response finally came through I was told the data could not be traced. I took that as a zero, but chose not to share my findings online. The season was developing into enough of a clusterfuck without me pouring fuel on the flames. Sullivan's house had been targeted by angry fans with a banner demanding that Brady be sacked. There was then an ongoing Twitter war between the fan responsible and Jack Sullivan over whether he had or had not been banned and had his away loyalty points rescinded.

In Moyes's first home game in charge against Leicester, West Ham fans showed what could be achieved if we did unite. Despite going behind early on we made a terrific noise and lifted the team visibly. Kouyaté equalised just before half time and we were unfortunate not to win. It showed we were much stronger united than divided, but the team had to play their part and respond. In that instance they did so admirably.

Around this time a new group was formed on Facebook, the Real West Ham Fans Action Group (RWHFAG), which was launched by two former members of the ICF. They were demanding changes from the board and their primary intention was to engage in a structured and organised way. They made five demands of the board and as those demands were met they would submit the next five, and so on. It was a good, well-timed move; it caught the imagination of fans who were at their lowest ebb for years. New manager David Moyes would have to do more than take a point off Leicester to win the fans' overall backing.

The popularity of the group was impressive; it gained 7,000 members in the first twenty-four hours. West Ham fans were desperate for proper representation and were getting on board in their droves. RWHFAG were addressing key matters like the preservation of the memorial garden, disabled transport, the badge, stewarding and the service within the stadium.

Other West Ham fans groups were available. For example, the West Ham United Independent Supporters' Association (WHUISA) had its genesis in the WHU's View campaign which had fought for a referendum on the stadium move back in 2011. It was a broad group of supporters, and at no point was it solely anti-Olympic Stadium. After its affiliation to the Football Supporters Association during the first season at Stratford, its membership grew to roughly 700 members. WHUISA was then, and still is, a strictly democratic group with all of its policies voted on by its members.

We thought that after the positive reaction against Leicester a trip to Moyes' former side Everton would motivate the team to its first win for him. We certainly were not expecting a 4–0 defeat that showed we had made no progress whatsoever. Hart still looked shaky in goal and the rest of the team were worse. We had a chance at 2–0, but Lanzini had his penalty saved by Jordan Pickford who was on his six-yard line by the time the ball was struck. Rooney, for the second time against West Ham, scored from the halfway line. There was no coming back.

The club finally agreed to sponsor the new supporters' club, funding premises at Stour Space for the remainder of the season. It was a shred of good news in a sea of desperation and woe.

Despite the fact that we had moved in to the London Stadium sixteen months earlier, rows over funding and the cost to the taxpayer continued to rumble on.

Following the publication of a report by accountants Moore Stephens, London Mayor Sadiq Khan insisted that he would be taking personal control of the stadium in order to try and recoup some of the £20 million annual losses.

The LLDC insisted that 'West Ham have a great deal', revealing that the cost of moving seats to and from football mode (initially budgeted at £50,000 per annum) was in the region of £12 million last year, largely as a result of the stadium hosting the World Athletics Championships. This was exactly what Tessa Jowell had said in 2006: 'Football would actually be much more expensive because we are absolutely bound to provide an athletics legacy. Running a parallel procurement is very, very expensive.'

The sums had been done twelve years before, but no one had listened. It was hardly our fault. But the board had presented a persuasive argument, and the government was determined not to be left with a white elephant.

The point that all supporters' groups continually miss is this: the stadium and structure of the stadium is not ours to control. If the LLDC decide to install a more cost-effective and better seating arrangement, that is for them to decide because it is taxpayers' money. West Ham could contribute, but why would they? Why would you pay your landlord to paint your kitchen when he should pay for it himself?

The loss at Everton was particularly hard to take given that the next three fixtures were Manchester City away, Chelsea at home and Arsenal at home. There were, however, signs of recovery at the Etihad. This was largely down to Hart being ineligible against his parent club, but overall we looked more solid. We had the front to go 1–0 up just before half time through Ogboner, but despite playing well for the whole game, City were irresistible, and won 2–1.

The question for Moyes now was whether to bring Joe Hart back in for the visit of Chelsea or retain the services of Adrián. If the spine of the team is vital, then a good goalkeeper is a must. Hart was vocal and marshalled his defenders, but he did not inspire confidence by deed. Adrián did. Moyes took the brave – and correct – decision to retain him.

In one of the best performances seen at the London Stadium,

Marko 'Arnie' Arnautović scored early on in his new central role and we held on for a memorable victory. It was similar the following Wednesday against Arsenal. Hernández hit the bar late on, but a 0–0 draw meant we had taken 4 points from Arsenal and Chelsea in the space of five days, which was exactly 4 more than we thought we would get.

Still the board would not shut their gobs. Sullivan continued to prattle on about transfer business in the press like it was something he knew about. In an interview with *The Guardian* he said:

> I'm very involved with bringing in the players ... I'm not involved in the strategy. The manager [Slaven Bilić] says he wants Fonte from Southampton and Snodgrass from Hull. My kids begged me not to sign them.

Nice one Dave, well done. Frank McAvennie later said on Twitter:

> How do you expect players to give you 100 per cent when you make comments like this? And especially about players still signed to the club! I think the board should stop using social media, it seems every time they post something it's totally wrong.

Couldn't have put it better myself, Macca. We've been trying to tell them to shut the fuck up, but they did not listen. They just couldn't help themselves.

The positive home performances were followed by an eventful 3–0 win away at Stoke. Lanzini won a penalty and was later charged with, and found guilty of, diving. It seemed harsh. To me, it looked like he went down to avoid getting clattered. But then, I am biased. Arnie scored against his former team and made no secret of his pleasure both to the home fans and to Mark Hughes.

I met Phil Whelans and Jim Grant in the Faltering Fullback pub in Finsbury Park before going on to the Emirates for the League Cup quarter-final against Arsenal. Given the three games that had gone before, it was disappointing that neither team showed any level of ambition, and hopes of a Wembley final were dashed yet again with an apology of a 1–0 defeat.

Rumours abounded that our home game against Newcastle may be switched to Christmas Eve, but thankfully it went ahead as scheduled, a rare Saturday 3 p.m. start. There the good news ended, though, as we lost 3–2, although it could have been closer, as André Ayew did miss a penalty.

At Bournemouth on Boxing Day we scored another 3 away goals, but it was only enough for a draw. We managed to snatch a draw from the jaws of victory, or rather referee Madley did, initially disallowing Bournemouth's equaliser, then changing his mind after consultation with the linesman. Still, as Il Fatso would have said, you had to respect the point.

We were scoring goals; there seemed to be no problem there. But defensive issues would take longer to sort out. With the transfer window approaching it was important that we bring in some decent names after the disappointments of the previous three windows. It was vital that we did not spend £10 million on an unproven championship striker from, say, Preston, or a non-league player for the stiffs, or a 36-year-old full-back most famous for attacking his own fans. It was also important the board kept out of the limelight.

But on 30 December in her hugely divisive column in *The Sun*, Karren Brady wrote:

> Other times, there has been an element of 'we must do something, anything' – and we've paid for ill-fitting players. Robert Snodgrass wasn't exactly a triumph, while Hammers fans could name several foreign players who added little. The obvious fact is we need one or two who the manager believes will be a real plus. But no bargains that fall apart under the Prem's pressure.

If you can't say anything helpful, say nothing at all.

63

PERFECT

TOTTENHAM HOTSPUR 1, WEST HAM UNITED 1
PREMIER LEAGUE, 4 JANUARY 2018
Rugby. Union or League. It's just egg-chasing.

The New Year started with a visit from West Bromwich Albion under the management of Alan Pardew. After bragging in the press that he would have turned us around instantly, he had been drafted in to replace Tony Pulis at the Hawthorns and had experienced the same sort of bounce you might get dropping a tennis ball into a bucket of treacle. They had not won in a staggering 19 Premier League games, and whinged about having to play so soon after their New Year's Eve game against Arsenal, whereas we had our game against Tottenham rescheduled after a saga involving transport issues.

They weren't complaining when James McArthur put them 1–0 up, but Andy Carroll decided to make a rare appearance and scored twice to win the game. It seemed to be a bit rich for Carroll to criticise fans for leaving early when he hardly ever turned up at all, and was about to take yet another three-month holiday. West Bromwich Albion's Jake Livermore dived into the crowd after being substituted and had to be restrained. Yet, despite the player's behaviour, which could have affected the safety of other supporters in the vicinity, the FA later confirmed it would take no action.

He had told the inquiry that someone had made a comment about the death of his child, which had sparked the reaction. He was advised never to do it again, and to allow security staff to deal with such incidents. One fan was removed from the stadium by security staff, but it was never established what was said and by whom. The FA accepted Livermore's version of events. Clearly, if someone did say something as Livermore alleges, they should take a long, hard look at themselves. It would be beyond banter, and completely out of order.

You may say football is tribal and it is about passion. But someone lost their child. When the world as you know it changes beyond your recognition and control, football is a welcome distraction. But it is just a game.

At half time I met Cássio Amaral, part of the administration team on the Hammers Brasil Facebook page, where West Ham fans in Brazil gather to share their experiences. Believe it or not, there are around 7,000 West Ham fans in Brazil. I joined primarily to help improve my Portuguese. So, of course the first question I asked everyone was, 'Why West Ham?!'. It was disappointing that a number of the replies detailed that their devotion to West Ham had its roots in the fact they had seen the films *Hooligan* or *Green Street*. Fucking hell. Cássio is a great guy, though. We had a long conversation in Portuguese and we have met up many times since.

Another S!HT contact, Trevor Drane, had procured me a ticket for the Tottenham game at Wembley only a few days later. I met him, Jim Grant and Jim's brother Pete in Marylebone. I could not believe my luck as the pub had my favourite beer, Proper Job, on draft. I am no beer snob, but I was getting thoroughly sick of the weak and tepid lager served before most football matches.

As it was my first sighting of West Ham at Wembley I wanted to make the most of it and enjoy every second. But on arrival, Wembley appeared to be one of the same monolithic, generic edifices as the London Stadium and the Emirates. The new Wembley did not have the soul of the old home of football, or of places like Upton Park, Highbury, the Dell, Roker Park, the Baseball Ground, Filbert Street or Ayresome Park, all of which were once alive with character and history but had all been bulldozed and concreted over in the name of progress.

Pedro Obiang concreted over Tottenham with a pile driver of a shot from thirty yards out to give us the lead. I celebrated with Trevor like we had won the FA Cup. That was special. It was a privilege to have been there to see it. But Tottenham equalised and the game ended 1–1. So after forty years of waiting to see us play at Wembley, it was a little bit disappointing.

We had drawn Shrewsbury away in the FA Cup. The BBC, as always sensing an upset, screened it live, but the only upset was in the millions of households that had to witness such a dire game. Young Josh Cullen was literally left looking for his teeth after a kick in the face. That was the most accurate shot of the day.

Many of the Upton Parklife gang went up to Huddersfield safe in the knowledge that a resident of Holmfirth just up the road, Chris Miles, would give them a place to crash. A fine day out by all accounts. West Ham won 4–1 with goals from Noble, Arnautović and a brace from Lanzini. He and Arnie were forming a good partnership, so it was about time one of them got injured.

The replay against Shrewsbury came within a few days and Lanzini played the whole 120 minutes of the game which went to extra time as we still could not break them down. A Reece Burke strike in extra time finally settled the tie, which had been hard work for all those who played in it – and harder still for those who had to watch it. It was thankfully made easier by watching with Colin Milne. We both ventured down to the new supporter's club premises at Stour Space and, as we had not previously been members, we signed up, paid £10 and had some proper beer and food. This was great, it was even bordering on a good matchday experience. Maybe we could build on this and make the London Stadium enjoyable.

On the anniversary of my father's passing, my Aunt Barbara, who had so generously sent me £200 in 2006 when West Ham reached the FA Cup final, passed away unexpectedly at the age of eighty-seven. Yet another link to the past, and to a different set of values that had gone.

After playing 120 minutes against Shrewsbury, Lanzini inevitably picked up an injury in the home 1–1 draw with Bournemouth. The injuries were staring to pile up again.

In the fourth round of the FA Cup, West Ham took to the pitch against Wigan at the JD Stadium like frightened mice against a team of lions. Wigan had beaten Bournemouth comfortably in the previous round and they looked like they had no issues with us, and we did not seem to be willing to give them any. We lost Pedro Obiang to a serious injury then Arthur Masuaku inexplicably gobbed at Wigan's Nick Powell and was suspended for six games. The fact that we lost the game 2–0 was almost forgotten in the post-match hubbub, as it was almost expected. And the loss of two more senior players was certainly more of an issue than the result.

I was invited to host the S!HT podcast in the absence of Phil Whelans, and what an absolute honour that was. What had not been explained to me was that I had to find guests myself, and I had a frantic weekend texting around trying to drum up interest. The biggest problem is always lack of notice, but James Kearns, author of the excellent West Ham blog 'The H List' and Colin Milne stepped in as familiar faces to ease my debut nerves. I didn't think I did too badly, but I haven't been asked to do it again.

By this time, the RWHFAG was gaining momentum. By 29 January the group had 14,000 members and they had started discussing a protest march, confusingly to be held in the month of March. At the end of January the RWHFAG had invited other groups to join them, in a bid to bring everyone together and show a unified front for the first time since the move.

A JustGiving page was launched supporting the march with a promise to give any unused funds to the #TeamIsla fund, set up to raise funds for Isla Caton, a young Hammers fan diagnosed in March 2016 with a rare child cancer called neuroblastoma. After only three days the group reached their £20,000 funding target and eventually hit £26,000. The planned march received a lot of media coverage and so other groups willingly helped team up to form the new West Ham Groups United (WHGU), on the basis they would be represented at meetings with the club. A new unified flag was launched to include all of the represented groups. Plans for the march became more elaborate as the group planned to hire ten hearses and lay wreathes at a mock funeral. A meeting was planned for 10 February, prior to the Watford game, to discuss objectives and allocate tasks. It was all looking promising.

As the transfer window closed, Diafra Sakho finally got his cherished move back to France and André Ayew went back from whence he came for £20 million. Unfortunately, the nature of modern-day football transfers is such that fees are rarely paid up front, so we were probably still paying Swansea for the initial transfer in August 2016. Because of the tremendous sums involved, it was impossible to know what was going on unless you were some sort of forensic accountant.

Crystal Palace had made a remarkable recovery under Roy Hodgson. After losing their first 7 games, they had climbed to 13th, still only 3 points above the relegation zone, but if you had offered them that in September they would have taken it. It was a measure of how far they had come that we were expecting to lose when they came to the London Stadium, such was our injury and suspension situation. In the end, our new signing João Mário, who had signed on loan from Inter Milan, slipped Hernández in to win a penalty Mark Noble converted to cancel out Benteke's opener. A draw was a good result.

January had been a shit month overall, but there was still time for one more embarrassing news story to add to our woes. Director of Player Recruitment Tony Henry was accused of pursuing a club policy not to sign African players.

According to an article by Matt Lawton, published in that shit-stirring rag the *Daily Mail* just before the end of the January transfer window, Henry admitted the agenda was being followed with the full knowledge of what the report referred to as 'club management'.

'We had problems with Sakho,' he allegedly said. 'We find

that when they are not in the team they cause mayhem. It's nothing against the African race at all. It's just sometimes they cause a lot of problems when they are not playing, as we had with Diafra.'

The club would not comment pending an investigation, which ended in Henry's sacking. In my opinion, this was not so much for what he said about African players, but for saying the policy was supported by the management. Maybe that was true. Maybe it wasn't. Either way, the whole unsavoury incident did not reflect well on a club already in crisis.

64

GOD'S PLAN

WEST HAM UNITED 2, WATFORD 0
PREMIER LEAGUE, 10 FEBRUARY 2018
People who express loud opinions on the train. Especially those about
how the Rothschild family is to blame for everything, ever.

The Henry story meant the hole I wanted to dig for myself as a West Ham fan was now getting deeper and deeper. It would have been nice just to have a few weeks with West Ham out of the headlines. But no, Karren Brady could not help herself. In her column in *The Sun* in 2017 she had criticised the Leicester chairman Vichai Srivaddhanaprabha following the sacking of title-winning boss Claudio Ranieri. She wrote:

> A fellow Premier League director reports that last night he bumped into the Leicester chairman at London's most-expensive wine shop … The Leicester owner told him they'd sacked Claudio Ranieri.
>
> He then casually settled his bill for wine and champagne. Since the sum was close to £500,000 I guess the compensation to his old manager is pocket change. At least the owner can drown his sorrows in style!

Just shut up, please. It emerged Srivaddhanaprabha was not best pleased by these comments and, as a result, West Ham's attempts to sign Islam Slimani from Leicester in January fell on deaf ears. Was there anyone left that our three stooges had not offended in some way?

Away form nose-dived, although the team was still suffering

from injuries and suspensions as we went down 3–1 at Brighton, and although Hernández scored the best goal of the game, it was scant consolation to suffer a double loss 6–1 on aggregate against a team that would only go on to win 9 games and score 34 goals. West Ham provided them with 22 per cent of their wins, 17.6 per cent of their goals and 15 per cent of their points. I liked Chris Hughton, but not that much.

The Upton Parklife contingent gathered at Stour Space before the Watford game. Jacqui excitedly arrived having represented the group at the WHGU meeting organised by RWHFAG on a barge on the canal. She was gushing about the plans for the march, and I was enthusiastic too: this seemed like good progress and a good way to get our points across to the board. But what were our points exactly? What was the purpose of the march other than to show we were basically unhappy?

I remember saying to Jacqui that all I wanted was for those idiots to shut up and get someone in who knew what they were doing to organise things. She thought I meant the organisers of the march. I meant SuGo. We talked about the organisers and the involvement of former ICF men I had never met either. I've met Bill Gardner, and a nicer more charming gentlemen you could not wish to meet, so I had no doubts they were all the same these days. But the association with the ICF was a problem for me. The ICF were that alcoholic uncle you were obliged to invite to weddings, the one who would always tip over the table and insult the waiting staff. Yes they were part of our history. But then so is the bombing of Dresden. It's not something to be particularly proud of. That said, they deserved enormous credit for galvanising everyone and putting forward the idea of the march, which, if I use David Gold's stadium approval figures, had around 90 per cent support.

I was part of the 10 per cent, though, as doubts filled my head about the march being a good idea. I had two main concerns. Firstly, that there was no specific agenda – everyone seemed to have different points they wanted to raise. Secondly, I could see that it would descend into violence one way or another. Not necessarily because of the involvement of former ICF members – those days were well behind them – but there did seem to be a simmering anger, a build up of flammable gas that would only need a tiny spark for it all to go off. For example, if fans of another team decided to infiltrate or, for example, if someone had wanted it to descend into violence to make their own position look better. Just as an example. I can't think who might have wanted that. But someone might.

I could see from that moment it would not work and I disassociated myself from it. I was upset. Upset because of what had become of my football club. Upset because it had come to this in an attempt to resolve things. Upset because I was just starting to enjoy my football experience again. We had found a good pre-match location and an amazing group of friends. But no sooner had I found it than there was a risk of having it torn away from me again. It seemed almost unimportant in the scheme of things that we beat Watford 2–0.

The WHGU seemed to be getting along, the march was planned to go ahead on 10 March prior to the home match against Burnley and was apparently approved by the police with full stewarding to keep order. But my decision to keep my distance seemed vindicated by the behaviour and comments of some members of the RWHFAG. There was widespread intolerance of any alternative view; it seemed to be a dictatorship focused on hating the board. Anyone who dared suggest anything to the contrary would be abused, called a 'snowflake' or a 'muggy cunt', and ultimately thrown off the group. Some left of their own volition and, in their absence, with no dissenting voices, the vitriol became worse.

On February 15, a tweet from RWHFAG proudly stated:

The ICF are celebrating their 40th anniversary this year and are having a get together for everyone that used to be involved. The ICF has nothing to do with RWHFAG. [The organisers] and everyone else made that clear.

Really? Wasn't that a bit like saying Paul McCartney has nothing to do with the Beatles? The group had everything to do with the ICF, as far as I could see. I couldn't decide whether people had seen through the thin veneer of this not being an ICF group, or if they joined up *because* they thought it was an ICF group. If it was the latter, then membership of 16,000 and £26,000 raised caused me deep concern about our fan base. I do believe that had it been as clear to other fan groups as it had been to me, they would not have joined the WHGU and aligned themselves so closely. Clearly, it wasn't obvious to the board, or they simply didn't care. Probably, it was a bit of both.

A meeting with the club was announced for the following week with representatives from other key members of the WHGU. The club wanted an opportunity to stop the march by negotiating a workable solution. Talking to the fans as part of the ten-point pledge should not, in my view, have taken this level of threat. It was clear that, whatever your thoughts on the ICF, the proposed march had rattled SuGo and got them thinking. The organisers deserve huge credit for that.

On 19 February, the meeting went ahead but SuGo did not attend, leaving it for Karren Brady. The WHGU put forward their list of issues. On 25 February, Karren Brady shared a 5,000-word open letter response to all groups which showed a willingness to at least try and address some of the issues. As I have said before, all I wanted was for the board to shut up and get professionals in – a director of football, and a decent press officer, for example – but Brady refused point blank to give up her column in *The Sun*.

At Anfield, as well as letting in goals scored by Liverpool in a torrid 1–4 defeat, West Ham fans scored an own goal in the stands by unveiling a banner which read:

BRADY, SULLIVAN & GOLD
   YOU HAVE DONE MORE DAMAGE TO THE EAST END
OF LONDON THAN ADOLF HITLER DID
   OUT OUT OUT

The banner was very professionally made, but whoever composed it had not considered the extent of the negative impact it might have in these days of instant news and social media. To align the board with Hitler, or imply they were in some way worse than Hitler, would understandably not go down well in certain sections, and was bound to be picked up by the press. Only Prince Philip can get away with making such sweeping generalisations.

The banner caused more wedges to be driven between those with a social conscience on social media, and those with none. Anyone expressing concerns over the banner was a snowflake. It didn't alter the fact the banner did a lot of damage to the campaign. Trying to explain why was a waste of time.

On 28 February, the WHGU were again invited to the London Stadium, but only representatives from RWHFAG and WHUISA could attend at such short notice due to the bad weather. RWHFAG explained to the club that the 5,000-word letter had only made things worse and the march would still go ahead.

It's not 100 per cent clear to me what happened after that, but there seemed to be a private meeting between RWHFAG organisers and the board, following which the RWHFAG leadership unilaterally announced the march had been cancelled.

Suddenly the club's written response was now acceptable and addressed all the important issues. Any funds unused from the Just Giving page would be donated to #TeamIsla, and the club would match this donation as long as no march happened. The involvement of this poorly young girl, no matter how well intentioned it may have been, was not well thought through. There would be a presentation on the pitch from a former player with one of those oversized cheques the bank won't accept.

RWHFAG reached this agreement without consultation of the other WHGU members. In that moment, WHGU ceased to exist. How could it continue when one group had taken such a massive decision unilaterally?

Also, at that very moment, the world of the average West Ham United fan caved in.

This sudden and unexplained change was greeted with widespread abuse aimed towards the RWHFAG hierarchy on Facebook, to which they responded furiously. Relevant questions were also asked, but the only answer was to come and ask face-to-face at the Podium. This was not helpful. Some level of engagement would have been useful; people were asking reasonable questions and being abused in response. WHUISA, the democratic alternative, announced they would try to resurrect the march, and other groups like KUMB and Crossed Hammers were also in support. RWHFAG's leadership reacted badly to this news. It was baffling. They had called for the march. The march had gained widespread support. People planned to fly in from all over the world to attend. It was a chance to show the board how people really felt. Did they think that everyone would just accept, on their say so, that these owners, with all their history of lies and deceit, would keep any promises made as long as the march was cancelled?

There had to be something more to it. The spite and vitriol aimed at WHUISA and its supporters was like nothing I had ever seen before. By 3 March there was an announcement in their page saying the ICF had taken over RWHFAG and the ICF say the march will not be allowed as 'leftie cunts' like WHUISA and anti-fascist organisations are not 'proper' West Ham.

I had to chuckle at the suggestion that the ICF had now taken over the RWHFAG, like they were not running it before? It was a cartoonish caricature of a response. I was also deeply offended by the insinuation that as I was not a fascist, I was not a proper West Ham fan. Explain please?

What I couldn't understand was why there was such insistence that the march should not go ahead in any way, shape or form. Why? What was at stake? It was no surprise that rumours of financial incentives were rife. To my knowledge no accounts have ever been published and no evidence of the appropriation of funds raised has been provided. Where, for example, had the funds raised for Isla Caton gone? A question which, at the time of writing, has still not received a satisfactory answer.

So now the ICF were taking control of the campaign and everyone had to do what they said. I rolled my eyes. The embarrassing uncle was on his tenth pint. The club is owned by everyone. Not the board, not the ICF, not WHUISA. It was an unholy mess. The drunken uncle was about to go too far.

Not surprisingly, all this menace and underlying threat did nothing to help team affairs and a six-pointer at Swansea was lost 4–1. That put Swansea above us on goal difference, as we hovered precariously over the relegation zone, 3 points clear but having played a game more than Crystal Palace who had slipped back into 18th.

WHUISA cancelled their plans to arrange an alternative march on the advice of the authorities. Perhaps I should elaborate on that: the authorities seemed to have no idea there was a march planned. Which begged the question as to whether the march was ever going to go ahead in the first place. Cue more abuse from all sides as Facebook and Twitter went into meltdown. WHUISA were, at least, a recognised organisation affiliated with the Football Supporters' Federation. They were not, and have never been, to my knowledge, associated with any political party, yet RWHFAG insisted WHUISA were 'lefties'.

Quite what this had to do with the price of fish was something of a mystery, and only went on to confirm that if you feed people enough lies they will accept it as the truth. Social media is a particularly useful tool for this; sometimes it is deliberate, sometimes people take jokes as the truth and the next thing you know it is being quoted as fact. It is really quite frightening.

A statement from WHUISA stated:

> Claims were [also] made that the group is affiliated with the Mayor of London's office … This is untrue. WHUISA is a resolutely non-political, democratic, completely independent organisation, proudly affiliated to the FSF and will continue to work for the benefit of all West Ham United supporters and to hold the board to account.

We believe that this commitment to transparency is a fundamental requirement of WHUISA's role as a voice of West Ham fans. All our work is done in consultation with our members so we hope if you are not already a member you will join us now for just £1.

At the end of it all, as the date of the cancelled march approached, all there was to show for the time and effort put in by so many people was a lot of hot air, a lot of insults, a lot of people getting hard-ons over badges and a lot of flags. Don't forget the badges and flags. Was it worth it?

65

THESE DAYS

WEST HAM UNITED 0, BURNLEY 3
PREMIER LEAGUE, 10 MARCH 2018
Cancelled marches. Especially when it's for no valid reason.

An opportunity wasted. A protest march against the board that could have had the support of thousands. Instead, a few determined stragglers made the effort. That enthusiasm and momentum would never be recaptured. Never. Not least because of a complete breakdown in trust in all directions.

Even when the march had been on, I had planned to be in the Truman Brewery with Phil and Jim. I have never enjoyed being told how to support my football club, never enjoyed being told I am not a 'proper' fan and never particularly enjoyed being called a snowflake. I've supported this club through thick and thin for forty years. I've done the miles up and down the motorway and shared in all the success and failures. If that means I'm not a 'real' fan, then so be it.

In the end, with the march off, the gathering at TruRib was larger than expected, with Upton Parklifers Gary Killington and Pete Ward joining us in an attempt to drink so much beer we would not care about any marches, and eat such spicy ribs from the rib man that we would be in the bog all afternoon and not have to witness a terrible game of football.

Inside the ground the atmosphere was fragile and fractious. One of the demands made was for more reference within the stadium to our history. To that end, giant flags were waved with each of the club's crests from its formation to date. Was that the best they could come up with? They might as well start playing music after goals. We played well in the first half and should have been leading comfortably, but this was not a team brimming with confidence. After we went 1–0 down, three people ran onto the pitch at different times, one taking the corner flag and planting it in the centre spot. Many people missed the significance of this. It was a hark back to the bond scheme protests in 1991/92.

More embarrassing were the scenes as fans gathered under the directors' box to vent their anger directly to SuGo. All three were ushered away from their seats, leaving Sir Trevor Brooking as the last man standing (or sitting). Sir Trev sat there wistfully wondering, like many others of his era, what had happened to his beloved club.

This was all very predictable. There was a lot of pent-up anger after the cancellation of the march. Whether you condone it or not, it was bound to overflow at some point. Unless we had been winning the game, perhaps. The FA has since charged the club with failure to control its fans and failure to ensure no unauthorised person enters the field of play. At the time of writing this matter remains unresolved, but I sincerely hope the board are not able to pass the buck to the stadium managers. The blame lays squarely with them because they tried to suppress the fans' emotions. When you try to control how other people feel, you must expect consequences and take responsibility for them.

The following weeks up until the Southampton game saw the RWHFAG group consistently heap bile upon WHUISA with the political agenda still mystifyingly at the fore. I remained confused as to what any of this had to do with anyone's political allegiances, any more than it had to do with the content of their record collection. I kept a lot of the messages directed at WHUISA, KUMB and Crossed Hammers and was going to recount them here. But as I read through them I started to feel physically sick.

I will reproduce only one here to give you the flavour; there is no need for any more.

ANTIFA Labour Sadiq Khan WHUISA you ain't dividing us
you left wing fucks

Needless to say, messages sent in private to the administrators
of these groups were not so polite or erudite. I have seen them.
I cannot un-see them.

Even though they had reached agreement with Sullivan
a few weeks earlier, they now mooted a static protest against
the board. I'm not sure what message this sent: were we now
unhappy about something else? Something that didn't warrant
a march, but warranted a standing around? It was all very confusing to a snowflake like me.

In preparation for the Southampton game on 31 March, the
club reinforced the barriers around the directors' area, in an
effort to prevent a repeat of the coin-throwing protests. There
were also more police and stewards in place to avoid trouble
inside the ground. Instead, we saw events happen before the
game with a small walking protest, a static RWHFAG protest
at Stratford concourse and an emergency meeting of WHUISA
members in Hackney Wick. The protests happened away from
the ground and attracted a few hundred people.

On the other side of the stadium at the WHUISA meeting,
the members were busy discussing whether or not the group
would support action against the club. Following a very interesting discussion, a unanimous vote of no confidence was
passed against the board for their inability to deliver a world-
class team or a world-class stadium – their original sales
pitch which fooled so many fans into supporting the stadium move. It was agreed to launch the United Campaign for
Change, a long-term strategy to 'help' the board deliver upon
their promises.

A united campaign would be great, but I suspected with
the number of different agendas out there, the only winners
would be the board. Until we focus and stop the hating, we,
as fans, will never achieve anything. The bond scheme was not
the same. There was one target, one objective. This is different.

There are many objectives, many targets, and some people see some issues as more important than others.

The home match against Southampton was approached with trepidation. It was clear we could not afford a repeat of what happened against Burnley. We should not have worried: 3–0 up by half time with an opener from Mario and 2 from Arnie while Mark Hughes, the newly appointed Saints boss, sat on the sideline unpacking a fresh bag of lemons.

The atmosphere was great; there was no fighting, no offensive banners, no coin throwing, no corner-flag planting. It showed that if the team performs, the fans stay happy; when the team does not perform, the fans will find ways to vent their frustrations. I often wonder what the sentiment would have been in March 2018 had we only just escaped relegation and played badly in our final season at the Boleyn, and finished 7th in our first season at the London Stadium. Would the stadium's shortcomings be overlooked?

The win against Southampton meant we took a giant stride towards maintaining Premier League status, but we were still only 5 points above the relegation zone with 7 games remaining. Of those 7, we had to play both Manchester clubs, Chelsea, Arsenal and bogey team Everton, which meant realistically we had to get wins against Stoke and Leicester, and that would still only give us 37 points and no guarantees.

We picked up an unexpected point at Stamford Bridge, then another against Stoke, which still left us a point down on target.

One of the promises made by Sullivan during the initial meetings was he would step away from the procurement of players and appoint a director of football. There were no signs this was happening. In fact, there were few signs anything was happening.

The situation with the supporters' club took an unwelcome turn as the original committee sought to dissolve the company, which would have resulted in the sale of assets meaning substantial payouts for outgoing committee members. The new committee tried to stop this. There were arguments over whether new memberships were valid in terms of having a vote at meetings. Again, fans turned against fans. And again, at the time of writing the matter has yet to be resolved and is the subject of legal action. However, there is real hope that this matter will be resolved with the supporters' club remaining in its new, club-sponsored accommodation at Stour Space.

Defeat at the Emirates meant Moyes was statistically the worst manager in West Ham's recent history based on win percentages. This was something the knee-jerkers on social media took great delight in. Those who wanted Moyes out put these statistics forward as actually meaning something, forgetting that win percentages take no account of draws or any potential handicap of having an interfering chairman.

A 4–1 defeat at home to Manchester City did nothing to improve his figures. The protests had calmed down, but the dire team performances could only go on so long as the memory of the home win over Southampton was fading fast. The scars caused by the events of the previous six weeks would take a lot longer to heal.

66

NO TEARS LEFT TO CRY

WEST HAM UNITED 3, EVERTON 1
PREMIER LEAGUE, 13 MAY 2018
Everything – and everyone.

The final away game of the season ended in an unexpected but welcome 2–0 victory over Leicester at the King Power stadium, with Mark Noble showing excellent technique to keep a low, long-range volley down and arrowed into the far corner. The result meant that with 38 points we were now mathematically safe. Stoke's earlier defeat at home to Palace condemned them to the Championship and West Bromwich Albion, despite a remarkable revival under Darren Moore, including wins over Manchester United, Newcastle and Tottenham, suffered the same fate.

That just left a straight fight between Swansea and Southampton, but Swansea needed a nine-goal swing on the final day to save them. They lost anyway.

Two years to the day after beating Manchester United 3–2 in the final game at the Boleyn, we faced them at the London Stadium on a Thursday night in the penultimate home game of the season. The 0–0 draw was entertaining, but had the air of a match between two teams who had nothing to play for.

Finally, Il Fatso brought his Everton team for the final game of the season. It was a relief that we didn't need anything from the game. The thought of needing to get a win against Allardyce filled me with dread. The look on his face would have been unbearable.

As it happened we went ahead early, and as usual he had no

plan B, so we went on to win 3–1. Moyes got his first win against a former team. We finished 13th on 41 points. As in 2006/07, looking at the final table, you would wonder what all the fuss had been about.

Facebook debates raged on about whether Moyes should stay. Personally, I could see no viable alternative and I felt he had probably done enough to warrant a two-year deal. Rafa Benítez's name continued to be mentioned, but I saw no value in that – he was synonymous with drab, defensive football. We could have got Alan Curbishley back a lot cheaper. I'm glad I didn't mention that earlier or SuGo would have done it.

I was still of the view that Moyes should be given a new contract when suddenly, without warning, Manuel Pellegrini was appointed.

Despite Brady's further attempts to poke sticks in hornets' nests by saying everything was fine at the London Stadium, it was just a few keyboard warriors and 'malcontents' making a lot of noise, the reaction to Pellegrini's appointment was upbeat. Why wouldn't it be?

I liked Pellegrini from his time at Manchester City. It was no coincidence the City fans had a banner calling him 'This Charming Man.' I always felt in press conferences he was gracious in victory and defeat, and I never saw him blame anyone else for his team's shortcomings. He didn't even react when Alan Pardew called him a fucking old cunt. Stay classy, Alan.

I liked Pellegrini's philosophy – he says he expects his staff to meet three key criteria:

1. Respect: for fellow players, staff, supporters, media etc.
2. Commitment: to the manager's plans
3. Performance: full commitment

If your manager has this philosophy, then surely this is something that we as fans can also take on board.

A director of football has been appointed in the form of Argentinian Mario Husillos, who has worked before with

Pellegrini. It bodes well that Sullivan will now withdraw from involvement in signings and we can sit back and enjoy the summer transfer window.

The shenanigans of the last year will not result in massive changes to the stadium structure. We can hire as many architects as we like, but ultimately the public purse will not stand further expenditure.

But we can all work towards improving the match day experience for each other by showing respect and hating everything just a little bit less.

Obviously, a winning team will help and the board deserves credit for taking the first step and appointing a manager with a proven track record, and, at the time of writing, for digging deep to provide the playing staff he requires. Maybe if they had done so for Bilić we would not be in this situation. But it can be no coincidence that the appointment of Pellegrini coincided with the arrival of American billionaire Albert 'Tripp' Smith on the board in September 2017. Smith purchased the remaining 10 per cent of the club still under the ownership of CB Holdings. All of this happened without any fanfare or major comment on the club website. The amount paid by Smith has not been disclosed. Whether or not he has bank-rolled the summer purchases is unclear. What is clear, however, is that there has been a sudden shift in SuGo's approach to handling the purchase of players and their comments in the press. Although Smith bought his share of the club well before the protests of spring 2018, the level of disquiet among the fans must have played a role and been part of a catalyst for change.

But some of us are keyboard warriors and malcontents. Brady's reference is to ordinary people frustrated at the perceived destruction of their club, who know of no other way to express themselves.

Our club has already been destroyed; there is no escaping that. Things will never be the same, we have to accept it. But they can get better, and to make that happen we have to start by respecting each other. Which is precisely Pellegrini's first point.

In a way it is strangely comforting that after the first four games of the 2018/19 season, despite the appointment of Pellegrini and Husillos, and the spending of close on £100 million in the summer, we can see no significant improvement. The club is sick, and the antidote cannot be bought. It will take more than a shedload of money to repair our broken hearts.

Writing this book has shown me that the last fifteen years have been one disaster after another, with consistent unhappiness among fans and protests against the board starting with WHISTLE and ending with RWHFAG and WHUISA. It shows that the more things change, the more they stay the same.

What has changed, however, is the level of bitterness and personal abuse afforded by the explosion of social media. I would like to leave my final words to a man I hardly know, but who I came across on Facebook via my old friend Adrienne Mann. There was a thread debating the intolerance among *Star Wars* fans. Can you believe that? *Star Wars* fans at each other's throats. Apparently, those who don't like the new film are leftie muggy cunt snowflakes. I am sure these people would be just as incredulous to hear that football fans of the same team could disagree so vociferously.

I would have claimed this for myself, but it is so wise, and so relevant that I have to give credit to Christopher West:

> There used to be a broad commonly-understood social stigma against being rude to other people in public.
>
> That blanket of civility has been fraying for some time (along with our concept of what is private speech and what is public, thanks to the Internet), and with the election of people whose defining characteristic (and political platform) is public rudeness, the tears in that fabric have only got worse.
>
> People have lost their shame about their own disrespectful behaviour, because they see others being rewarded for it.
>
> I believe this will change. The pendulum will swing back and our society will self-correct, but the further this goes in the wrong direction, the more painful and awkward that correction will be.

We will always have our ups and downs. There will always be arguments among people with common objectives and beliefs. But if we respect one another we can achieve anything we want. The board will always be the board, and we have to make it known when we are unhappy. But I believe the democratically elected and representative WHUISA can do that moving forward, and we owe them a debt of gratitude for standing firm in the face of terrible abuse. I suppose the basic tenet is: don't say anything on the internet that you would not say to someone's face.

Respect everything and everyone. Hate nothing and nobody – unless of course it's an irrational hatred.

ACKNOWLEDGEMENTS

There are many people I would like to thank, without whom this book would not have been possible. Apart from my amazingly patient wife giving me up most evenings for four months while I buried my head in this thing, a supportive family is vital for anyone who has a major project to complete. Especially when you have to combine it with a full-time job. My mum, Mary Banks and sisters, Sylvia Prior and Lynn Cooper, have always supported me in my writing projects; this time Mum also lent me her laptop when mine went on strike. It's been a hard couple of years for us all and I like to think we are closer for it.

Long-term friend Stuart (the QPR Fan) Davies, and new friends from the STOP! Hammer Time group, Jacqui Hughes and Gary Killington for their proofreading, constructive feedback, support, encouragement and assistance with timelines.

Phil Parkes is a club legend and a very busy man but did not hesitate to accept the invitation to write the Foreword. Thanks also to Marie Parkes for brokering the deal.

Perry Fenwick, Pete May, Jeremy Nicholas and Brian Williams for their positive comments.

When I had the initial idea for the book I contacted Iain Dale at Biteback and he said, 'What took you so long?' (or words to that effect). It meant a lot and I know it has been a wrench for him to leave Biteback, but I also know he will not need my wishes of good luck to be a success in whatever he does going forward, but he has them anyway. Olivia Beattie and Stephanie Carey at Biteback gave me positive and patient feedback when my confidence was at its lowest and I felt like I was pushing a rock up a hill, and I thank them for that.

Jim Grant wrote the excellent poem, 'Seventh Heavenshire', which features in this book, with his permission unquestioningly given. Thanks also to my talented wife, Elaine Banks, for taking my portrait to accompany my author bio at the end of the book. She said she has always wanted to shoot me.

And the following, in the random style of the founders walls at the London Stadium, without whom the book would have been possible but a lot less fun to write (in no particular order):

James McFadyen, James Milne, Craig Climpson, Philip Pitt, Ben Parry, Trevor Drane, Matt Liston, Adrienne Mann, Jeff Hatton, Reece Barber, Dave Hirst, Christine Nickerson, Nick Grant, Gary Stewart, Rebecca Bailey, Mark Prior, Jeremy Nicholas, Simon Smith (and his amazing dancing bear), Rob Chapman, Dave Moore, Stephen Carr, Phil Whelans, Graham Patterson, Michael Brennan, Dave Springer, Cate Mallett, Colin Milne, Dave Quinn, Dave Witts, Nigel King, Kevin Williamson, Clare Kendall, Chris Miles (and Stanley), George Mann, Jim Dolan, John Schofield, John Webster, Nathan Byrne, Robin Cotgreave, Trudy Smith, Luke Stoneman, Amy Gardiner, Derek Thomson, Bruce Halligan, Rosemary Parry, Cassio Amaral, Lisa Davies, Steven Tait, Matt Skitt, Sam Prior, Lawrence Connell, Brian Williams, Vanessa White, Beccy Curry, Liam Tyrrell, Phil Nice, Don Peretta, Jon Fenton, Mark Latimer and everyone else who posted their irrational hatreds on my Facebook page. If I have missed anyone I offer you a Gallic shrug and say, 'meh'.

Finally, thank you to everyone who helped in any tiny way, by confirming details or jogging my memory.

If I am honest, with it being fifteen years since the last book, I had forgotten quite how much work is involved – least of all for me as the author – but also for everyone associated with the project. Great team, well done everyone. I'm proud of you all, as well as the end product, and I'm so happy to have you in my life.

AUTHOR BIO

© Elaine Banks

Robert Banks started supporting West Ham as an impressiona-ble six-year-old after seeing them win the FA Cup in 1975. He has written three bestselling books charting his personal trials and tribulations as a Hammers fan struggling to come to terms with life in general: *An Irrational Hatred of Luton* (1995), *West Ham Till I Die* (2000) and *The Legacy of Barry Green* (2003). He started his football writing career contributing to the fanzine *Over Land and Sea* and frequently wrote for *Hammers News*. He is now a regular guest on the podcast *STOP! Hammer Time*. He lives with his wife, Elaine, and plans to retire to Brazil, though probably not from the proceeds of this book.